A Voice of Their Own

The Authority of the Local Parish

William A. Clark, S.J.

D1531265

A Michael Glazier Book

LITURGICAL PRESS
Collegeville, Minnesota

www.litpress.org

A Michael Glazier Book published by the Liturgical Press

Cover design by David Manahan, O.S.B. Photo courtesy of W. P. Wittman Photography Limited.

1	2	3	4	5	6	7	8

Library of Congress Cataloging-in-Publication Data

Clark, William A. (William Anthony), 1958–
    A voice of their own : the authority of the local parish / William A. Clark.
       p.   cm.
    "A Michael Glazier book."
    Summary: "Examines 'community,' 'intimacy,' and 'authority' in the church at the formative, local ecclesial level; examines contributions of several theologians; concludes that a deeper appreciation for the enormous, practical authority of local communities can help ground a renewal of the church's self-understanding"—Provided by publisher.
    Includes bibliographical references and index.
    ISBN-13: 978-0-8146-5218-3 (pbk. : alk. paper)
    ISBN-10: 0-8146-5218-2 (pbk. : alk. paper)
    1. Fellowship—Religious aspects—Christianity. 2. Community—Religious aspects—Christianity. 3. Church—Authority. 4. Authority—Religious aspects—Christianity. 5. Church. I. Title.

BV4517.5.C52 2005
262'.2—dc22

2005011785

**Dedicated to the Memory
of Two Lives Devoted to God's People:**

Msgr. Philip Murnion
(1938–2003)
Pastor, student of parish life, and friend
who, unbeknownst to either of us,
gave this book its start on the day we first met

Sr. Bernadette Laflamme, R.S.M.
(1932–2005)
Educator, pastoral caregiver, and woman of God,
who never stopped teaching her nephew

"Let us listen to what all the faithful say,
because in every one of them the Spirit of God breathes."
St. Paulinus of Nola (Epistola 23)

Contents

Preface

This book grew from a deep personal interest and involvement in the life of local Catholic communities, both parishes and "small Christian communities." The relationships I have formed in a variety of communities over many years have profoundly shaped my own understanding of the life of faith. With a growing awareness of that fact have come some basic questions. How does such an influence, repeated in the lives of countless Christians, impact the life and faith of the church as a whole? Is my own community experience something of a fluke, or can it really be fundamental to the church? If such relationships are an important factor in the way Catholics understand themselves and their beliefs, should we not acknowledge the practical authority they have in the church? Would not such recognition allow us to make more conscious and effective use of this resource? I have tried here to explore these questions using a variety of theological, pastoral, and sociological tools I have received from many generous mentors. I hope that my use of them will assist in some way the thought and work of others who have experienced the influence of intimate community relationships in the church.

One of my fundamental assumptions is that behind official structures are always complex networks of persons responding to, challenging, and supporting one another, and so allowing the structures to accomplish their purpose. That is true in academic pursuits, and it is true in the church. It is appropriate, then, to begin by thanking those communities whose response, challenge, and support have been particularly foundational for this book: the Clark and Laflamme families for life and faith, the Society of Jesus for companionship in the Spirit, Immaculate Heart of Mary Parish in Fairfield, Maine, for still being my home. To the particular parish communities to which I refer frequently throughout the text I owe my very deep and special gratitude: St. Joseph's Parish in Biddeford, Maine, for their unfailing welcome and appreciation; St. Thomas Aquinas Church in Kingston, Jamaica, for constantly challenging me to love; St. Matthew's Parish in Dorchester, Massachusetts, for so willingly sharing their heart with me in the initial stages of this project.

The original version of this work was prepared while I was a doctoral student at Weston Jesuit School of Theology in Cambridge, Massachusetts. The guidance, confidence, and encouragement I received from friends and faculty there were absolutely essential in the completion of this project. I offer special thanks to Roger Haight, S.J., Margaret Guider, O.S.F., and James Keenan, S.J., for their interest, ideas, challenges, and assistance over several years of field work and inquiry leading toward this project.

For the past four years my professional home has been at the College of the Holy Cross in Worcester, Massachusetts. I owe many thanks to my colleagues in the Department of Religious Studies for their encouragement and confidence, and their good practical advice in matters large and small. My very special thanks go to Dr. Alice Laffey for her unflagging concern and interest in the progress of this work. I would also like to acknowledge the College's Committee on Fellowships, Research, and Publication, which provided me with resources to expand my observation and interview data at St. Joseph's in Biddeford in June of 2002. Mark McDougall, my student research assistant that summer, also made valuable contributions to the collection and analysis of that material.

Several colleagues at other institutions have generously served as readers and consultants at various stages of my work. In particular, I would like to thank Brian McDermott, S.J., of the Georgetown University Jesuit Community, and the late Msgr. Philip Murnion, founder of the National Pastoral Life Center, for reading and commenting on the original version. Dr. Richard Gaillardetz of the University of Toledo and Rev. Richard Lennan of the Catholic Institute of Sydney, Australia, have been particularly diligent readers of the revised text.

A version of Chapter Six was previously published as "The Authority of Local Church Communities: Perspectives from the Ecclesiology of Karl Rahner," *Philosophy and Theology (Marquette University Journal)* 13:2 (2001) 399–424. I am grateful to the editor, Dr. James South, for permission to make use of this article in revised form.

Finally, to my Jesuit brothers in the several communities where I have lived and worked in the time during which the various parts of this work were developing: the Silvera Drive community in August Town, Kingston, Jamaica; the Weston Jesuit Community—especially the residents of Hopkins, Faber, and Zipoli Houses—in Cambridge, Massachusetts; the Heythrop College community in London, especially the residents of Garnet House in Clapham, all gave me welcome, support, and patience as I conceived this project and worked toward its completion. I am particularly grateful to the Jesuit Community at Ciampi Hall at the College of the Holy Cross, my current home, for so readily making me a part of our common life and work.

You are all the face of God for me. May you be blessed as richly.

College of the Holy Cross
Worcester, Massachusetts
January 28, 2005

Introduction

Church and the Local Community

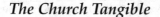 *The Church Tangible*

Saint Robert Bellarmine famously observed, "The Church is a human community as visible and palpable as the community of the people of Rome, or the Kingdom of France, or the Republic of Venice."[1] By themselves these words offer a number of interesting possibilities for understanding the social dimensions of Christian faith. They depend on the radical and troublesome Judeo-Christian notion that the People of God (and God's very self) are enmeshed in human history. They could even be understood to suggest that the form of this historical involvement can shift and evolve according to the historical period and location of the church. As political bodies, the three examples given could hardly be more disparate and still be familiar to their sixteenth-century European audience. Bellarmine, however, in the midst of intense Reformation-era controversy about how to identify the "true church," had something quite narrowly juridical in mind. He therefore accompanied his statement with a definition of the church that lays all the stress on external professions and structures, and virtually none on the lived experience of believers.

Christians in other eras, however, have often understood the church more theologically. They have grasped that it is more than the language

---

[1] See Robert Bellarmine, "Controversiarum de Conciliis, Liber III: Qui est de ecclesia militante toto orbe terrarum diffusa," in Justin Fevre, ed., *Roberti Bellarmini Opera Omnia* (Paris: Louis Vivès, 1870) 2:318.

of its laws and traditions, broader and deeper than the structure of its offices, doctrines, and rites. They have located their origins as a people in the descent of the Holy Spirit upon the apostles at Pentecost, or in the less spectacular memory of the disciples gathered around Jesus their Teacher, or even in the struggles of the Exodus community of the Israelite people wandering in the desert. In each of these images of the church coming into being, the dominant feature is one of *relationship* and *covenant:* God draws his people together and binds them to one another by binding each of them to himself. At its most fundamental, the church is a community of living faith. This faith is what allows its laws, traditions, offices, doctrines, and rites to become theologically meaningful rather than mere cultural curiosities.

A part of Bellarmine's emphasis on "visible and palpable" realities, however, remains crucial even for this alternative point of view. We recognize living faith, like most other human qualities, not so much in the abstract as when we encounter it in concrete times and places. The faith that is the driving force of the church becomes real when we see it directly affect the conduct of actual persons in particular relationships with other specific persons. Just as we may not quite grasp a "global economy" until we have met our new Asian coworkers, or may not be concerned with "global warming" until we have lived through an unexpected drought, so the global community of faith makes itself known most truly in our local communities and circles of acquaintance. This is as true for the bishop gathered with colleagues on a visit to Rome as it is for the little girl learning the "Our Father" from her grandmother. It is as necessary and lifegiving for the nursing-home resident developing a "personal" bond with a priest on the Eternal Word Television Network as it is for a college student asking challenging questions of the chaplain. However broad the implications or varied the international experience, it is in the face of the concrete and local that Christians—with few exceptions—encounter, live in, honor, or reject the church.

A Crisis of Authority

This local quality of the Catholic Church is wed to its more celebrated universal aspects by a powerful system of shared values, knowledge, and authority that more often than not seems to overshadow the local communities. Front page church-related headlines do not generally focus on the doings of a particular parish, but on papal journeys, conferences of bishops, or controversial Vatican statements. Yet a large number of ordinary Mass-going members of the church are likely to have only a vague sense of their relationship to such structures. ("Who's that guy?" asked one devout, elderly, lifelong Catholic woman at the *end* of a parish Mass at which the bishop had unexpectedly presided!) Most of the time this vagueness has not been particularly important. It is made up for by an unexpressed conviction on everyone's part that "the church," whether local or universal, stands for an identifiable set of decent, just, and holy values that each in her or his own sphere depends on and seeks to uphold. Even some of the more severe collisions between local expectation and administrative fiat have usually caused no serious disruption of the equilibrium. A couple, denied a dispensation to marry, drops out of sight. Parishioners, irate over the bishop's refusal to replace an incompetent pastor, transfer to a neighboring parish. Alumni saddened and angered by the closure of their parish school form an association and establish scholarships to other institutions. Individuals or whole groups may wander away, but the basic relationship between local community and central authority remains and offers no serious challenge to the faith of most Catholics.

It is, however, precisely this relationship that was attacked in the scandal of sexual abuse and coverup that broke into public consciousness in 2002. The crimes uncovered had not taken place in some distant chancery office, but in the local rectory. The priests involved were not just the odd misfits that land at the occasional unlucky parish, but some very dynamic and popular priests at one parish after another. The victims were not anonymous urchins of some sort, but sons and nephews, daughters and nieces, friends and neighbors of loyal and active parishioners. Once the perception was generally adopted that diocesan bishops would often dismiss, minimize, or cover up such terribly tangible sins as these, the unspoken conviction that the whole system operated on strong and shared values was seriously compromised.

The predictable response of many—we may never know how many—was to walk away. Attendance and contributions in areas most directly affected by the scandals declined noticeably, in some cases even drastically. Yet, the structure that had been disrupted was not the simple parody that some too easily imagine—a hierarchy of power and privilege resting on the contributions of the ignorant and powerless. Rather, the threat was to something much nearer to home for most Catholics, and it is to this threat that they have responded. A common saying shortly after the revelations of abuse began to multiply ran something like this: "I will never contribute to the diocese again, but I love my parish."

Local communities and personal networks had identities, traditions, and resources of their own, and many of them began to make this very plain. Parishioners began to educate themselves rapidly about structures and policies beyond their communities that had barely entered their consciousness before. They began to demand an accountability and transparency that had rarely crossed a mind previously. They began to make lists of criteria and principles that should be followed in reform. They began, all this is to say, to exert authority.[2]

The questions about authority that this devastating chapter of U.S. Catholic history underscores have, in broad strokes, been in the consciousness of the whole church for decades. The Second Vatican Council was celebrated for having shown the way toward episcopal collegiality, a responsible and participative laity, and appreciation for the riches of cultural diversity. However, it was followed up by poisonous arguments over liturgical change, lay "rebellion" and clerical "intransigence" with regard to the understanding of sexuality, and a steadily renewed centralization of leadership appointments and crucial decision-making. This contrast between Vatican II's promise and its actual implementation has inspired a greater attention to the quiet authority of local communities, by factions both "conservative" and "progressive," almost without regard for their sometimes diametrically opposed readings of the Council documents. Whether we speak of the activities of radically political base communities on the one hand, or parishes encouraging fervent supporters of Tridentine rites on the other hand, disappointed Catholics have been looking to local communities more explicitly than ever in the decades since the Council. As *social* foundations for Catholicism, the importance of such local groups is thus perhaps self-evident. To emphasize their *theological* importance is the purpose of this book.

Ecclesiology from Below

The idea of listening closely to Christian communities and observing their circumstances for the purpose of producing distinctive theological contributions is actually as old as the New Testament itself. Luke, acknowledging that many had already done what he was doing, relied on

[2] Two public examples of this phenomenon, from opposite ends of the ideological spectrum, can be seen in the websites of "The Voice of the Faithful" (*http://www.votf.org/*) and "Your Catholic Voice" (*http://www.yourcatholicvoice.org/*).

"those who were eyewitnesses from the beginning" while still "investigating everything accurately anew" for the aid of his "excellent Theophilus" (Luke 1:2-3). In the second part of his narrative, the Acts of the Apostles, he frequently describes circumstances in which the apostles (as close as the early church had to a "central administration") were scrambling to keep up with events taking place in new communities distant from Jerusalem. Reluctant apostles are persuaded of the sincerity of the converted Paul (Acts 9:26-27); a bemused Peter is forced to admit that the Spirit has come upon the Gentile Cornelius and his family (Acts 10:44-49); the church at Antioch (Acts 11:19-26) and its missionaries Paul and Barnabas (Acts 13:44-47) forge ahead in preaching to the Gentiles and precipitate a crucial decision by the apostles (Acts 15:1-12). After centuries of general Christian use of the New Testament, we tend to forget or discount the fact that virtually every book or letter originally addressed a specific community with theology created for its specific circumstances, and only later passed into the general Christian tradition. This is particularly obvious, of course, in the letters of Paul, but across the New Testament biblical scholarship can provide from the writings themselves quite detailed descriptions of the communities that inspired them.[3]

In recent decades the practice of theologizing based on the particular situation of a local community has been revived in a variety of ways. In the 1960's and 1970's liberation theologians such as Ernesto Cardenal and countless others devised a whole tradition of listening to the poorest communities of believers in Latin America and elsewhere.[4] The intention of these theologians was to take the perspectives of ordinary Christians on gospel teaching and Christian doctrine with theological seriousness for perhaps the first time since the early church. There followed efforts to transport this attempt at listening into the North American context, efforts that produced the well-known contributions of Robert Schreiter, James and Evelyn Whitehead, and others.[5] Particularly over the last decade and a half a movement that has flourished largely among Protestant theologians and pastors has produced a large

---

[3] A classic example of this genre is provided by Raymond E. Brown, *The Community of the Beloved Disciple* (New York: Paulist, 1979).

[4] See Ernesto Cardenal, *The Gospel in Solentiname.* 4 vols. (Maryknoll, NY: Orbis, 1976–1982).

[5] See Robert Schreiter, *Constructing Local Theologies* (Maryknoll, NY: Orbis, 1985); James D. Whitehead and Evelyn Eaton Whitehead, *Method in Ministry: Theological Reflection and Christian Ministry* (New York: Seabury, 1980).

literature in the field called "Congregational Studies."[6] Scholars in this field use a variety of social science tools to compile the raw material both for effective pastoral discernment on practical questions and for local theological reflection. In Roman Catholic circles the field of practical/contextual theology has gained prominence with a variety of similar concerns, though less tied to specific congregational settings.[7]

Though we shall see that these initiatives are not precisely the same, this attention to local communities does invite an approach to theological reflection about the church that has come to be called "ecclesiology from below." When the *comunidades de base* began to organize the poor in Latin American rural villages and urban *barrios*, the literature that was generated in the 1970's and 1980's often noted that the term "base" had a variety of connotations. Among these was the notion that these small cells were "basic" to the church, that they organized at the most intimate level those who also made up the membership of the church's parishes and dioceses.[8] Some theologians, such as Leonardo Boff, were bold enough to call these communities a "new way of being Church," but also compared them to the primitive Christian communities of the first century. Boff complained that the church had moved away from its early self-understanding as the "community of the faithful" toward a more clerical and structural view. This shift, though perhaps historically necessary, has now "left no room for the responsible participation of all people in the affairs of the Church."[9] Elsewhere in his writing the implied opposition between the "popular church" and the "hierarchical church" is somewhat more nuanced,[10] but it was taken up precisely as opposition by the Vatican curia. Speaking to bishops in Boff's own

[6] See Nancy T. Ammerman, et al., *Studying Congregations: A New Handbook* (Nashville: Abingdon, 1998).

[7] See Stephen B. Bevans, *Models of Contextual Theology* (Maryknoll, NY: Orbis, 1992).

[8] Jose Marins, Teolide Maria Trevisan, and Carolee Chanona, *The Church from the Roots: Basic Ecclesial Communities*, Reprint Edition (London: Catholic Fund for Overseas Development, 1989) 29.

[9] Leonardo Boff, *Church: Charism and Power. Liberation Theology and the Institutional Church*, trans. John W. Diercksmeier (New York: Crossroad, 1992) 128. The section containing this passage is headed "A New Way of Being Church." The phrase is also used as a chapter heading by Marins et al., 2.

[10] See, for example, Boff, *Church: Charism and Power*, 126, where the two conceptions are presented as "two expressions of the one Church of Christ and of the apostles" and described as complementary.

Brazilian homeland in 1990, Joseph Cardinal Ratzinger rejected the idea of a church built up from a popular base, which he claimed necessarily meant that "the Church is not conceived episcopally but congregationally." The disaster that the future Pope Benedict XVI feared was the loss of the "all-embracing reconciliatory character of the Church." "The Church," he concluded, "becomes a group held together by her internal agreement, whereas her catholic dimension crumbles away."[11]

The lines of theological and pastoral controversy are very clearly drawn in exchanges like this. Yet the phrases "from below" and "from above" need not generate mortal combat within the church. As they were presented in 1971 by Karl Rahner (in an essay on method in christology), these terms sought to clarify two basic *types* of theological approach without extensive comment on the ultimate conclusions these approaches may yield.[12] The approach from below uses concrete, historical human experience as its starting point, and incorporates in its method all of the tools developed by the human sciences for the study of that experience.[13] In the case of christology the starting point is thus Jesus of Nazareth as historical person. The approach from above begins, rather, with established doctrine. It appeals first to the teaching authority of the church and its various sources and, in the case of christology, moves forward from Christ as divine person. Rahner points out that this second type in a sense includes the first, since the divinity of Christ is a doctrine that could not have been formulated without the disciples' prior experience of Jesus as a man.

Roger Haight has applied these same approaches to ecclesiology, contrasting the argument from authority with the critical examination of church history. Haight sees the first as attempting to clarify the church's predetermined doctrine about itself by presenting it systematically. The second, on the other hand, seeks "to arrive at a theological understanding of the Church" that cannot be set forth at the outset.[14] As Rahner did in his original essay, Haight draws the contrast between the two types very boldly, but notes that "a fuller account would display a great deal which

[11] Joseph Cardinal Ratzinger, *Called to Communion: Understanding the Church Today*, trans. Adrian Walker (San Francisco: Ignatius Press, 1996) 81–82.

[12] Karl Rahner, "The Two Basic Types of Christology," in idem, *Theological Investigations* 13 (New York: Seabury, 1975) 213–23.

[13] Joseph A. Komonchak, "Ecclesiology and Social Theory: A Methodological Essay," *The Thomist* 45 (1981) 274.

[14] Roger Haight, "Towards an Ecclesiology From Below," in Jeremy Driscoll, ed., *'Imaginer la Théologie Catholique': Permanence et Transformations de la Foi en*

they share in common."[15] Although the conclusion of the exercise is that the ecclesiology from above has dominated to the detriment of a more balanced understanding of the church, each of the two types still has its contribution to make, and they are not ultimately to be set against one another.

Local Community and Universal Church

Approaching the study of the church "from below" does not actually require us to focus on the local community. "From below" refers most especially not to the "lower level" of the church's structure, but rather to the historical roots of the church, or to the direct encounter with the church today in very tangible human experiences. From that base the method "ascends" toward a fuller understanding of the church in its relationship to Christ. On the other hand, one of the important features of the ecclesiological approach from below is that, since it does begin with concrete human experience, it tends to open a more appreciable role for the local church community within an overall understanding of the universal church. A word about how these terms—"local" and "universal"—will be understood in this book will be helpful in imagining their relationship to each other.

The church is *universal* by virtue of being accessible to all times and places through the presence and action of the Holy Spirit. Therefore the universal church is not merely the central structure of the worldwide ecclesial institution, but rather the church considered in its fullness, with all its aspects. On the other hand, this same church is *local* by virtue of being visible and tangible in many particular places and times. These local manifestations of church can be delineated in a variety of ways: culturally, geographically, politically, and so forth. In this book I will focus on the community gathered in a distinct location, whether that community be a parish, a base community, or some other cell group. Though these communities can be called "churches" by analogy to the universal church (and in other contexts there can be good reasons for so

---

Attendant Jésus-Christ. Mélanges Offerts à Ghislain Lafont. Studia Anselmiana 129 (Rome: Centro Studi S. Anselmo, 2000) 413–14.

[15] Ibid. 414. For a "fuller account" of the ecclesiology from below and its relationship to more traditional methods see Roger Haight, S.J., *Christian Community in History, Vol 1: Historical Ecclesiology* (New York and London: Continuum, 2004) 17–66.

referring to them), I have preferred "local communities" for two main reasons. First, this term avoids confusion with the familiar application of the term "local church" to a diocese. Second, it provides an emphasis on the idea of *community*, which will be a major consideration in what follows here. The term thus simplifies reference to a key idea employed in this book: that the church is made present and becomes "event" in the communion of persons tangibly experienced in a particular location.

This focus on local communities is therefore not exactly what Cardinal Ratzinger was complaining about with his claim that ecclesiology from below conceives the church "congregationally." Christians experience the church directly and concretely in such local settings regardless of their ecclesiological perspective. It is in these communities that the impact of any universal doctrines, structures, or rules is "realized." In an ecclesiology from below, therefore, local communities, both past and present, are heard as primary voices in a conversation that leads toward a theological understanding of the church even on the universal level.

This is why Rahner claims that these local communities are not mere "parts" of the universal church, but are the way in which "the whole Church becomes tangible."[16] Nor is this an example of mistaking a part for the whole.[17] Rather, Rahner deliberately presents a paradox based on the firm understanding of the local community as the site of the universal church's eucharistic celebration. The perspective from below, therefore, need not limit ecclesiological insight to a strictly local view. Neither does it imply that the dependence of the universal upon the local is not reciprocal. On the contrary, its logic can be as expansive as human experience itself, and so can lead toward a vision of the church present and active in the world, even beyond the administrative and denominational boundaries that often restrict our view. As Haight points out, though such an ecclesiology must necessarily be elaborated from a particular perspective (here, the Roman Catholic Church in North America), its proper object is in fact "the whole Christian movement."[18]

---

[16] Rahner, quoted in Richard Lennan, *The Ecclesiology of Karl Rahner* (Oxford: Clarendon Press, 1997) 72.

[17] For such an objection see John Paul Vandenakker, *Small Christian Communities and the Parish* (Kansas City, MO: Sheed and Ward, 1994) 206, in his discussion of the "criteria for ecclesiality" to be applied to Small Christian Communities.

[18] Haight, "Towards an Ecclesiology From Below," 432. This, of course, raises a question about the focus of this book on the Roman Catholic Church; see my remarks in this Introduction under "The Authority of Local Communities."

Of course, an ecclesiology from below could be constructed that actually would conceive "church" primarily as the congregation, understanding it essentially in terms of the spiritual links among members of the particular community. Ecclesiologies of this sort tend to minimize the importance of the historical continuity and unity that only broader institutions (Scripture, tradition, hierarchy, law, etc.) can maintain. Yet a complete understanding of the social, historical, and theological context of any local Christian community necessarily depends on and includes these broader institutions. For this reason, using the ascending approach by focusing first on particular local communities requires us to avoid conceiving those communities in isolation from one another, or basing their ecclesial status on "internal agreement" in the way that Ratzinger rejected. Yet the local church community can be understood as a window onto fundamental aspects of the church as a whole that are customarily less emphasized. Among these fundamental but neglected aspects are the lay believers who make up the communities, and the concrete circumstances within which the communities exist.

Lay ministry and responsibility have, of course, grown rapidly in the church since the Second Vatican Council, even at the diocesan level. For all this, however, the official governing structures of the church are clearly still the domain of the ordained clergy.[19] As I have already mentioned in connection with the leadership crisis the U.S. church is now experiencing, the average lay person neither participates in nor particularly understands these broader structures. Oddly, this remains true even though it is these very structures that are the ordinary referent for the term "the church." Despite that fact, lay Catholics generally relate to the church first through their experience of the local community. Not only is this the almost exclusive setting in which they encounter the church in any personal way, but it is also the setting in which they have the greatest opportunity to see themselves as vital participants. Certainly, aspects of the organization and leadership of the local community are them-

---

[19] One of the many indicators of this is the ordinary use of the terms "lay" and "laity" themselves. They mean, of course, "non-clerical, non-ordained," but the inadequacy of a purely negative definition of the bulk of the church's membership will be very clear as the discussion of local authority unfolds. For an early appreciation of the problem and some positive solutions, see Karl Rahner, "Notes on the Lay Apostolate," in *Man in the Church. Theological Investigations* 2, trans. Karl-Heinz Kruger (Baltimore: Helicon Press; London: Darton, Longman & Todd, 1963) 319–30.

selves part of the broad legal structure of the church, yet these structures would be unnecessary and meaningless without the lay persons who form the communities that the structures regulate. To speak, then, of the local community is largely to speak of the laity in the church. To begin an ecclesiology at the point of the local community is to make of the laity central figures in the discussion of the church's meaning.

Similarly, ecclesiology from below requires taking seriously the church in its concrete reality, as opposed to whatever cultural, organizational, or theological abstraction of it one might prefer. In *Gaudium et Spes*, Vatican II laid claim for the church to "the joys and hopes, the fears and anxieties of the people of this world."[20] In owning such a statement the church understands itself as inescapably part of the world that it serves, no matter what aspect of its mission or membership we consider. From this point of departure, the "local community" can be taken to be any regularly gathered group of Christians, whether they be a Brazilian base community, a North American parish, a Benedictine priory, or the pope with the cardinal prefects. Clearly, each of these gatherings functions and contributes differently within the communion of the universal church. Yet in each case it is in the local community, the church *here* and *now*, that the ideal of church meets the realities of human life, is understood in their light, and is shaped by their demands. The local community is the place where the church moves from concepts, teachings, and policies to concrete actions with observable effects, and back again.[21]

The Authority of the Local Community

What follows is an examination of the ecclesiological role and authority of the concrete local community of Christian believers, within the broad structure of the church. In the course of seven chapters,

[20] Second Vatican Council, "Pastoral Constitution on the Church in the Modern World (*Gaudium et Spes*, 7 December, 1965)," in Austin Flannery, ed., *Vatican Council II: The Conciliar and Post-Conciliar Documents* (Northport, NY: Costello; Dublin: Dominican, 1996) 1:903.

[21] This interaction between "concept" and "action" at the local level relates to the ongoing discussion of the idea of "reception" of church teaching, and the lay role in this process. For a review of this question see Richard Gaillardetz, "The Reception of Doctrine: New Perspectives," in Bernard Hoose, ed., *Authority in the Roman Catholic Church* (London: Ashgate, 2002) 95–114.

presenting several distinct approaches to the main premise, I will examine the reasons for understanding these communities as essential to the universal church and as exercising their own proper and inherent authority. Through the local community, the Spirit of Christ works to ground the mission and authority of the universal church in the intimate person-to-person communal relationships out of which the church originally grew as a human reality.

In clarifying this point I will touch on a number of other vital questions, each of which has already inspired multiple major studies. I do not intend here to completely evaluate or even fully summarize the larger theological discussions on authority, communion ecclesiology, local and universal church structures, and other relevant topics that have been in progress for a long time. In putting forward my own view I will merely borrow perspectives that help to highlight the inherent authority of local communities, with gratitude to the many prominent scholars who have done this work and, hopefully, with correct attention to the meanings they intend.

I should also underscore what will already be quite plain, that I make my argument within the Roman Catholic context. There are two primary reasons for this. First, my own personal experience, as both member and leader, is focused on this church, and such concrete experience is at the heart of the method I will employ. Second, while a number of other Christian communions have a lengthy heritage of emphasizing the local community, the Roman Catholic Church has long been in reaction against the splintering tendencies that weak central authority encourages in some other communions. It is the Roman Catholic Church, then, that is in particular need of addressing the issue of balance in the direction of the local community. What I say on the topic, however, is also relevant to a more general Christian discussion of the meaning of church, since the problems of the relationship between local and universal have been among the most important and divisive issues for the whole church since the time of the New Testament.

The six main chapters of this book correspond broadly to three distinct approaches. I have based the first two primarily on sociological observations that have a theological impact. Chapter One begins "on the ground," with a look at three particular communities whose vitality and struggles have directly fed my own reflections. Each in some fashion is wrestling with its cultural milieu in ways that help expose the sources of its community values and its understanding of faith. Saint Joseph's Parish is an old working-class, ethnic community in a New England

mill town, proud of its heritage and yet facing enormous change. Saint
Thomas Aquinas Parish is a small community in a Caribbean capital,
sharply divided between comfortable middle- and upper-class "pillars"
and the many poor who live near the church. Saint Matthew's Parish,
once similar to Saint Joseph's, is now a varied community of recent immigrant Catholics struggling to knit themselves together, to survive and
grow, in an inner-city environment new to many of them. Brief sketches
of these parishes will introduce some of the characteristics of church as
seen from within the local community and the interrelationships that
constitute it. These will provide the setting for the more general discussion of the church understood as intimate community, and of the type of
authority with which this community is empowered.

Today, of course, the whole notion of "intimate community" is a
problematic one. The "Catholic neighborhood" of earlier times is replaced in American cities by a more anonymous urban environment, or
completely displaced in more diverse suburban settings. Further, increasing numbers of people perceive a certain incompatibility between
reinforced cultural boundaries, on the one hand, and a spirit of Christian inclusiveness and an ever-broadening dynamic on the other. The
situation is made all the more complex by the modern mobility of huge
numbers of people and the increasing irrelevance of older ideas of
"rootedness." The problems become particularly acute when the community ideal is associated rather mechanically with the structural concept of "parish."[22] Over the last fifty years these difficulties have led
many pastoral and theological commentators to suggest that the idea
of intimate community is no longer appropriate to the discussion of
local church. On the other hand, the ongoing base community movement, from its beginnings in Latin America to new forms (both sponta-
neous and institutional) in many other places, seeks to revitalize the
community ideal within the shifting context and with new structures.
Chapter Two uses the earlier parish sketches, and other data from a variety of sources, to conclude that the idea of "community" remains a
crucial one. The work of grasping its contemporary meanings in the
most local manifestations of the church is not only worthwhile but essential to an overall understanding of the church.

---

[22] Karl Rahner recognized this problem early in the conciliar period and addressed it in several aspects in "Peaceful Reflections on the Parochial Principle,"
in *Man in the Church. Theological Investigations* 2:283–318.

The next two chapters introduce a more properly theological approach, but one that still relies heavily on the insights of social theorists
as a tool. Chapter Three takes a closer look at the concept of "intimacy"
and its relationship to "authority" and related notions. Though we tend
to use the word "intimate" most commonly for strictly personal relationships in the sense of "closely familiar," it also carries a primary sense of
"inmost" as essential or intrinsic. As a verb it speaks of making something known or familiar.[23] All these senses make it a helpful description
of local church community. The actual condition of face-to-face relationships in many communities may in fact be quite poor. Regardless of this,
the local community is that dimension of the church—and the only one—
in which we can come into close regular contact, and become familiar in
both comfort and challenge, with other Christians *as such*. Properly respected, this aspect reveals more deeply the inmost foundations of the
church. Intimacy as an essential quality of the church is rooted in the relationship of love and closeness between Jesus and his disciples. The
Gospel of John makes clear that this love reveals the kinship between
Christ and the Father that they share with the whole church, and that is
mirrored in relationships of love among the members of the church.[24]
From an empirical point of view, intimate community will take a variety
of forms, and may be honored more in the breach than in the observance.
From the theological point of view, however, intimate community is constitutive of the church, its mission, and its hope, whether or not it is fully
manifest in concrete, limited, and sinful human situations.

Having introduced the related concepts of "authoritative" and "authenticity" in this chapter, I turn more directly to the theme of authority
itself in Chapter Four. The work of a variety of sociologists and theologians leads to the view that genuine authority rises upon a deep foundation of authoritative meanings and values held within a community.
Sociologically, authority is not so much imposed by heaven as it is necessarily embedded in the flow of human history and social function.
Its proper exercise as a bonding force in a community (and therefore
as part of the intimacy of the community) requires an authentic engagement with the values that underlie it. This in turn implies a deep

[23] See *Oxford English Dictionary*, 2d ed., s.v. "intimate, *a.*" See also ibid., s.vv.
"intimacy" and "intimate, *v.*"

[24] "As the Father has loved me, so I have loved you; abide in my love. If you
keep my commandments, you will abide in my love, just as I have kept my
Father's commandments and abide in his love." (John 15:9-10, NRSV)

understanding of, and respect for, the community itself. For the Christian, the gospels present Christ as the very embodiment of such authenticity, shared intimately with his disciples. Recognizing the Spirit of Christ as our own authoritative standard, then, suggests an important role for the local community within the authority of the church.

Regardless of how one understands authority, of course, such an application of the concept to the local church is theologically controversial. To understand what is at stake in this controversy, the next two chapters turn directly to the work of three influential Catholic theologians. A lively debate concerning the relationship between the local and the universal church, which began in earnest with the Second Vatican Council and has continued right up to the present time, has concentrated on the relative roles of episcopacy and papal primacy. Nonetheless, the concepts and arguments involved are equally applicable and vital to the focus on local congregations. Examining the most relevant points of this discussion is the work of Chapter Five. Here I will first consider the case for the "temporal and ontological priority of the universal Church." This was the formulation of Cardinal Joseph Ratzinger, taken up in important recent documents of the Congregation for the Doctrine of the Faith and supported by various papal statements. It is meant to forestall what is understood as a "one-sided emphasis on the local church."[25] Predictably, it has also inspired some fears that the practical development of "recentralization" of church administration during the papacy of John Paul II is receiving official theoretical buttressing. One of the most eloquent recent spokespersons for this opposing view has been Cardinal Walter Kasper. His objections to Ratzinger's formula have relied on the notion of the simultaneous, interdependent nature of the universal and local church.[26] Discussion

[25] Congregation for the Doctrine of the Faith, "Letter to the Bishops of the Catholic Church on Some Aspects of the Church Understood as Communion," *Origins* 22 (June 25, 1992) 108–12. Kilian McDonnell, O.S.B., "The Ratzinger/Kasper Debate: The Universal Church and Local Churches," *Theological Studies* 63 (2002) 228, notes that the phrase "temporal and ontological priority," which appears in this CDF document, was seen in its initial forms in individual writings of Ratzinger, specifically *Church, Ecumenism and Politics* (New York: Crossroad, 1989) 75, and *Called to Communion* (San Francisco: Ignatius Press, 1991) 44.

[26] Kasper's principal responses to Ratzinger are contained and developed in *Leadership in the Church: How Traditional Roles Can Help Serve the Christian Community Today,* trans. Brian McNeil (New York: Crossroad/Herder & Herder,

of the relevance of this stance to the position of specific local communities will form the conclusion of Chapter Five.

Certainly Kasper is very far from being the lone post-conciliar voice in support of a deeper theological appreciation of the local church. A wide range of others will be heard from time to time in the course of these chapters, including those of Boff, Jean-Marie Roger Tillard, and John Zizioulas. In Chapter Six, however, I will return to and dwell in particular on the work of Karl Rahner, which for the past fifty years has helped to form the foundations for much of the reevaluation of Catholic systematic theology. Even though Rahner himself did not fully develop the method "from below" in ecclesiology, some of the most basic attitudes of his theology do orient it toward this ascending viewpoint. Beginning from his basic assumption of the individual human person as radically open to grace (which he understands as God's own self-communication),[27] Rahner builds "a theology characterized by its emphasis on identifying God as central to all human experience."[28] His theology therefore has a concrete and pastoral bent,[29] and his writings on the church emphasize history, an understanding of the dynamics of change in the church, and a realistic hopefulness about the future of the church. All of this is gathered in the central theme of Rahner's ecclesiology: church as sacrament. The chapter will first summarize Rahner's basic approach to the meaning of local church community. Then, making use of some of his most helpful images, I will turn to connections between his treatment of local church and some of the general themes of his ecclesiology. In thus filling out a picture of the local community as People of God, as the church in history, and as the presence of Christ, I will also be able to return to some of the central ideas that emerged from the observations of specific communities in Chapters One and Two, in order to place them in a broader theological context.

2003). See also Killian McDonnell, o.s.b., "Walter Kasper on the Theology and the Praxis of the Bishop's Office," *Theological Studies* 63 (2002) 711–29, and idem, "The Ratzinger/Kasper Debate," 227–50.

[27] Karl Rahner, "Concerning the Relationship Between Nature and Grace," in *God, Christ, Mary and Grace. Theological Investigations* 1, trans. Cornelius Ernst, o.p. (Baltimore: Helicon Press, 1961) 312–13.

[28] Lennan, *The Ecclesiology of Karl Rahner*, 7.

[29] Ibid. 6. Lennan laments the current tendency to regard such theology as "vaguely old-fashioned."

Practical theology, while it takes seriously the realm of ideas and encounters them on their own terms, ultimately pursues improvement in the life of the church. A study of local church community such as this must end where it begins, with the local communities themselves. Chapter Seven, therefore, takes the form of a brief discussion of the obstacles to be overcome and the outcome to be hoped for by local church communities seeking to claim and live their inherent authority. However differently they are composed, these communities are the location in which virtually every church member has had her or his faith established, shaped, nurtured, and challenged by receiving and living it in common with other believers. In this process faith has grown and developed, and its peculiar shape has become the property of the wider church through the communion that central structures mandate and promote. Some members go on to become intimately familiar with the workings of these central structures, but all continue to encounter the church most regularly in some form of local community. It is my hope that looking at the church from the point of view of these communities will allow the weight of their actual authority to be more consciously appreciated and so become a more widely acknowledged force for ongoing renewal in the whole church.

Allow me to make two final notes with regard to the text itself, each of which bears on the understanding of my main point. First, it has been customary to use an upper case letter for the term "Church," especially when it refers to the "whole Church" or the "universal Church." Readers will already have noticed that I am not following this custom, except in proper names and direct quotations. This decision is prompted by a basic assumption of the book itself: "local" and "universal" are not names for two different churches, one less important than the other. Rather, the local church is the concrete presence of the universal church. Because the two realities "interpenetrate" each other, there are points in the text at which it would be very confusing to employ two different forms of the word. I use the lower case for clarity and simplicity.

Finally, although I have not identified individuals, I have retained the actual names and locations of the three parish communities to which I refer throughout the text. After long consideration, I came to the conclusion that to mask them would do damage to the very thing that I most wanted to pay attention to, which is the life and stories of concrete communities. Readers should keep in mind, however, that what I provide here are mere "snapshots," and in no way meant to be definitive evaluations of these communities. In the first place, each of these communities deserves at least a whole volume to tell its story with all the nuances and diversity of viewpoints that rightly exist. There simply is not room for all that could, and perhaps should be said in the scope of the one chapter and various subsequent references that are dedicated to them here. Second, the stories themselves show that there is a dynamism in the lives of these communities, as there is in all things human, which does not allow them to stand still at whatever point in their history I have chosen to highlight. Although their experiences are always instructive in some way for the wider church, the only way truly to know these communities is to live with them, to listen to them attentively, and to keep going back for more.

Chapter One

Church, in Three Places

The institutional structure of the Roman Catholic Church is an enormously complex global organization that is itself only a part of the even more massive tangle of beliefs, stories, connections, affinities, and aversions that constitute Christianity worldwide. It is easy to despair of ever really coming to "know" such a phenomenon. In our age, on the other hand, it is even easier to accept the stuff of headlines, sound bites, and video clips as if they were the full reality of the church. The technology that brings us endless streams of information also inserts added layers of distance and interpretation between us and the sources. It is not surprising that we find it increasingly difficult to feel connected and committed to the institutions that nonetheless dominate our lives. In regard to the church, this state of affairs is further exacerbated by a theological tradition that for centuries thought of the church itself almost entirely through its legal structures, with an emphasis on the papacy—especially since the Protestant Reformation, and even more in the past century and a half. So it is that, forty years after the Second Vatican Council described it as "The People of God," the term "The Church" still immediately conjures pictures of men in robes and mitres, carrying their crosiers down marble-paved aisles.

Yet the church is born, breathes, grows, flourishes, and fades in far more intimate settings, too. On a brief visit to a rural parish in Honduras, Central America, some years ago, I was reminded of this continuous life cycle within the church when I accompanied the parish priest on his semiannual visits to a few of the one hundred fifty villages that made up his pastorate. We drove to one isolated house and celebrated the baptism

1

of several children in families who gathered from a considerable distance in all directions for this special sacrament of beginnings. On muleback and on foot we moved on to a small mountain village, where a rift between the two catechists appointed and trained to lead the weekly community worship had widened into a schism that all the pastor's admonition could not heal. On the return trip we stopped at a cluster of riverside houses whose residents had only recently begun to gather for worship, and celebrated Mass to inaugurate their newly-formed church community. In each of these local groups, for better and for worse, I saw church acting and speaking. As a theologian, I began to reflect on the possible meanings of these experiences for the church as a whole.

Listening theologically to a local Christian community is not an exercise in detachment. It requires connection to a living network of personal relationships. It begins in earnest not when the social statistics about a community have been absorbed, but when the listener has become enough a part of the network that his or her own imagination begins to respond to the visions and struggles of the members of the community. Whether a person be an ordinary community member, an academic researcher, or a pastor, lacking a share in that communal imagination will have its deadening effect on any project. It will guarantee at best a "one size fits all" result, an admission that, in the end, the particular community does not much matter. Conversely, to imagine from the particular community's point of view means that genuine listening has already begun.

Such has been my experience of the three parishes I am about to describe. Years of membership and participation in each of these communities, followed by further years of close correspondence with many parishioners, have provided a variety of opportunities for observation and analysis. They may appear here as "models," "types," or "cases" that perhaps offer some useful insights about other local communities. Yet they do not perform this function as part of some "master plan" over and above them. Rather, they have value as cases because they have shared historical eras and geographical regions with similar communities whose lives can be viewed together for the discernment of various patterns. Of themselves, on the other hand, the individual parishes are in fact uniquely interwoven relationships—personal and institutional, contemporary and historical, human and divine. Like the spiritual mysteries they celebrate, they must be seen from the inside to be grasped, and those who understand them best do not necessarily have the opportunity or acquired skill to share their knowledge broadly.

Such sharing requires viewing the communities' meaning and role against the background of the larger church and world, and also requires use of some particular systematic approach.[1] The collected impressions of these local church communities can then become useful tools. With them, theological reflection can analyze less observable features of the members' own understanding of their parishes. Not trained in theology, these Christians nevertheless make it clear, through their words and actions over the course of years, that they strongly associate a variety of particular meanings with the word "church." Some of these focal meanings will be my starting point here as I try to open a small window on each of the communities. The aim is not merely to share interesting anecdotes, but to underscore the expectation that the experience of a remarkable local community, listened to and considered respectfully, can lead to a deeper understanding of the universal church.

Saint Joseph's Parish

Microcosm in an Old Mill Town. The terms "congregation" or "gathered community" tend to have more resonance for Protestant Christians than for Roman Catholics. The first instinct of Catholic ecclesiology is to view the church as a universal whole. A frequent, but unfortunate, consequence of this starting point is that particular local groupings of Catholics come to be seen as mere subdivisions of that whole. Often forgotten is that each parish or other local community, even when created legally

---

[1] In gathering data I have drawn on some of the qualitative techniques of ethnographic study in order to develop detailed descriptions of the communities in their various aspects. In addition to notes and journals kept of informal observations and conversation, these studies have involved several programs of systematic observation, various courses of interviews, and occasional simple surveys. In the case of both St. Matthew's and St. Joseph's parishes some of the results of the studies have been formally presented on several occasions: William A. Clark, "Church As Classroom: Parochial School Students and the Parish at St. Matthew's" (Unpublished course paper submitted to Prof. Polly Ulichny, Department of Education, Boston College, 1993); Clark, "Ecclesiology and the Life of a Parish Community: Listening to the Voice of the Church On Stanton Street" (S.T.L. Thesis, Weston Jesuit School of Theology, 1994); and Clark, "Crossing Borders, Defending Borders: The Sacred Space of an Old Immigrant Community" (paper delivered to the "Theology and Religious Reflection" section of the American Academy of Religion, November 21, 2004).

by episcopal fiat, corresponds to a particular community of human persons that in a sense must create itself, either before or after any official structure comes into being. On the one hand, such a community receives both its general *raison d'etre* and its specific Christian faith from outside itself (either from ancestors or from the larger Christian community that establishes it). On the other hand, each particular community must make these things its own by the thoughts and actions of its own members. In so doing it plays an active part in the shaping of the tradition that other new, and renewing, communities will receive in turn.

From the mid-nineteenth century through to the end of the twentieth the old Yankee town of Biddeford, Maine, came to be known as a Catholic, Franco-American enclave. The story of how this came about is one of many that can be told of mill towns all over New England and the northeastern U.S. Beginning in the mid-nineteenth century, young men and women from Quebec farms responded to the same prosperity and opportunity that drew immigrants to the U.S. from so many European locales. They began arriving in New England towns for work in the burgeoning textile mills. At first the pattern was one of seasonal or short-term work with the intention of returning—with some added economic security—to family, culture, and language in Quebec. Soon, however, that pattern gave way to the formation of a transplanted French Canadian community of increasingly permanent status. The members of this community were, assuredly, only generically aware of the broader picture of which they were something of a microcosm. Despite elegant words written about them in the parish anniversary book, decades later, they reserved little time for thinking about their place within the sweep of American immigration, their "essentially religious" character as a nation, or any comparison with the ancient Israelites.[2] Specifically, they knew their *own* community, their own dreams and immediate needs, their own families, and the stories, songs, prayers, and practices they preserved.

"*Qui perd la langue, perd la foi*—those who lose their language lose their faith," went the saying ingrained in the French Canadians, surrounded and ruled by Protestant English-speakers as they had been for over a century. The Irish had preceded them to Biddeford, and the French-speaking Catholic Canadians of necessity joined them in wor-

---

[2] *Mémorial du Cinquantenaire de la Fondation de la Paroisse St-Joseph de Biddeford, Maine* (1922) 3.

ship at St. Mary's parish church. Nevertheless, the Quebecois knew that, as soon as they were numerous enough and organized enough as a community, they would have to have their own church. Unlike some other immigrant communities—the Irish themselves, for example—the Francophone (French-speakers') solution to the second-class citizenship with which they were met in their new home was not to fight their way into a place in society beside their Yankee "betters." Rather, they tended to endure their second-class status externally (as, indeed, they had been doing in Canada) and put their considerable social energies into the maintenance and enhancement of their own Francophone subculture. For a very long time thereafter in Maine, "Frenchmen" were the butt of jokes in general society largely because they were not eager to assimilate. Meanwhile, however, their communities thrived internally, and Biddeford was a classic example.

Church: Sign of Continuity, Sign of Change. The most visible early sign of that flourishing in Biddeford was the formation of a new parish expressly for the Francophone community, named for St. Joseph, patron of Canada. The church was understood from the beginning to be the very heart of the community's existence. As an essay in the parish's fiftieth-anniversary program explained in 1922:

> When we look back on fifty years of parish life, we look back on as many years of generous sacrifice for God and his Holy Church. The virtues of justice, probity, and order which make for honest citizens and happy peoples take their origin from parish life. For it is the holy ark where pious traditions are preserved; it is the corner stone of family life; it is the buttress that assures the solidity of worldly government.[3]

The St. Joseph's parish community first gathered for Mass and devotions in 1870 in a building acquired from a local Methodist congregation. There was no question, though, of remaining for long in a made-over Protestant meeting house. A site was purchased and a predictably French Gothic church was planned. The project, however, entered a long process of troubled fundraising and delayed construction, marked by a locally famous contention between the French-born pastor, Jean-François Ponsardin, and the new bishop of Portland, James Augustine Healy.[4]

[3] Ibid. 21.
[4] The series of events is described in Albert S. Foley, s.j., *Bishop Healy: Beloved Outcaste* (New York: Farrar, Straus and Young, 1954) 153–68.

Healy was the first bishop of African-American descent in the U.S., his Irish father having married a former slave in the south, and there were very likely racial overtones in the fight between pastor and bishop. From the very beginning St. Joseph's was a symbol of a Franco-American separateness, over against various forms of mixing, which in some ways contributes to the community's understanding of church to this very day. The classic understanding of the church as a "perfect (i.e., complete) society" was grasped here less as a teaching about the universal church than as a description of its microcosm in Biddeford.

The church building, which was eventually completed in 1883, remains a monument to a certain national brand of Catholic triumphalism. It is situated on a rise only two blocks from the current site of the Irish parish from which it broke off. Its enormous belfry and steeple was once, at 235 feet, the tallest structure in the entire state, and still dominates the city's otherwise humble skyline. It contains three large bells that are still rung, loudly and long, before Sunday Masses and during weddings and funerals. Scenes of the life of Christ on canvases in the clerestory are by nineteenth-century French artists, and the fleur-de-lis emblem adorns the oak pews installed in 1970 as it did the original dark-stained benches. The style of the building is reminiscent of the enormous parish churches of rural Quebec, built to gather the entire population of their small farm communities. There is no mistaking the origins of the population who built the church. Yet there were concessions to their new environment as well. Notably, the building is faced in the familiar, available, affordable red brick of New England, like the huge and now largely vacant mill complexes nearby, rather than the stone of many of its notable Quebecois models.

Despite such slight accommodations, though, St. Joseph's, for the greatest part of its history, existed as a well-defined enclave within quite strict boundaries. The English-speaking Yankee world intruded primarily via the mills and work life. There were, indeed, a few priests assigned to the parish in the early decades who seem to have been "emissaries" from the Irish-dominated establishment (a Father Hurley in 1884–1885; a Father Healy in 1889). By and large, though, the Irish continued to be seen as another people entirely, despite their Catholicism. After the establishment of a second French parish in Biddeford, St. André's, in 1899, even the Francophone community on the east side of the city was somewhat beyond the pale. The parish helped to sustain a nearly-complete set of separate social structures, of which the centerpiece was the parochial grammar school and, eventually, a high school.

There were also social and recreational clubs, mutual assistance, and devotional societies for every age group and both genders. For these practical, working-class people, being French-Canadian, being Catholic, and being members of the St. Joseph's community became practically one and the same thing.

The desire of the first generation of St. Joseph's parishioners to build an institution that would help them preserve their cultural purity, and so also their strong faith, was admirably fulfilled by the parish for a long time. The church and the parish schools sustained a lively sense of French Canadian identity for many decades, and the city itself became largely identified with the Francophone community in Maine. Even at the beginning of the twenty-first century animated French conversations can still be heard on the street, and it is not unusual to meet middle-aged adults who are fluent in this "mother tongue." Yet both the language and the sense of connection with the French Canadian homeland have shifted significantly over time. A striking indication of change can be seen in the souvenir booklet that was printed to celebrate the parish's seventy-fifth anniversary in 1945. While still written entirely in French (the last of its kind), it contained a tribute to the young soldiers and sailors of the parish who were *"au service de la patrie."*[5] The U.S., no longer Canada, had become "the homeland." A genuine Franco-*American* community had come into being and, more and more, blended with the neighbors it had feared, even while retaining its distinctive identity. The parish that had served and been understood as the point of continuity for the community, holding it together by preserving the bond with the homeland, had also become the place where smooth, if glacially slow, assimilation could be fostered.

Eventually the parish would itself come to represent the very changes that were transforming the community, as it channeled the renewed insights of the Second Vatican Council to the people. The universality of the church is no mere doctrinal abstraction, but a concrete personal and interpersonal experience. For a long time it had manifested itself at St. Joseph's primarily in the somewhat ambiguous phenomenon of national parishes existing side by side. The Irish had carried their faith from across the Atlantic and had been there to greet the Francophones when they arrived. The French Canadians, in turn, established their

---

[5] *Paroisse St-Joseph, Biddeford, Maine, 75ᵉ Anniversaire Programme—Souvenir* (1945) 77.

own parish, with its links back to Quebec and, more remotely, to France. It was a process going on in much of the U.S., especially the northeast. By 1970, however, when the parish celebrated its centennial, the concrete and immediate experience of the church's universality was shifting radically. The people of St. Joseph were rapidly being forced to see more plainly that the church was about more than continuity with their own culture of origin and the social coherence of their own ethnic neighborhood.

The centennial book produced in that year chronicles the earliest phases of the transformation. A rather upbeat history of the parish high school ends abruptly with the bald announcement that the building will henceforth house the grammar school.[6] What had happened, in fact, was the closure of the forty-year-old St. Louis High School by order of the Bishop of Portland who, like his predecessors, was Irish-American. The quite sudden decision was part of a general diocesan response to changing economic and personnel conditions. At least among the younger diocesan clergy there was also a widespread, if temporary, uncertainty about the compatibility of parochial education with the Council's broadminded attitude toward modern culture. The announcement of the closure, however—coupled with the news that the "Irish" Jesuit high school twenty miles away in Portland would remain open—gave one final powerful jolt to the ethnic identification of the parish community. Many parishioners remember the event with great bitterness over thirty years later, and it still occasionally surfaces in conversation with a defiant "us against them" tone of voice.

Other changes, however, were less easily attributed to "outsiders." The centennial book was printed almost entirely in English, which, despite Masses in French after Vatican II, was clearly becoming more and more surely the daily language of the community. (Today only one Mass, Saturday evening, is still offered in French for the benefit of senior parishioners.) The post-conciliar renovation of the church took place in the centennial year as well. The work included the removal of the old high and side altars, the replacement of marble and tile flooring with carpet, and the installation of a new tabernacle to the left of the main altar. The anniversary book reports it all quite cheerfully, but many of these changes would be lamented, and would be reversed thirty years later by some of the same active parishioners. In the early nineties two

[6] *St. Joseph Parish Centennial, Biddeford, Maine* (1970) 44.

additional changes eroded the social boundaries of the parish even further. The grammar school was amalgamated with those of the other two Catholic parishes in town, one of which was the original Irish parish, ending the clear ethnic mission of that institution as well. At about the same time some of the administrative functions of the three parishes also merged, foreshadowing a time probably not too distant in which only one parish will serve the entire city.

After 1970 the experience of the church's universality no longer came to St. Joseph's merely as a comfortable affirmation and support of a familiar identity, but also as a sometimes deeply upsetting challenge to the community's chosen social separation. Without very careful analysis of the root causes of change, many members of the community resented the loss of control that the parish seemed to be experiencing in so many ways. The changes, though, like the ones that had brought the French Canadians to Biddeford in the first place, were not entirely imposed, but reflected in important ways the shifting attitudes of the community itself. Through all these developments, moreover, this local church community was struggling to renegotiate its identity within the universal church and to reappropriate its Catholic faith for yet another new setting. In all of this it was demonstrating that the specific tasks of the church's overall mission of continuity remain in the hands of local communities.

Owning the Church. In a basement room now used for catechism classes at St. Joseph's still hang the elaborately engraved and framed income reports for two of the many church bazaars held in the last decades of the nineteenth century. They represent the intense dedication of the working people who provided the funds for the building of St. Joseph's church. The fight between Father Ponsardin and Bishop Healy had centered on the accounts for the building project and Ponsardin's general lack of regard for the bishop's prerogatives where the property was concerned. Regardless of the bishop's eventual "victory" in the battle for control, however, there has never been any doubt in the minds of the people of St. Joseph's as to whose church this really is. The building was bought and paid for, maintained and restored, by the ongoing commitment of the community of which it is a visible sign. That community "owns" the church in many different senses, even if not in the sense of possessing the title deed.

Yet to claim that the local community in a particular place shapes and defines in great measure the church as it is understood there is not to claim that the community is or ought to be autonomous. While it is a

primary way in which the spiritual reality of the church is literally embodied, there is nothing quasi-magical or even necessarily especially
virtuous about a local church community. It is human. It does, and must,
respond both to the larger structures of the church and to its own cultural and historical context; this is both its strength and its weakness.
Moreover, like all human structures, the local church community requires effective leadership and vision. For all these reasons, the period
of gradual decline in morale and participation that the St. Joseph's community experienced in the 1970's and 1980's was almost inevitable, and
a good mirror of what was happening elsewhere. The coincidence of the
internal sea change brought about by Vatican II, on the one hand, and
the even more immense social changes of the 1960's, on the other hand,
brought initial excitement. Yet it also brought confusion, contention,
enormous leadership challenges, and gradual loss of group morale. In
the mid-nineties, a new pastor arrived to find a crumbling infrastruc-
ture and a fatigued, diminishing, and divided congregation. It was all
aptly symbolized in the rainwater buckets in the church aisles, the roped-
off "falling-plaster zones," and the peeling paint on the rectory.

At the local level such sights can be signals either to throw in the
towel or to rouse the community to urgent action. Predictably, it was the
arrival of the new pastor, an energetic man who had spent part of his
childhood as a member of the parish, that decided the question in favor
of action. Able both to listen and to challenge, he recognized the signs as
a call to renewal of parish identity and pride. Standard parish histories
might read as though such a leader were entirely responsible for the
positive changes that followed. But while this priest had built a reputa-
tion as the dynamic pastor of a rather avant-garde parish in another
Maine city, it was clear to him that no preconceived agenda would accomplish the revitalization St. Joseph's required. He would allow the
community to evolve in the direction its own conservative history most
strongly suggested. During his pastorate St. Joseph's re-emerged as what
many would consider a vibrant "neo-traditionalist" parish.

The unspoken, largely unnoticed negotiation between pastor and
parishioners over the character of the parish has played out over the
course of ten years. As it had at the beginning of the community's history, the church building has again become the symbol of vitality at St.
Joseph's. The first project was the construction of a new daily Mass
chapel in a portion of the church basement, which had once served as
additional Sunday worship space. The idea at this point was not restoration, but a practical renovation. Rather than echoing the original

arrangement of the lower church, the new chapel featured a tasteful but homey atmosphere with carpeted floor, indirect lighting, dark wood furniture, and individual padded chairs. There were various practical innovations intended to increase its flexibility and usefulness for a variety of church functions. Organized resistance among some of the parishioners to the exclusion of a tabernacle from the design (in favor of the single tabernacle already located in the upper church) was instructive for future efforts. Largely, however, the response to the chapel was very positive. The community's energy and enthusiasm began to build.

With the next phase, exterior restoration, the theme of rectifying past errors began to emerge. A decorative slate roof matching the original design replaced inadequate asphalt shingles installed in the 1970's. Neglected damage from a lightning strike in the steeple, and long-deferred repointing of the bricks, were attended to. When the work was completed, an outdoor parish celebration included a telescope trained on the detailed shingle work and gilding of the steeple. By the time the final phase of physical renewal was undertaken—in the main worship space—attention had turned fully and pointedly to "restoration" rather than "renovation." The once-hailed post-Vatican II remodeling had come to represent the malaise of the era that followed it. For the pastor and for the consultant hired to design the restored space, emphasis was on removal of features introduced in 1970 that were both dated and out of harmony with the building's original gothic style. Red and green carpets, '70s style paneling, and squarish, light oak altar furnishings were all to be banished. Meanwhile, parishioners—the older ones in particular—emphasized the return of what they most missed from the previous era. Support for the project was very high, but points of tension emerged precisely around the various ways in which the "restored" church would not be sufficiently like the "old" church. The life-sized crucifix and an unobstructed view of the tabernacle in the center of the sanctuary were most frequently mentioned. As one parishioner put it, "Why call it a restoration if you are not going to put it back the way it was?"

What was happening to St. Joseph's, however, was not a simple return to the past. It is true that the social revival that was accompanying the physical rebuilding brought back many familiar kinds of activities, from parish suppers to service organizations. Many parishioners also expressed satisfaction that, unlike specific nearby parishes that they would readily name, they did not have to contend with architectural novelty and liturgical experimentation. Yet this very comparison was one indication of the new group consciousness that was evolving. The community that only a few years earlier had made a newly ordained assistant priest feel unwelcome for not being able to speak French was now far less focused on its ethnic and physical boundaries. Instead, it was becoming more widely known for its "traditional" atmosphere. A considerable number of people, including young families and many with little personal stake in the Franco-American identity, began to attend church at St. Joseph's. They came even from outside the official boundaries of the parish, those invisible lines that earlier generations would have felt the guilt of disloyalty for crossing.

The "old time" gatherings and activities, as well, did not return merely on their old terms. The parish found one opportunity for social outreach to the wider community in providing low-cost luncheons for bereaved families. The frequent funerals had once seemed only an occasion for lamenting the passing of the most loyal of St. Joseph's parishioners, but now are an opportunity for strengthening bonds as well. A parish Knights of Columbus council was created, despite the fact that a long-standing, though insufficiently active, citywide organization existed. This council promptly established a "Squires" circle for boys of the parish, which had never existed before, and which was soon thriving, adding a distinctive note to what some considered an insufficient multi-parish youth outreach. Most novel of all in this "revival," the large Victorian rectory, gradually restored with the same vigor and taste as the church building, was opened as the venue for several high-profile parish events, including a completely public open house at Christmas time. This, of course, would have been an unheard-of mingling of clergy and laity in the "old days."

Saint Joseph's has used the energy and vision of its pastor. Yet it has neither been remade in his image nor attempted a simple return to the past (neither of which could ever account for the current vigor of the community). Rather, the community has made a run at holding onto its old identity within an entirely changed context. Along the way it is demonstrating that the church is more than just a bulwark *against* change (though it can certainly preserve and nurture some cherished, but challenged, traditional values). Neither is the church merely about discipline imposed from another time and place (though traditional devotions do indeed flourish at St. Joseph's, from rosary before Mass to weekly eucharistic adoration). At St. Joseph's and, undoubtedly, parishes like it in many places, the church is emerging as an *intentional* community. It is no longer built up so much by the natural growth of a stable population (though there are still many who were originally members by *heritage*) as by the deliberate commitment of numerous individuals. Further, what seems a new development is actually very congenial to the understanding of leadership that St. Joseph's parishioners have long held: leadership is *local* and *familiar*, but "outsiders" (geographically, ethnically, socially) are readily welcomed and cooperated with, to the extent that they are able and willing to enter into the network of relationships that constitute this local church community.

Saint Thomas Aquinas Parish

Class and Gospel in Jamaica. Saint Joseph's demonstrates a church community whose identity has long been tied to its ethnic cohesion. By contrast, the story of St. Thomas Aquinas in Kingston, Jamaica, suggests that a local church community can also draw its identity from the very tensions and lack of cohesion that characterize it. From the point of view of ecclesiology, a local community may offer a keener understanding of the situation and meaning of the church through its reaction to adverse conditions than to favorable ones. In the end, both alike are part of the human reality that contains and shapes the proclamation of the Gospel for us today just as it did for Jesus and the first disciples.

The island of Jamaica in the Caribbean has been fertile soil for the growing of such crops as sugarcane and bananas. It has managed a rather less abundant harvest of Catholic Christians, if we allow population statistics to be the guide. Three hundred fifty years after Protestant English raiders booted the Catholic Spanish from the island that they themselves had taken from the native Arawaks, Catholic believers comprise about five per cent of the total Jamaican population. The rest, overwhelmingly Christian and very largely the descendants of slaves who were first evangelized in the eighteenth century by Moravian, Baptist, and Methodist missionaries, tend toward various mainline Protestant and Evangelical churches.[7] A continuous official Catholic presence was not reestablished in Jamaica until 1792, when the government granted permission for a resident priest to serve the small population of Spanish merchants who had settled on the island. These were soon after joined by French-speaking planter-class refugees from the

---

[7] Francis J. Osborne, *History of the Catholic Church in Jamaica* (Chicago: Loyola University Press, 1988) 170–72.

slave-led revolution in nearby Haiti.[8] Although a small number of slaves owned by Catholic masters were baptized, from then on (though for changing reasons) the Catholic Church in Jamaica was seen by most people as a foreign, and generally upper-class, institution.

Despite its quite clearly marginal status on these counts, however, by the late twentieth century the church in Jamaica had established a high profile for itself. Many fine parish church buildings and an enormous Byzantine-style cathedral in Kingston were presided over by an archbishop. For over a century Catholics both lay and religious had contributed to the maintenance of a growing network of excellent schools. From the beginning these institutions had enrolled Catholic and non-Catholic students alike and had served the children of all social classes (although separately at first). The concern of the church for education and various other social services gradually expanded its exposure to the broad spectrum of Jamaican society. Although it never grew to include a very considerable percentage of Jamaicans as formal members, the church became increasingly known and attractive to many.

Eventually, while retaining its popular associations with the more educated and well-to-do, the Catholic population began to reflect the complex mixture of ethnicities, races, and social classes that came to characterize Jamaican society. The national motto, "Out of Many, One People," while evoking this complexity, is somewhat optimistic in its suggestion of harmony. The distinctions within this rich mix are still of great social importance, particularly when it comes to economic class, and this has held true within the church as well. Wealthier Jamaican Catholics have typically looked to the church and its institutions as buttresses for their own social position, upholders of strong discipline in areas such as work ethic and sexual mores, and the providers of dignified and refined ritual. These same functions have suggested to many middle-class members that support of the church comports with their own desire for social advancement. For the very poor the dominance of wealthier persons within the church has also signaled a potential source of material assistance. At the same time, less educated persons often find in the rich symbols of Catholicism a deep spiritual connection that can nevertheless take quite superstitious forms. Despite the overwhelmingly Protestant cultural milieu, Catholic pictures, objects, and gestures show up with great frequency in "Revivalist" churches,

---

[8] Ibid. 143–51, 173.

Jamaica's version of the Afro-Christian syncretism to be found throughout the Caribbean.[9] All of this helps to explain the existence and circumstances of St. Thomas Aquinas Church in Kingston, which sits at a literal crossroads of these various class groups.

"Aquinas Centre," as it was originally known and is still often called, was built on the fringe of the academic campus at Mona, northeast of the center of Kingston, in 1962. That year—also the year of Jamaica's national independence—the campus achieved its status as the University of the West Indies, after having been a college of the University of London since 1948. Aquinas was built on an open, flexible plan, to serve the Catholic population of the university—students and faculty—in a variety of ways. The work of early pastors established a pattern of regular sacramental worship in the ground floor chapel, with the upstairs rooms serving as chaplain's residence and meeting facilities. Administratively the center was at first a chapel of Sts. Peter and Paul parish, the main church being about two miles away. For many Catholics associated with the university, though, Aquinas became the ordinary place for Sunday Mass and their primary church community, engaging in a range of services, activities, and outreach projects. As others from the nearby area began to join them, the archbishop came to recognize the wisdom of establishing St. Thomas Aquinas as a separate canonical parish. It received territory carved out of Sts. Peter and Paul parish and membership drawn from that territory as well as from those personally associated with the university. This arrangement both acknowledged the reality of the community that had begun to form and set the stage for the development of that community according to a dynamic that has been intense with both inspiring creativity and maddening difficulty.

Kingston is remarkable for the close physical proximity of many comfortable, even wealthy, Jamaicans to those who are quite desperately poor. In general, "uptown" (literally higher up the slopes of the "bowl" in which the city is built) and "downtown" (the area of the original eighteenth-century town near the harbor) designate rich and poor sections respectively. However, in many parts of the city a class of people with a dramatically different lifestyle is only a turn or two down the road from anyone. So it is at Aquinas. The church building itself is situated on a spacious piece of property it shares with the

---

[9] See Edward Seaga, *Revival Cults in Jamaica: Notes Toward a Sociology of Religion* (Kingston: Institute of Jamaica, 1982).

convent/retreat center of the Ursuline Sisters. Backed on the east by a steep precipice, the property faces the university's hospital and medical school campus across a busy road to the west. This campus is contiguous to the main academic campus and to the quiet neighborhoods of comfortable ranch-type houses where many students, faculty, and other professional people live. North of the church is a small "yard" (a cluster of simple houses on a single property) and a busy commercial area. It is the neighborhood to the south, a "squatters'" settlement called Mona Common, that provides the sharpest contrast. A tract of public land completely filled with simple houses built without title, it is crowded with hundreds of inhabitants. It is characterized by the hand-to-mouth existence of much of its population, the largely outdoor living dictated by the inadequacy of most of the houses, and a predictable propensity for violence.

The proximity and neediness of Mona Common have tied this neighborhood in particular to St. Thomas Aquinas Church. The original core of the church community consisted largely of university-connected persons and other residents of the areas beyond the campus. Though they were neighbors, the desperately poor families and individuals who were moving onto Mona Common land at about the same time that the Centre was built were rarely seen as members of Aquinas. By the time the Centre became a canonical parish, however, it was already deeply involved with the Mona Common neighborhood (and to a lesser extent with the neighborhood in the river valley below the precipice, called Tavern). The quality of this relationship, though, has been changeable over the decades, depending on the efforts of particular parishioners and the emphases of various pastoral leaders. Older parishioners share many stories of assistance given and received between individuals. One pastor in the 1970's is said to have physically put himself in the path of bulldozers that were sent by the government to clear the squatters off the land. Under his influence a social service center was built on Mona Common. However, some residents of the very neighborhood it was intended to serve came to see this effort as an intrusion. To many church members it was only a distant curiosity. Eventually the center succumbed to the combination of a suspicious fire and the later effects of the devastating Hurricane Gilbert in 1988.

In the meantime others pursued smaller-scale outreach efforts at the church itself, including a small reading class and a charismatic-style prayer group. Following the hurricane, when large numbers of Mona Common residents took shelter in the concrete church building, a renewed period of direct ministry to the residents of the Common began. It was based largely on the people's expectation of material assistance, greatly reinforced in the wake of the hurricane. It was also strengthened, however, by the development of new relationships between parishioners and residents. A number of young men were employed doing odd jobs at the church and for some of the wealthier church members. Two stalwarts of the parish began a sewing class for women and girls. The government included the church in negotiations (which ultimately failed) toward a planned relocation of the squatter community. Through all of it there was a growing hope that residents of the Common would accept the invitation to worship at Aquinas and become increasingly a part of the church community themselves. The pastoral team undertook a formal effort at evangelization among a group of teenagers, and about a dozen were eventually baptized and welcomed officially into the church.

Yet there has always been caution, hesitation, and even opposition to these connections. Whereas individuals might be welcomed to the church and dealt with kindly there, the report that a middle-class member of the parish has visited the Common itself is often met with a curious mixture of alarm, awe, and amusement. This is as true on the part of residents of the Common itself as it is on the part of outsiders. This reaction arises from the extreme divergence of lifestyles, and their associated values, between the majority poor and the much smaller percentage of middle- and upper-class persons in Jamaica. The divergence takes in everything from language (Jamaican Patois versus standard English) to work ethic (freelance day labor versus steady employment) to styles of worship (energetic sound and movement versus decorous structure). The social separation, of course, reinforces the differences and thereby strengthens itself. In an atmosphere of economic hardship, crime, violence, suspicion, and genuine fear inevitably accompany this separation. In the end the class division provides the context for the church's understanding of its own work at Aquinas.

Church: Source of Help, Source of Interference. Observing the interaction between Aquinas and its neighborhood quickly suggests the notion of "church as helper." The Christian tradition itself, of course, enshrines charity as a primary value for church communities, but it is individual communities that must receive and embody this value. As the early story of St. Joseph's parish showed, that reception might take place through a chiefly *internal* focus on the needs of community members.

At Aquinas, however, the situation demands that the community's out-reach embrace a very wide variety of people, many of whom have only a peripheral connection with the church itself. In recent years, despite a more security-conscious outlook that includes higher walls, stronger fences, and brighter lights, important outreach programs have tended to survive regardless: a fund providing assistance for children's school fees, the sewing class, scouting and youth groups, and both emergency and developmental assistance given to various individuals.

However, the complexity of the situation guarantees that, while the idea of "church as helper" is always taken on and appreciated in some way throughout the community, it will never be a simple notion at Aquinas. For every social class, the local church is also at times a hin-drance, an external force that imposes itself between persons and their wishes or expectations, a "stumbling block." It is the community as a whole—rich and poor, core and marginal members alike—that must continually wrestle with this paradox and draw its self-understanding as church from the midst of the struggle. This profound and immensely important work simply cannot be dictated from a "higher" level of au-thority or by any set of general norms.

The members and associates of the parish have various kinds of rela-tionships to this complex identity. The more comfortable and educated members include faculty, students, and employees of the university (who are frequently non-Jamaican), professional and business people from nearby neighborhoods, and a variety of foreign visitors, often vol-unteer workers on longer or shorter stays. They are good and generous people who generally understand themselves as "helpers," reaching out to the poor in and around the church. Their actual activity can range from broad involvement with church projects as "active mem-bers," through regular and generous work as "parish leaders," to deep personal involvement with the lives of poor people. Because, for many of them, this outreach confirms and structures an important part of their own self-understanding, and contributes to a stronger commu-nity, they are also "helped" by the church. In both its practical unfold-ing, therefore, and its effect on their lives, the essentially personal nature of the helping church is displayed.

This, however, is only part of the story. The church is a place where these relatively well-to-do members are more or less forced to face a class of people with whom they can experience intense discomfort. It can sometimes appear, therefore, as an obstacle to the "reasonable" so-cial arrangements that the upper and middle classes might desire. The consequent frustration can be seen in passive or active opposition to potentially revolutionary ideas such as the "preferential option for the poor." It is displayed when traditional upper-class Jamaican disgust with "indiscipline" is triggered by incidents as diverse as the occasional use of Jamaican Patois in a homily or perceived permissiveness regarding the marital and family arrangements of the poor. At Aquinas the fear of the crime and violence associated with Mona Common (both in imagination and in objective reality) can become coupled with sometimes intense resentment toward residents of the Common who are seen to be "taking advantage" of the community's generosity. Even among the most dedicated church members from the wealthier classes, all of these considerations can lead to what might elsewhere be called "ministerial burnout"—the need to step back from church outreach activities for a time, or even permanently.

By the needy, likewise, the "church as helper" is experienced in a variety of ways. Because of its conspicuous location Aquinas attracts a large number of people begging for money for various needs both real and apocryphal. Successive pastors have devised different arrangements for responding to these requests, ranging from budgeting a ten per cent tithe of all income to simple refusal. Most of the time, however, a network of "informal clients" has existed, "regulars" who know they can get at least some assistance by going to the church. Although most of these are seen rarely, if ever, at worship services, they play a conspicuous role in the way the church functions and understands itself. Sometimes they directly affect the way in which members of the community relate to each other. In some sense, then, they too are "members" of the community. A similar, though somewhat distinct, group might be called "personal protégés," people who become attached to one particular pastor, staff person, or church member, and through them may even become very much involved in church activities. The nature of the relationship is such, however, that the protégé does not come to be seen by the community as a regular member, and should the particular patron depart the scene for some reason, the protégé will probably drift away also. There are needy persons, of course, whom the whole community comes to accept as regular members because of their habitual attendance at worship and participation in activities. This status suggests that the help such persons receive from the church is of a more complex kind that includes their recognized place in the community's social structure. Maintaining this place, moreover, has involved their ability to be skillfully deferent toward the wealthier and better educated members, and this ability in turn has involved a certain aspiration on the part of these members to the lives and values of the middle and upper classes themselves. These are, then, the "good, needy Catholics" that many community members argue should be the primary (or even the sole) beneficiaries of the church's outreach efforts.

This description of the various ways in which poor persons seek help from the Aquinas church community helps make it clear why many of these same people also find in the church an obstacle as well as a help. For those who are merely seeking material assistance of whatever kind, Aquinas appears a logical place to turn. It is well understood that churches in general, and Catholic churches in particular, make material charity an important part of their mission. Further, in the case of Aquinas both the well-kept grounds and the constant presence of obviously well-to-do people encourage the conviction that this community has considerable resources to dispose of. As long as the requested aid is given, these assumptions and cues point toward the church as helper. Yet the very same things represent graphically one of the major negative features of the lives of the poor: the enormous and apparently unbridgeable gap between themselves and wealthier Jamaicans. If ever a request is refused, this fact turns hope into scandal almost instantly, and the resentment that is seldom far below the surface will often enough issue in a curse, or in some more clever gossip about what does and does not go on with "di Cat'olic."

A more ominous complex of neglect and marginalization is sometimes encountered by residents of Mona Common and other poor neighborhoods served by Aquinas who have genuinely attempted to be recognized as fully active members of the community. In such cases the problem is as much, and more, a failure to respond to cultural needs for a certain type of worship and to the ordinary human need for involvement and influence as it is an inability to satisfy particular material needs. Community members from the poorer neighborhoods are generally much less likely than other members to have grown up in a Catholic household or, even more certainly, among many Catholic neighbors and friends. The overwhelmingly Protestant evangelical flavor of the predominant Christian culture supplies for them, prior to their active involvement at Aquinas, a set of expectations about "what church ought to be." Disappointments and misunderstandings are almost inevitable under these circumstances. One young woman thanked the coordinator of a parish retreat program, who had gone to considerable trouble to invite well-known speakers for several consecutive nights of lively music, prayer, and reflection, by saying, "We're moving ahead; now if we could only get someone who can *prrreach!*" Some persons, including those who experience satisfying protégé relationships, may be able successfully to modify their expectations in the light of the community's actual strengths. This happened to some extent, for example, in the baptismal preparation program for teens. Yet the process is seldom thoroughgoing, and those who are dissatisfied will often seek the remedy elsewhere (as did the young woman in search of Pentecostal-style preaching).

The local church is fundamentally a personal community. With regard to parish outreach activities this becomes particularly clear in the Jamaican context. Here enormous financial and logistical difficulties present themselves whenever one attempts to go beyond simple, direct assistance of needy members and neighbors toward the establishment of structured charity. There are, indeed, a few outstanding examples of this having taken place on the island. Yet it is interesting that the established institution then, by its very nature, takes on a life of its own and becomes, both in perception and in organizational and legal fact, a different entity. In the end outreach that is genuinely an effort of the local church community seems, also of its own nature, to rise and fall with the efforts of one or a few key individuals. This fact makes the "church as helper" both a very powerful and a very fragile image, entrusted in large measure to the work of the local community. At Aquinas, as in nearly every local community of which I am aware, stories abound of those individuals whose lives and perspectives have been deeply affected by the assistance given to them by one or a few particular representatives of the community. Also plentiful are stories of those who have turned away, either from this particular community or from the church altogether, because of being rebuffed (or thinking they have been) when looking for assistance from the community.

Whether the church appears to such people as "helper" or as "obstacle" depends very much on how the community is employing its resources for outreach at any given time. When the community is most carefully responding to the actual needs of the real persons in and around it, the aspect of a "helping" church comes through. When, on the other hand, the community has focused its attention more on its own internal coherence and security (as it must sometimes do), it may appear as an obstacle to people with particular needs. Whether or not such people succeed in finding help, their understanding of what the church is will be shaped in some measure by the proclamation they hear in the community's attitude toward them. The understanding of church held by the active members themselves will be shaped in similar fashion: the community that is constantly reaching out gives a very different impression to its members about what it means to participate in a Christian community than the one that is entirely inwardly focused.

Stealing the Church. The road frontage of Aquinas's property includes a broad lawn, quite lush during the rainier seasons of the year, with a large tree in the center. In addition to buffering the center itself from the noise of the street, the lawn serves as a parking place for the vehicles of the well-to-do who attend Mass on the weekends. It is also, of course, an attractive playground, and at various times the young men and boys from Mona Common have been welcomed to play soccer and cricket between the road and the tree. In recent years, however, during the same period as the addition of new walls and fences around the property, a large sign with prominent white lettering has appeared, affixed to the tree at the behest of the church council: "Please! No ball playing on the lawn!" The sign is an emblem of the tensions inherent in the community's composition. It underlines the unsurprising tendency of most Aquinas parishioners to judge the community based on how well it responds to the reality of their particular social class. The typically indignant exclamation of one impeccably dressed woman as she encountered ballplayers at the church door—"Ugh! These dirty boys!"—is matched by the equally class-conscious cry of a disgruntled Mona Common woman—"Is pure 'big people' up ah church! [There are only big shots at church!]" Accompanying the remarks in each case is the suggestion that the "other group" has violated the speaker's entitlement to church property.

Themes of *property* and *theft* have been quite conspicuous generally in discussions at Aquinas, and this seems to mirror trends in Jamaican society as a whole. The issues have ranged from internal disagreements about the boundary of church grounds as opposed to convent and retreat house grounds, to the perennial problems of neighbors tapping utility lines or allowing their goats to graze on the church flowerbeds, to outright burglary and even armed robbery in the churchyard. From the point of view of people with fairly abundant material resources, who contribute to the church from those resources, all of these issues are part of a constant battle to maintain their common property amidst a sea of people who do not respect their stewardship. This approach accounts for the indignation of members from this segment of the community at those times when they have perceived staff and pastors as actually encouraging some of the depredations they have struggled hard to prevent.

On the other hand, those persons with very few material resources tend to approach the world—church property included—with a kind of "hunter/gatherer" mentality that seeks the means of survival wherever they can be found. This approach is sometimes quite openly buttressed with a version of the familiar "finders' keepers" proverb, liberally applied. On one occasion the pastor had to mediate a serious rift between two active parishioners, one a university professor and the other a young mother from Mona Common: the mother's son found a winning raffle ticket that had been dropped by the professor's daughter at a church fair, and proceeded to claim the prize of a resort weekend. Both parties defended themselves with what they took to be inviolable moral principle. Each also suggested that the other's class seemed to think it "owned the church."

These apparently trivial, mundane issues do, then, lead to the direct question at Aquinas, "Who *does* own the church?" Is one group or the other attempting to steal it away? The answer, of course, is entirely bound up with one's idea of what the church actually is, and who are its legitimate members. One part of the community takes the church implicitly as institutional support for middle- and upper-class values, even to the extent of taking real offense at finding the pastor doing yard work, for example. There is plenty of history, custom, and even doctrine to support this approach. The church in Jamaica, as elsewhere, has provided prominent educational and social structures, promoted honesty, discipline, marriage and family values, and established a connection with power structures both on and off the island. Genuine membership in the community seen from this point of view is established by a parishioner's longstanding record of activity and giving, either of money or of time. These criteria are understood as class-neutral, which is why wealthy members of the community can be quite enthusiastic about those of far more modest means who "join in" and "do their part" in expected ways.

Of course, these same values establish the church community's responsibility for the neighborhood in which it is located. The mass of poorer people is not forgotten, but neither is it usually understood as an actual part of the community. Many of those very people, however, consider Aquinas to be part of the structure of their lives. It is physically "next door," they have often—even if not regularly—participated in either Mass or prayer meetings there, and they have also received material help and encouragement. They are not happy to be seen as outsiders. In a move that strikes many of the more comfortable parishioners as sheer opportunism, they may describe themselves as "members" even by virtue of how often they have been given assistance by one of the priests or parishioners. They tend to see the church first and foremost as a set of practical relationships within which they obviously have a place and a certain influence. Those who look with suspicion on their claim to membership are "fighting against" them.

The implicit question of genuine membership lingers on at Aquinas without real resolution. In the meantime, at the administrative level, the question of ownership faces another familiar complication. Legally the land and building belong to the Archbishop of Kingston. Ordinarily this important fact stays in the background and does not impose itself very noticeably onto the life and struggles of the community (despite a former archbishop's occasional indulgence in the proclamation, "I am corporation sole!" in the midst of property-related discussions). From time to time, however, the community is reminded that, regardless of how it comes to understand itself, it must also account for its place in the wider church. Renovation projects involving more than a few hundred dollars have to be reviewed at the archdiocesan level. Archdiocesan meetings and gatherings may be scheduled to use the facilities, and generally take precedence over other community plans. On one occasion the archbishop arrived unannounced and toured the property with a group of persons who were seeking a location for a major Marian shrine in the archdiocese. All such incidents raise a basic unsettling question: does the community that has gathered at the Aquinas Centre property, however it may decide to describe itself, ultimately owe its existence to structures and persons that are ordinarily quite outside its day-to-day struggles for definition and effectiveness? In one way or another the question confronts all local Catholic communities.

Saint Matthew's Parish

New Immigrants in the Inner City. "Globalization" is a recent buzzword in our culture. The reality of intense intercultural exchange, challenge, and development, however, has been a part of the church's history in various ways for most of its existence. Dimensions of this are quite evident in the stories of St. Joseph's and Aquinas. Saint Matthew's parish, in the Dorchester section of the city of Boston, adds yet another strand to the network, for here Euro-American immigrant history and contemporary Caribbean realities have met to create one more unique community.

Founded as a "mission church" in 1890 by up-and-coming Irish residents freshly arrived from in-town Boston, St. Matthew's was part of the transformation of Dorchester from a separate rural town to an urban annex. As the Irish began arriving and putting their permanent mark on the area, parish churches sprang up all over. The buildings, of course, were an emphatic statement, part of the reinvention of Boston as an Irish-American, Roman Catholic city, a character that clings to it today despite more than a century of newer immigrations and further transformations. In this way St. Matthew's and its numerous sister parishes throughout Boston figure in an ongoing large-scale movement that has brought ethnicities and religions from across Europe and around the world into close proximity with one another, for better and for worse.

St. Matthew's is also another reminder that large-scale changes happen in the small-scale settings where both their causes and their consequences are lived out by real people. Unlike the French Canadians in Biddeford at the time of St. Joseph's founding, the Irish in Boston by 1890 were a huge and influential, if not yet dominant, group. It would be easy to think of them only as the more established classes often did—as an undifferentiated mass. The parish churches of Boston, though, provided focal points, that might otherwise have been missing, for neighborhood cohesion and tangible expressions of daily faith, as the people organized, saved, and built.[10] Eventually, all over Dorchester, people would as easily refer to their parish as to their street address. St. Matthew's came into existence because the working-class Catholics clustered around Codman Square built themselves an identity and had determination and material means enough to express it in a parish church of their own. From the opening of its temporary wooden chapel in 1891, through provision of an impressive rectory and its occupancy

---

[10] Note Jim Castelli and Joseph Gremillion, *The Emerging Parish: The Notre Dame Study of Catholic Life Since Vatican II* (San Francisco: Harper & Row, 1987) 11: "The history of Catholic parishes often seems a history of fund raisers and new buildings, and for a time it was common to joke about the Church's 'edifice complex.' But it was the Catholic people who demanded the buildings for churches, schools, and meeting halls to provide the symbols and instruments of a worship community. Buildings and, therefore, finances posed a problem for the church in both urban and rural areas."

of a completed church basement for Mass, to the dedication of its new church nearly a quarter-century later and the addition of adjacent school and convent buildings, the community slowly took shape. Like all parishes, St. Matthew's was officially created by the act of a bishop (in Boston, an emphatically Irish bishop). Yet its appearance was also a central part of a local community's coming into existence.[11]

The grand new Romanesque church building, which the parishioners of St. Matthew's were able to complete and dedicate by 1923, escaped the kind of large-scale 1970's remodeling undertaken at St. Joseph's in Biddeford. Ironically, the building conveys to this day a certain permanence and stability, partly because the community that might have paid for massive renovations began to evaporate at just the time it would otherwise have been called on to do so. Just as the community's emergence illustrated the expansive feel of the American church in the first half of the twentieth century, so its disintegration mirrored the apparent suddenness of profound change in the second half. Postwar prosperity encouraged the suburbanization of the parish's traditional population, and a new immigration, this time of mostly Protestant African-Americans from the south, began. The year 1964 marked both the arrival of the first African-American Catholics in the parish and the last year of numerical growth St. Matthew's would see for a long time to come. Shortly thereafter, amidst Boston's dramatic struggle over the issue of court-mandated busing for public school integration, racial tension joined economic advancement as a motive for "white flight" from the neighborhood. Today a few parishioners recall times in the late 1960's and early 1970's when every house on a given block was offered for sale.

By 1982, when the fourth new pastor in nine years arrived at St. Matthew's, the neighborhood had undergone a thorough transformation. Far from the desirable residential area the nineteenth-century Irish had sought, south Dorchester was now the "inner city"—an area of poverty and crime neglected by the wider municipality and abandoned by many of the "mainline" religious communities that had once served

[11] Charles R. Morris, *American Catholic: The Saints and Sinners Who Built America's Most Powerful Church* (New York: Vintage Books, 1997) sets the Irish ascendancy in the much larger context of the religious response to the potato famine of the 1840s, the American church of the mid-nineteenth century, and the cultural impact of massive immigration to the U.S. The significance of local experience on the shape of the overall phenomenon is nonetheless evident in his account, as for example in his description of the Irish town of Skibbereen (ibid. 26–29).

it. The membership of St. Matthew's itself had fallen so low that the future of the parish seemed in doubt. Yet still another immigration was in process. The neighborhood began to receive in substantial numbers many traditionally Catholic people from the Caribbean and elsewhere and, small as it was, the Catholic community at St. Matthew's was there to welcome them. A vibrant St. Matthew's community began to reemerge as these newcomers, particularly the Haitians, gradually became the dominant and defining group. Like their predecessors in the neighborhood, these immigrants brought their devotion to Catholicism with them. Yet, although they moved into solid buildings that spoke of permanence, they brought a very different expression and a different set of needs. St. Matthew's was about to receive a new community character.

Church: Place of Gathering, Place of Division. The peculiar current shape of the St. Matthew's community comes in large part from the rich mixture of cultural and linguistic characteristics in its membership. After years of truly multicultural ministry, during which large parish celebrations would often employ as many as five languages, it is now most widely known as a Haitian parish. Yet within this community itself lie divisions somewhat similar to those seen at Aquinas in Kingston: some Haitians are more comfortable with standard French, others with the Creole dialect, a distinction that, in Haiti as in Jamaica, has class implications. To this is added the growing differentiation between those who arrived in Boston as adults and those who have been raised, entirely or in part, within the English-speaking, and African-American influenced, popular culture. Moreover, St. Matthew's still retains a considerable non-Haitian community, including immigrant West Indians and some Euro-Americans, both longtime residents and others attracted to the parish from outside the area for a variety of reasons. There even remains a tiny Spanish-speaking contingent.

Each of these linguistic groups and subgroups has a different history within the parish, a different reason for being present in it, and undoubtedly a different perception of it. This diversity contributes to the existence of remarkable centers of creativity and openness within the community structure. Frequent and enthusiastic spiritual gatherings of Haitian people bring a distinctive liveliness to the parish, whether the devotions and energetic singing of the Haitian youth group, the long weekly prayers and benedictions of the Creole charismatic meeting, or the numerous special occasions marked with great musical efforts and spoken tributes at the noontime Sunday Masses. The Sunday liturgy of the English-speaking segment of the community is marked by a sense that the congregation's members know one another well and happily participate in the rites of the Eucharist together, along with "local rituals" such as holding hands across the aisles during the singing of the "Our Father" (invariably to a tune composed by a parish organist more than twenty years ago). The parochial school is another locus of creative energy, running at near capacity with neighborhood students from many different nationalities and including on its staff several teachers who have held their posts for decades. To varying degrees over the past twenty years other social outreaches (parish visiting, direct assistance, adult education, neighborhood development, etc.) have also been organized and managed by a combination of outside volunteers, concerned parishioners, and regular parish staff.

What from one point of view appears as rich diversity, though, from other points of view can also be seen as the source of threatening division and struggle. Overall, the parishioners of St. Matthew's have been able to move beyond simple ethnic and linguistic factions. As the balance between Haitian and non-Haitian populations has shifted, however, some of the older parishioners who are used to identifying St. Matthew's as "multicultural" have grown increasingly defensive. At the same time the divisions within the Haitian community have become more significant for the parish as a whole.

Furthermore, there are signs that important fault lines lie elsewhere as well. For example, separate groups with their own natural leaders, advocates, and points of view cluster around different degrees of parish participation: the "actively involved," the "Sunday regulars," the "occasional participants."[12] Another overlapping set of distinctions relies on different physical "centers of gravity" on the parish compound, suggested by a pupil who described St. Matthew's parochial school as being equipped with "a church and a gymnasium for the students."[13] Though without quite this naïveté, other members of the parish community also tend to view the purpose and function of the whole parish from the point of view they themselves usually (often quite literally) occupy. For a community that has not constructed but inherited the physical structure of

[12] There are, of course, cliques and factions within each of these levels as well. Anecdotes in Castelli and Gremillion, *The Emerging Parish*, 116–17, pointed predictably toward the frequency of such cliques among staffs of U.S. parishes in the 1980's.

[13] Clark, "Ecclesiology," 48.

its parish, such a strategy may provide the sense of "ownership" of the church in this place that might otherwise be lacking. The school, the rectory, the church, and the former convent buildings have all fostered their own particular subcommunities.

It seems that all of these lines of tension converge in a series of on-going struggles within the parish that can most readily be called "turf battles." Subgroups and their leaders are accustomed to controlling certain physical space, segments of time, and group activities; struggles for any part of this "turf" come into play when resources must be shared or plans made in common. The view from the parish school, for example, focuses naturally enough on the needs of the parochial students and on the perceptions of the faculty, staff, and parents, not all of whom are "Sunday regulars" at the church. This view has sometimes come into direct conflict with the perception of the pastoral associates who until very recently occupied offices in the rectory building. These staff members tend to see their work as more involved with "the whole parish." By this, they refer primarily to the Sunday worshipers, whose contact with the church is focused on that one day of the week and for whom the church building itself is, of course, the primary point of reference. Many of these parishioners, in turn, tend to see the rectory as foreign territory. This has been especially true in recent years as several short-term pastors have tried to limit the public use of the priests' residence, reversing an old habit of ever-greater access. The changed attitude has brought about something of a competition among staffers and volunteers for regular contact with the pastor and for a limited number of keys to the rectory door. Meanwhile, a few parishioners still mourn the social-action-oriented subcommunity that was once fostered when the former convent—now converted to archdiocesan rather than parish use—was being used as a Haitian multi-service center.

It is noticeable here that cultural tensions and turf battles are sometimes exacerbated by two other kinds of tension. One of these is based on variation in the quality of personal connection between parishioners and leaders, and the other on variations in spirituality and religious expression. The Haitian community and other recent immigrants at St. Matthew's generally prefer a spiritual style that is heavily dependent on traditional devotions and personal piety. (Interestingly, these features would also at one time have characterized the old Euro-American community of the parish, even though the current style is more demonstrative and charismatically oriented than was ever dreamed of in this church in days gone by.) On the other hand, many of the resident priests over the years (all non-Haitian but three), and many of the volunteers and staff members who followed them, have demonstrated a social justice-oriented spirituality. Such variation can cause divergence in everything from liturgical pet peeves to the setting of major priorities for the community.[14]

Amid all the variety, the pastor of the parish remains a key figure in the structure of the community, though in ways perhaps rather different from those envisaged by a traditional understanding of a pastor's expansive authority. It has been well demonstrated at St. Matthew's that the style of the pastor's availability and personal interaction with parishioners has a tremendous effect on the overall operation and "feel" of the community. The Irish-American pastor whose twelve-year tenure coincided with the firm establishment of the Haitian community in the parish dealt well with people on an informal, one-to-one basis. He used this method both to discover the needs of the parishioners and to attract volunteers. In his day an apt image of the parish social structure might have been a hub (the pastor) with many spokes but no outside wheel to connect them. His successor, pastor for only three years, shifted toward a more organizational style, with a council, committees, and job descriptions, even while continuing the availability and personal touch of his predecessor. The first Haitian pastor then arrived, along with the whole population of his previous parish, when a neighboring church building was closed due to structural problems. The merger of the two communities occurred suddenly and without adequate community preparation. Quite abruptly a distinction between those connected with the new pastor and those in opposition to him took hold as one of the defining (if not always plainly stated) qualities of parishioners and subgroups. Several years after this pastor's death, a long period of very unsettled clerical leadership is now ending with the appointment of another American priest. This pastor, however, will also continue to lead yet another neighboring parish, also largely Haitian, where he has already been at work for several years. Clearly, the patterns of alignment and influence will soon shift again.

---

[14] This divergence in spiritualities as it impacts liturgy was noted as a frequent characteristic of American parishes in the 1980's by Castelli and Gremillion, *The Emerging Parish*, 41. The Notre Dame study discussed by them indicated that ethnically concentrated parishioners in the northeast were particularly likely to favor traditional devotions and that, generally, parish staffs were more supportive of participatory liturgical styles.

In spite of such important changes, the differing styles of the pastors have never on the whole outweighed the broader structural features of the community. In many respects the styles themselves have been greatly influenced by the pastors' interaction with the community they encountered upon arrival at St. Matthew's. While the shape of the local church at St. Matthew's has been acknowledged, encouraged, and guided variously by the clergy throughout its history, the community has "gathered" itself in very concrete ways and has both created and coped with its own divisions. In doing so it has demonstrated, just as St. Joseph and St. Thomas Aquinas parishes have done in their turn, the human reality of church.

Reclaiming the Church. At the time of St. Matthew's centennial as a separate parish, former parishioners and generations of past parochial school students were invited back to the massive church on Stanton Street—newly cleaned, repaired, and painted—for a Mass in celebration of the event. As people packed into the building prior to the ceremonies, comments and stories could be heard all around about how good the church looked, how little it had changed, how much people remembered about the times they spent there. As the Mass began, the racial mix in the church was more visible than it had been for decades, and the liturgy was a multicultural tour de force—undoubtedly quite *unlike* what most of the visitors remembered about St. Matthew's. However, the dinner that followed took place at a function hall in a different part of town and was dominated by Irish-American alumni from the Boston suburbs; relatively few Haitians or other current parishioners turned out. Visitors who had once been parishioners had come and been warmly received, but they had not stayed long. St. Matthew's is no longer their home.

The history of St. Matthew's illustrates a process of successive communities forming around or within a pre-existing structure and then laying claim to it and stamping it with their own features. Even in its founding, the parish was a reclaiming of the already familiar structures of church by a community that was evolving in its patterns of urban life, in its social status, and in the kinds of functions it would henceforth require the church to fulfill. In Dorchester the Irish had not looked toward the church so much to receive, succor, and organize the desperately poor as they had once had to do. Rather, they came to see the church as an important feature of neighborhood stabilization and identity, a group statement of "having arrived." As the process continued further, most of the original St. Matthew's community eventually dissolved itself, dispersing to various suburbs where the social and religious needs of its former members would be redefined yet again. They left behind them not their former church community, but rather the buildings it had constructed and used. The communal continuity that is so appreciable in a place like St. Joseph's in Biddeford was quite dramatically broken at St. Matthew's.

The Caribbean Catholic immigrants who eventually arrived in south Dorchester, after most of the Irish had already moved out, did not have the tasks of their predecessors of urging the canonical process to legally create the parish or of saving their pennies to build the physical plant. Yet they no less than the founders had to find the way to live their Catholic religious tradition in changed circumstances—changed, in fact, even more radically and suddenly than those their predecessors had known. For the sake of their own identity they had to maintain some sort of continuity both with their particular cultural traditions and with the structures of the church, while also learning to adapt to a radically new context. In the process these parishioners, too, had to reclaim the church for themselves.

On the material level they began simply by arriving in the parish in their numbers. The same physical plant that had been in place for over sixty years and was being maintained by the remnant of the old community gradually became the spiritual home of the immigrants. For over a decade they slowly moved through the stages of being treated as clients, as visitors, as "step-children," and as partners, until it became clear to most that St. Matthew's was "their church." Surviving significant moments of challenge to this assumption—the unprepared merger with the neighboring Haitian parish and the initial inclusion of St. Matthew's on an archdiocesan list of parishes recommended for closure—ultimately served to strengthen the community's sense of ownership. The spiritual process ran parallel to this physical one as more and more of the vitality of the parish centered on meeting the needs of the new immigrant community. Worship, as well as the social and outreach activities of the parish, took on the distinctly Caribbean flavor that was there to greet the former parishioners who attended the centennial Mass.

The relative permanence of buildings (especially those built specifically to impress) suggests falsely that the communities they house are similarly stable. St. Matthew's demonstrates that, in fact, communities come and go at varying rates of speed. Nonetheless, these evolving networks of relationship are not merely passing phenomena of no importance. Rather, they both carry and benefit from crucial elements of the church's own long-term continuity. Some of these elements cling to the people themselves as they move from one context to another (particular stories and traditions, personal faith and understanding, ways of prayer and special devotions). Others await them in their new surroundings (longtime parishioners, differing customs, physical structures), and still others are indeed "universal" (sacraments, doctrine, Scripture, hierarchy). Together such things are the stuff of which the living tradition of the whole church is made. In each place and time, however, they are reclaimed and rewoven as circumstances demand and their interrelationships, relative importance, and practical meaning change before they are passed on in turn. The work that has been done by St. Matthew's new parishioners to construct a spiritual home over the past twenty years has in fact been an essential contribution to the life of the whole church.

The Church in Three Places

These glimpses at actual local church communities illustrate the struggle and the reality of church "ownership" far beyond questions of corporations and deeds. It is easy enough to understand the sociological influence of communities such as St. Joseph's, Aquinas, and St. Matthew's on the identity of the larger church. The shape of these communities certainly affects what the church "looks like" on the visible level, and perhaps even what the church might be "mistaken for" were one to have only a single community as an example. The argument I will make in the following chapters, however, is that the influence of local community life on the church is also actually *theological*. Its effects are not limited to externals, but are deeply embedded in Christians' understanding of themselves and of God, helping to form the ways in which believers speak and act at the very heart of their faith. The Christian relationships shaped by the community context mold the reception of formal church teaching in ways that are, while only rarely unique, nonetheless peculiar to each community. This is because each community receives the teaching within its own particular interpersonal network and lays claim to it as part of the expression of that network rather than in some abstract sense. If the church's age-old reliance on the safeguarding presence of the Holy Spirit is not at work here, it can hardly be at work in an effective way at any other level of the church's existence.

Originally I planned to make this point with reference to only one community. In its own way each of the perspectives on church found in the three could be elaborated from any one of the cases. The experience itself of these three communities, however, showed me that the impact of their lives and struggles on the understanding of church and mission is multiplied, expanded, and enriched with the addition of each new perspective. Although a careless look at the vast expanse of the worldwide church across the centuries might pass over their importance as they individually recede from view, in such gems as St. Joseph's, Aquinas, and St. Matthew's consists the whole mosaic of the church's life.

Chapter Two

The Problem of Community

Saint Joseph's, Saint Thomas Aquinas, and Saint Matthew's are outstanding examples of centers of Catholic activity. The brief glimpses the preceding chapter was able to offer show them to be points of contact for many people, across various ethnic, racial, and generational lines. In them the church has for many years wrestled with some basic puzzles about its identity: How to both value continuity and effectively meet change? How to reach out in help and friendship while continuing to respect the differing realities of people's lives? How to bring people together in faith despite the many real-world issues that divide us? Within each of these struggles, and the divisions they imply, lie the questions that are the focus of this chapter: Is the term "community" really an appropriate label for such a parish church or other local Christian gathering? How does a parish or other local body of Christians operate as a "community"?

Intuitively and from the point of view of a most basic definition of community, the first question hardly seems worth asking. In parish churches persons are indeed connected to one another through a variety of shared goods and circumstances. Moreover, from God's covenant with Israel to the friendship of Jesus and his apostles to the worldwide history of believing peoples, "community" is a central concept for both Judaism and Christianity. On the other hand, it is also clear that "community" has many meanings and connotations, both religious and secular, which do not necessarily complement one another. It is connected, for example, both to the *koinōnia*—the deep personal communion—experienced by the early church[1] and to the needs and values of popular and business cultures now at the beginning of the third millennium.[2] Even further, almost without regard to what particular perspective one takes, the reality of community seems to be undergoing a severe test in our times. Because it will remain central throughout the rest of the book, I will pause in this chapter to examine the idea of community more closely in its relationship to local churches.

The Church as Community Today

"Community" in the Law of the Church. Canon 515 of the 1983 *Code of Canon Law* follows the lead of Vatican II's *Lumen Gentium* in referring to the parish as a community: "A parish is a definite community of the Christian faithful established on a stable basis within a particular church."[3] Interestingly, however, the Code does not carry this term through to the level of the diocese, even though Vatican II had gone to some lengths to call to mind the ancient image of the church community as "God's holy people . . . in the same Eucharist, in one prayer, at one altar, at which the bishop presides, surrounded by his college of priests and by his ministers."[4] In the preparation of the revised Code, the word *"communitas"* replaced the word *"portio"* (portion of a diocese) used in an earlier draft. The commission that made the substitution explained that they chose *"communitas"* as more expressive of a "dynamic interaction among many persons united under the same pastor." *"Portio"* was nevertheless deemed appropriate in describing the

---

[1] On *koinōnia* see Christopher O'Donnell, "Communion—Koinonia," in idem, *Ecclesia: A Theological Encyclopedia of the Church* (Collegeville: Liturgical Press, 1996).

[2] Frances Hesselbein, et al., eds., *The Community of the Future* (San Francisco: Jossey-Bass, 1998), a collection of essays from primarily non-religious sources on the concept of community for the twenty-first century, is one of a variety of recent works on the topic. See also Howard Rheingold, *The Virtual Community: Homesteading on the Electronic Frontier* (Reading, MA: Addison-Wesley, 1993).

[3] Canon 515, *The Code of Canon Law: A Text and Commentary*, ed. James A. Coriden, et al. (New York and Mahwah, NJ: Paulist, 1985) 415.

[4] Second Vatican Council, *Sacrosanctum Concilium* 41, in Austin Flannery, O.P., ed., *Vatican Council II: The Conciliar and Postconciliar Documents* (rev. ed. Northport, NY: Costello Publishing; Dominican Publications, 1996) 1:15.

diocese in relation to the universal church, because "the communitarian aspect appears more in the realm of the parish."[5]

The canon and its background give a clear affirmation, not only of the use of the term "community" itself, but especially of the essentially interpersonal dimensions of the term. Here current church law moves away from assigning a merely functional significance to the most local manifestations of church. At the same time the law subtly raises an important question about the pastoral function of the modern diocese. In taking this approach the Code implicitly defers to the ancient understanding of *koinōnia,* and to the importance of the interpersonal elements in the ministry of Jesus and the early church. I will consider more closely both the concept of *koinōnia* and these interpersonal dimensions in the next chapter. For now it is enough to emphasize that an interactive community of shared goods, circumstances, and values is very much at the heart of the definition of "parish." Concrete support for this notion is clear in the experience of the actual parish communities we have already met.

Contemporary Challenges to Community. Despite firm legal and scriptural foundations and positive indicators of local support, however, it is still evident that the ideal of local Christian community is under severe pressure today from both inside and outside the church itself. Studies such as Robert Bellah and colleagues' *Habits of the Heart: Individualism and Commitment in American Life,* and Robert Putnam's *Bowling Alone: The Collapse and Revival of American Community,* have garnered great attention during the past two decades. This attention alone is an impressive measure of our collective concern at the apparent growth of individualism and the concomitant diminishment of "social capital."[6] The studies themselves help to sharpen that concern. Part of the project of Bellah and his associates, for example, was to examine contemporary American religious

---

[5] F. Coccopalmerio, "De Paroecia ut Communitate Christifidelium," *Periodica* 80 (1991) 22. It should be noted that Vatican II's Decree on the Pastoral Office of Bishops in the Church *(Christus Dominus)* 28 does apply the description *"portio"* to the parish, but specifically in the context of the sharing of priests in the pastoral work of bishops rather than in defining the parish *per se.*

[6] Robert N. Bellah, et al., *Habits of the Heart: Individualism and Commitment in American Life* (updated ed. Berkeley, CA: University of California Press, 1996); Robert Putnam, *Bowling Alone: The Collapse and Revival of American Community* (New York: Simon & Schuster, 2000).

practice. Their results pointed out the strength of a religious individualism that ultimately "suggests the logical possibility of over 220 million American religions, one for each of us."[7] This increasing pluralism, in turn, makes the "community of memory," as they describe the traditional religious congregation, a concept "hard for Americans to understand."[8]

Under these circumstances congregations tend to model one of two types. One makes few specific demands on its members, emphasizing instead an "empathetic sharing" by loosely associated individuals. The other privatizes morality and faith in another way by making them the property of a sect that sees itself as set apart from society at large.[9] (Bellah also points out the irony that the insistence on moral or doctrinal purity makes these apparently strong sect communities as fragile and dependent on individual decision as their "empathetic" counterparts.)[10] In contrast to these extremes, what Bellah and his colleagues term the "religious center," made up of "mainline" Protestant denominations and post-Vatican II Catholicism, has generally "tried to steer a middle course between mystical fusion with the world and sectarian withdrawal from it."[11] However, the intellectual life of this sector has become "over-specialized," and at the same time the entire sector has experienced a growing loss of self-confidence in the face of the broader culture. This combination has produced congregations Bellah describes as afflicted with "quasi-therapeutic blandness" that "cannot effectively withstand the competition of the more vigorous forms of radical religious individualism, with their claims of dramatic self-realization, or the resurgent religious conservatism that spells out clear, if simple, answers in an increasingly bewildering world."[12]

Robert Putnam's work quantifies the late-twentieth-century decline of American "social capital"—the value derived by society as a whole from connections among individuals—in areas as diverse as "political participation" and the overall sense of "reciprocity, honesty and trust" in society.[13] Relatively optimistic that the decline he documents is part of an ongoing historical cycle of collapse and renewal, Putnam none-

---

[7] Bellah, *Habits of the Heart,* 221.
[8] Ibid. 227.
[9] Ibid. 232.
[10] Ibid. 245.
[11] Ibid. 237.
[12] Ibid. 238.
[13] Putnam, *Bowling Alone,* 19, 11.

theless takes the current phenomenon as a serious social challenge. Examining a series of potential reasons for it, he attributes at least part of the blame to each: "pressures of time and money," "mobility and sprawl," "technology and mass media," and an overall shift in values from one generation to the next as the twentieth century concluded.[14] With regard to religious communities Putnam notes a forty-year decline of about ten per cent in those who *claim* membership, but a much greater decline in the same time period—from twenty-five to fifty per cent—in rates of actual participation. The statistics indicate that the decline is "attributable largely to generational differences,"[15] but Putnam also observes that

> active involvement in the life of the parish depends heavily on the degree to which a person is linked to the broader social context—having friends in the parish, in the neighborhood, at work, being part of a closely knit personal network . . . . [T]hose supporting beams for religiously based social involvement have themselves been weakened in recent decades.[16]

Putnam does report that the decline is somewhat compensated for by the continuation of "the historically familiar drama by which more dynamic and demanding forms of faith have surged to supplant more mundane forms."[17] Nonetheless, his analysis is in harmony with Bellah's discussion of sectarianism when Putnam notes that "the community building efforts of the new denominations have been directed inward rather than outward."[18]

Some of the ways in which these problems play out in local Catholic church communities are suggested and illustrated by the struggles of the two American parishes among our three examples. The cities in which St. Joseph's and St. Matthew's are located differ enormously in size and many other features. The local cultures of both, however, once rested solidly on the tightly defined "Catholic neighborhood." Over the past fifty years both parishes have seen this foundation eroded and replaced by a more heterogeneous and anonymous standard. The change

---

[14] Ibid. 11–12.
[15] Ibid. 72.
[16] Ibid. 74.
[17] Ibid. 79.
[18] Ibid.

in neighborhood living has in turn forced a rethinking (more dramatic at St. Matthew's but no less real at St. Joseph's) of an easy equation between parish and ethnic group. Under such circumstances, increasing numbers of people even perceive a certain incompatibility between reinforced cultural boundaries on the one hand and a spirit of Christian inclusiveness and global awareness on the other.[19] Closely connected to this rethinking is the further complication of the modern mobility of huge numbers of people. Saint Joseph's experiences this mobility in the outward migration of many young singles, the influx of young families without previous ties to the community, and the growing seasonal migrations of its retired senior members. At St. Matthew's mobility has taken the form of the virtually complete replacement of now-suburbanized Irish Americans by newly arrived Caribbean immigrants who themselves must be ready to follow job and housing markets.

Much of the change and mobility in American society to which the people of these parishes have responded was accompanied by welcome economic growth and opportunity. Yet it has also been related to the virtual disappearance of the fairly unified Catholic subculture that once shielded local church communities from the most damaging effects of such social storms. In the culture at large these developments together have tended to separate and isolate individuals from one another, leaving them, as Karl Rahner put it over forty years ago, "to the tender mercies of anonymous, vast, soulless and brutal collective powers."[20] They have brought with them such unwelcome phenomena as the diminishment of the sense of "home,"[21] the separation of elderly members of the society from the daily lives of the younger and more active, the subsequent loss of "roots" and sense of permanence for younger generations, perhaps especially in the area of religious faith, and a seemingly related commodification and commercial exploitation of youth.[22] Even when it addresses religious community directly, as Bellah and company note,

---

[19] See Bellah, *Habits of the Heart*, 228–30.

[20] Karl Rahner, "Peaceful Reflections on the Parochial Principle," in *Theological Investigations* 2, trans. Karl-Heinz Kruger (Baltimore: Helicon; London: Darton, Longman & Todd, 1963) 288, hereafter cited as "Parochial Principle."

[21] Ibid. 289.

[22] See William J. Bausch, *The Parish of the Next Millennium* (Mystic, CT: Twenty-Third Publications, 1997) 18–23, for a particularly grim assessment of this phenomenon as part of the cultural background for the immediate future of U.S. parishes. Bausch's broader and very negative evaluation of "The Way

American culture has since the nineteenth century generally emphasized "ethical communities in a dangerous and competitive world"
rather than "the stable harmony of an organic community."[23]

The cultural mainstream has grown ever more suspicious of authority
and tradition during the same post-Vatican II era in which the church attempted to adopt a greater openness to the world at large. The resulting
debate about the desirability and underlying motives of change in the
church has, for forty years, fueled the growing polarization between "tra-
ditionalists" and "progressivists." The polarization, in turn, has had a direct effect on the context in which all local communities operate, and is
sometimes directly reflected in the evolving shape of these communities.
We have already seen this at work in the emerging identity of St. Joseph's.

Related to this prolonged acculturation process, the precipitous drop
in the number of persons taking up clerical and religious vocations has
been a cause of great anxiety to many Catholics, both clerics and laity.
The overall reluctance to fill the resulting leadership gaps with trained
lay persons has increased the necessity all over the country for parish
closures and mergers of various sorts, with mixed but surely momen-
tous effects on the local communities involved. This restructuring has
generally increased the size of the congregations and of the workloads
for which pastors are responsible. Therefore it has also engendered
among the clergy a tendency toward specialization (endemic in the
culture at any rate), which some have found restrictive and unhelpful
to communities.[24] Under such conditions a legalistic or mechanical association of the term "community" with the old structural concept of
"parish" runs the risk of completely destroying any interpersonal content the community concept may still hold. Over the last fifty years
these difficulties have led many pastoral and theological commentators
to suggest that the idea of intimate community is no longer appropriate
to the discussion of local church.

The inclusion of the Jamaican St. Thomas Aquinas Church among
those introduced in Chapter One carries us a little further in thinking

---

We Are" (preceding a far more optimistic view of the resources and prospects
for contemporary parishes) can be found in pp. 7–66.

[23] Bellah, *Habits of the Heart,* 222.

[24] Myra Lambert, s.s.c.m., and Linda Hatton, s.s.c.m., "Women Religious as
Pastoral Leaders," *Chicago Studies* 37:2 (1998) 138, address their unsatisfactory
experience of priests as "sacramental ministers."

about the challenges to the idea of "local church community." The problems of community are not restricted to the United States. The class distinctions that are such an important feature of life at Aquinas are, in part, the lingering result of the slavery system, abolished nearly two centuries ago yet in countless ways etched into the national culture and memory of Jamaica both openly and covertly. More obviously today, they are also in part the result of the overall failure of Jamaica to find a way to general prosperity in a world economy. For both reasons the rifts they create within a given church community such as Aquinas are profound, even when there is evident Christian desire to move beyond them somehow. The cultural differences between persons, though they are sometimes softened by personal contact, are often enough even more pronounced, as virtually any member of the parish community, encountering another member for the first time, is able to determine intuitively the other's class position on the basis of skin tone, manner of speech, or style of dress. Economic pressures familiar to middle-class Americans afflict the wealthier classes in Jamaica in similar ways, rearranging community priorities and diminishing energies. For the lower classes, the endemic social solvents of poverty and violence are exacerbated by a globalization that has disrupted some reliable sources of semi-skilled labor and has also included the expansion of the drugtransshipment "industry" into ghetto neighborhoods that had previously escaped serious involvement. For many people there is a growing conviction that emigration to the U.S. or Canada, with or without one's family (and certainly without one's church community) is the only rational response to a bad situation.

The Response of the Church and the Persistence of Community. Considering all of these problems, we are left confused about the continued practical possibility of local church community. The social analysis suggests two apparently contradictory dangers, of "communization"[25] on the one hand and of individualism on the other. Whereas the threat to community of "anonymous collective powers" is palpable, the too-obvious parry of a more militant individualism is clearly not the route by which to preserve Christian community. The massive Notre Dame study of U.S. parishes in the 1980's showed that this confusion affected the heart of parish community in the U.S. in the decades following Vatican II. The study found, on the one hand, that active parish

---

[25] See Rahner, "Parochial Principle," 287–88.

members were just as likely as inactive Catholics to practice "'pick and choose' Catholicism," following or rejecting church teaching according to their own personal lights. On the other hand, it found that "American Catholics have adopted the rhetoric and vision of Vatican II which view the church as the People of God, and in many parishes, though certainly not all, the ideal of parish community has become a reality."[26] Here is a cultural conundrum of some importance: there is a yearning and expectation for "community" in the church, but we have also absorbed cultural expectations of individualism to such an extent that we find it very difficult to accept a corporate stance or teaching. Interestingly, this struggle continues at the same time that broader church structures (dioceses and the Vatican) are increasingly visible in their manner of regulating local community life. This interposition of the larger structures is obvious most recently in the tightening of liturgical regulations through the revised General Instruction of the Roman Missal. Increasingly cautious personnel policies adopted in the wake of the clergy sex abuse scandal, and the widespread diocesan programs of parish restructuring underway in many areas, are two more examples.

Efforts to address this confusion within local communities tend toward opposite ends of a long continuum, and so require careful balancing. At one extreme is the return of an old-style authoritarian structure no longer capable of commanding the respect of the whole community. At the other is deterioration into barely structured individualism. Either extreme, of course, would seriously damage true Christian communion. Maintaining the balance depends on the mutual respect of the clerical officeholders (pastors, chancery officials, and bishops) and the lay members. The clergy exercise enormous influence over all aspects of the parish. They bear a proportionate responsibility for encouraging

---

[26] James Castelli and Joseph Gremillion, *The Emerging Parish: The Notre Dame Study of Catholic Life Since Vatican II* (San Francisco: Harper & Row, 1987) 4. The Notre Dame survey found the most popular reason for attendance at mass was the apparently individualist one that "I enjoy the feeling of meditating and communicating with God" (ibid. 132 [Table 11]). Mark Searle, "The Notre Dame Study of Catholic Parish Life," *Worship* 60 (1986) worries on the basis of this and other Notre Dame data about the "practical ecclesiology of voluntary association" (332), the lack of appreciation for "the one eucharist symbolizing the unity of the church" (318), and "a decline in the sense of Catholic identity and the rise of cultural individualism" (324).

the conditions that allow the personal networks and subgroups within a parish to flourish. Lay parishioners, on their part, determine by their attitudes and actions whether legitimate structures and leadership (either clerical or lay) will receive respect at all.

Community trust and stability are seriously challenged when decisions from beyond the local structures are seen to disrupt the personal networks and interrelationships upon which the community relies. This was St. Joseph's experience during the rapid changes of the 1970's, especially with the closure of the parish high school. At Aquinas, too frequent changes of leadership and priorities during the 1990's painfully challenged established patterns of interaction among different classes of people and fed a sense of insecurity. Saint Matthew's in that same decade was caught in an early wave of the sex abuse scandal and saw a pastor removed with little explanation. Within a few years the unplanned merger with the neighboring parish, the death of another pastor, and the threat of closure during the archdiocesan reconfiguration process followed the first trauma. Yet all three parishes are still much more than the "communities of the like-minded" or "withdrawn islands of piety" that Bellah's team fears.[27] This suggests that the expectation of community at the local level—a dynamic and sustained interpersonal sharing of spiritual and material goods—can, in fact, be met. Such community, however, is neither a matter of official intransigence nor one of laissez-faire pastoral styles. It is, rather, the result of a complex interaction of culture (both secular and religious), personalities, and structures of power and relationship (again, both secular and religious).

How that interaction is structured is less important than that it be allowed to take place. To a large extent the essence of church at this level is more in the interrelational reality than in its form. This point can be made theologically, legally, historically, and sociologically. Karl Rahner underscores it theologically by suggesting that there are many natural characteristics, in addition to physical domicile, that could serve as organizing principles for pastoral care.[28] In the legal realm, Canon 518 allows for non-territorial parishes "based upon rite, language, the nationality of the Christian faithful within some territory or even upon some other determining factor."[29] James Castelli and Joseph Gremillion

---

[27] Bellah, *Habits of the Heart*, 223, 224.

[28] Rahner, "Parochial Principle," 296.

[29] James A. Coriden, Thomas J. Green, and Donald E. Heintschel, eds., *The Code of Canon Law: A Text and Commentary* (New York: Paulist, 1985) 518.

use American church history to point out ways in which a sense of interpersonal exchange and responsibility for parishes has continued even when structures of governance and relationship have shifted. This was true, for example, in the ending of lay trusteeship in U.S. parishes in the latter part of the nineteenth century, or in the postwar establishment of suburban parishes without the benefit of the ethnically and religiously cohesive urban neighborhoods of earlier times.[30] In a more qualitative fashion, the parish case studies here demonstrate a similar fluidity of form in the patterns of interaction and a similar constancy of the community ideal.

The context for understanding this persistence of the community ideal continues to broaden and change rapidly. In order to understand more clearly how the church is community in our own times we also need to recognize how many overlapping, yet distinct, social groups lay claims on us. This multiple membership has gained attention for decades and often appears as a detriment to the idea of church as community. Rahner notes that, moving frequently and participating in so many varied pursuits, modern people "cannot possibly have the farmer's sense of 'belonging.'"[31] Gregory Baum uses a similar insight to declare that "this search [for a community that fulfills all our needs and in terms of which we are able to define ourselves] is illusory, especially in our own day when to be human means to participate in several communities and to remain critical in regard to all of them."[32] It is certainly true that contemporary believers in industrialized countries find themselves drawn into distinct religious, residential, work-related, social, and recreational "communities." In any one of these they encounter people very different from themselves in other respects. This is undoubtedly the reason why so many regular parishioners no longer look to the parish to meet their overall social needs, as earlier

---

[30] See Castelli and Gremillion, *Emerging Parish,* 16, on the shift in lay participation from administrative leadership to religious societies within parishes; see ibid. 201 for comments on the survival of community life in suburban parishes. Jay P. Dolan, *In Search of An American Catholicism: A History of Religion and Culture in Tension* (New York: Oxford, 2002) 185–86, describes the coincidence of the church's suburbanization and the flowering of lay movements in 1950's America.

[31] Rahner, "Parochial Principle," 297.

[32] Gregory Baum, "The Church of Tomorrow," in idem, *New Horizon: Theological Essays* (New York: Paulist, 1972) 141.

generations might have done.[33] In Jamaica the social aspects of church life appear to have remained much stronger than in the U.S. Nonetheless, at Aquinas the mixing of traditionally distinct Jamaican class communities is clearly a challenge to most parishioners and causes many to look elsewhere for many of their social needs. At the same time, the continuing value of a definable faith community remains clear. It is evident in the willingness of parishioners in all three sample communities to struggle with their differences of language, culture, and material need.

Redefining Local Church Community. Two things now seem clear. There is, first, serious reason to regard interpersonal community as constitutive of church life at the most local level. Yet, second, the contemporary cultural challenges to that assumption are numerous and powerful. For both these reasons, redefining what community actually is and demands of us in the concrete must be an ongoing task, precisely within our local communities. Theologians and social scientists have been proposing, for some time now, various theoretical perspectives and tools for such a redefinition in both religious and secular spheres. Evelyn Whitehead, for example, suggests that rather than being a closed and self-sufficient unit, a community is a group characterized by a common orientation to life, opportunities for personal exchange, and some level of agreement about membership, values, and goals.[34] Bellah and his associates propose an integrated understanding of public and private life concerned with "reconstituting the social world" that has deteriorated.[35] Peter Drucker and associates discuss business practices that emphasize "communities of value," and thus address the decreasing significance of geography to our patterns of association.[36]

That the redefinition is now happening in local churches, on a very practical level, is suggested in many ways. Already in the 1980's about half of American parishioners cited a wide range of non-geographical criteria for choosing a parish, indicating that the "voluntary" parish

---

[33] Castelli and Gremillion, *Emerging Parish*, 59–60.

[34] Evelyn Eaton Whitehead, "The Structure of Community: Toward Forming the Parish as a Community of Faith," in eadem, ed., *The Parish In Community and Ministry* (New York and Mahwah, NJ: Paulist, 1978) 42.

[35] Bellah, *Habits of the Heart*, 275–96.

[36] Dave Ulrich, "Six Practices for Creating Communities of Value, Not Proximity," in Hesselbein, et al., *Community of the Future*, 155–65.

was becoming a reality.[37] We have seen how this notion of moving beyond officially established boundaries has helped St. Joseph's redefine itself from the ethnic enclave of the past to the "traditional" parish of today. At St. Matthew's, on the other hand, it is precisely that ethnic character that draws Haitians in particular from near and far. They gather in a community that is already the result of the joining of two canonical parishes and recent close cooperation (including sharing a pastor) with a third. In Jamaica, even at its founding Aquinas went beyond the territorial principle by including in its official membership all those who were associated with the university. Many parishes, of course, have proven to be just too large and varied for the formation of meaningful "communities of value." Even in these circumstances, though, parishioners continue to seek practical ways of experiencing interpersonal religious community. The "small Christian communities" that have flourished in many areas, both within parish structures and independent of them, are further testimony to this search.[38]

The resources a congregation is able to bring to the task of defining and building a Christian community depend on everything else in the life of that community. The stories of the sample parishes show the extent to which the experience of community and church are shaped by events and circumstances that seem purely secular. The tremendous shifts in the makeup and functioning of these parish communities over the years have been the result of vastly changed social circumstances and of the differing histories and social positions of older and newer members.[39] Through the several decades since these changes began to take place, the people of the parishes have reacted to their concrete situations and evolved ways of being church that allow the communities to survive despite their ongoing struggles and provide an intimate setting in which their members can practice their faith.

The parishioners themselves have brought with them very different kinds of problems. They have also brought a rich variety of resources, including skills, values, and perspectives carried with them from previous

[37] For the Notre Dame statistics see Castelli and Gremillion, *Emerging Parish,* 55 (Table 4) and 75.

[38] Philip J. Murnion and David DeLambo, *Parishes and Parish Ministers: A Study of Parish Lay Ministry* (New York: National Pastoral Life Center, 1999) 18; John Paul Vandenakker, *Small Christian Communities and the Parish* (Kansas City, MO: Sheed and Ward, 1994).

[39] Murnion and DeLambo, *Parishes and Parish Ministers,* 9–10.

experiences of community: the love and discipline of extended Franco-American families, Jamaican intuition about personal survival and personal dignity, the determination of Boston's Haitian immigrants. There is a sense in which the cohesion of these communities is "external" to the parishes themselves. Nonetheless, that cohesion is a resource that the church community has honored, and has used to great effect in forming the identities the parish communities have taken on.

Conversely, however, the local church community can only exercise a meaningful influence when individual parishioners experience it also as an ongoing part of their day-to-day lives.[40] The literature of the small Christian community movements around the world has noted this with special emphasis. The very purpose of these movements is to enhance this sense of belonging when parish life *per se* cannot. One such movement in Africa, for example, insisted that "these smaller communities in which the ordinary life of the people takes place" ought to be seen as basic to the church.[41] Another understood its mission as forestalling the departure from the church of lay people who had not yet developed a sense of belonging.[42] In the U.S., Jesuit researcher Thomas Sweetser has found that successful small communities have members with a common purpose who make real demands on one another, an insight corroborated and developed extensively by the work of Bernard Lee, s.m.[43]

Contributing to the community in response to such demands connects strongly to one's sense of belonging. This has been suggested by statistical links between parishioners' participating in liturgy and embracing the idea of church as community,[44] and between the presence of lay leaders in a parish and an overall high rate of parish participation.[45] As Michael Place has written, "In a sense, a parish is an abstraction that exists only in concrete expression."[46] Particular interpersonal relation-

---

[40] Putnam, *Bowling Alone*, 72–74.

[41] Bishop Patrick Kalilombe of Lilongwe, Malawi, in Vandenakker, *Small Christian Communities*, 121.

[42] Vandenakker, *Small Christian Communities*, 115–16.

[43] Thomas Sweetser, s.j., *Successful Parishes: How They Meet the Challenge of Change* (Minneapolis: Winston, 1983) 53–54; Bernard Lee, s.m., et al., *The Catholic Experience of Small Christian Communities* (New York and Mahwah, NJ: Paulist, 2000), particularly 77–147 (Chapters 4 and 5).

[44] Searle, "The Notre Dame Study," 328.

[45] Murnion and DeLambo, *Parishes and Parish Ministers*, 4.

[46] Michael Place, "Parish Pastoral Councils," *Chicago Studies* 37:2 (1998) 145.

ships and the ways in which they overlap with one another, specific ways of participating, and the sense of belonging that these enhance are important parts of that concrete expression. The structural arrangements of a parish or a small Christian community can encourage such expression, but ultimately the human network itself is the true heart of the community.

This discussion may now lead us to some basic conclusions regarding the possibility of experiencing church as community today. Although we speak readily of community as an important meaning and goal of church, two opposing forces present tremendous obstacles for us today. These forces are perhaps best represented by the images of "faceless corporation" and "alienated individual." As these models, seemingly in spite of our best intentions, come to dominate much of our social thinking, we instinctively trust less that institutional mechanisms can maintain genuine social cohesion. Instead, a third model has gained currency, using the images of "network" or "web" that have become so much a part of our vocabulary via computer technology. Increasingly, people base the coherence and meaning of their lives on the more flexible networks of relationship that the institutions, at their best, serve.

These networks can encompass, embody, and share the institutions, their roots, heritage, and traditions, among many persons who are interrelated in a variety of ways. They thus recreate, in a more intentional and adaptable form, the communities that used to be taken for granted. At St. Joseph's in Biddeford great-grandsons of Canadian immigrants now make the personal choice to "connect to" their Franco-American heritage in the parish of their ancestors. At St. Matthew's in Dorchester the immigrant Haitians sustain their faith in a church that was there to greet them only because a small remnant of the earlier community refused to abandon it. At Aquinas in Kingston the bonds of friendship that have formed across class lines hold a naturally fractious community together despite sometimes bitter struggles. All of this seems due less to the staying power of old structures themselves than to the personal interconnections that encourage people to carry on. The growing personal networks that result carry people beyond traditional boundaries almost despite themselves, and so serve to challenge an easy narrowness with the breadth of Christian vision.

Of course, this model of community interaction, with its emphasis on personal connection, can also further dampen specific institutional commitments. The network approach lends a helpful flexibility in a geographically and socially mobile and pluralist society. Yet the flexibility of a network allows a person to avoid potentially enriching and strengthening challenges by distancing oneself without completely disassociating. The more extensive the network, the more options exist for this kind of mobility, and the less necessary it is to submit fully to the demands of a given institution. Breadth of connection substitutes for depth of relationship, the opposite temptation of the depth without breadth that can accompany an uncompromising institutional loyalty. In the end neither leads in very healthy or true directions, yet networks rather than geography increasingly bind the world together. The church must learn how to view and interpret its own structures accordingly if it is to remain intelligible to the people who form it. It is likely that in so doing it will discover that once-indispensable arrangements can be dispensed with after all, and with very good pastoral results. On the part of the individuals in their networks the challenge is to understand that greater depth leads to greater human richness, stability, and meaning. It leads, in a word, toward a fuller encounter with God.

The Context of Local Church Community

The image of a network, it might be objected, contributes to making community boundaries rather indistinct, resistant to clear definition. The concept can be extended outward to include even those who, far from sharing their lives in common with members of a parish, come into contact with the community only when taking advantage of its social outreaches.[47] Yet if we are to consider the local church as the human society it surely is—and one, moreover, that is called to a mission beyond its own survival—we must admit that this vagueness represents the way human relationships work in a pluralistic world. Significant and influential contact takes place with and among people of widely varying backgrounds and motivations. Sorting the community from the context in such a situation, while surely possible, is not a simple affair. The distinctiveness of church community, in fact, must emerge from considering and engaging the broader context of the particular community and the way its network of relationships is formed. The ele-

---

[47] Searle, "The Notre Dame Study," 331, concerns himself with this question of community identity in discussing certain results of the Notre Dame survey and calling for "theological reflection and ecclesiological clarification of Catholic community identity in a pluralistic society."

ments of this context are virtually innumerable, and can be very particular to the community in question. That is why a close theological analysis of particular communities becomes so valuable.[48] I will touch briefly here on some of the primary categories for this kind of analysis.

Christian Tradition. From the point of view of ecclesiology the first element of the local church community's context is the Christian faith tradition itself, arising from the identification of persons or groups in some way with Jesus Christ. This tradition's influence on individuals and cultures remains pervasive even in our time. True, some may think it advisable from a sociological point of view to consider faith tradition as secondary to broader and more secular social forces such as the general cultural bonds within an immigrant group. The content of Christian tradition is diffuse and its impact difficult to quantify. However, as long as we are still meaningfully speaking of a local *church* community, the Christian tradition and its spiritual effects must shape every level of the context in which the community exists. Thomas Sweetser touches on this necessity when he writes:

> A successful parish demands good organization and management skills, but it is also a faith community that exists in response to the Lord's call. Therefore a parish could go through a process of writing a mission statement and formulating goals and still not be in touch with the Gospels or be attentive to the urgings of the Holy Spirit. A parish could establish its goals for the coming year and miss the whole area of social justice because the majority of parishioners, or at least the more articulate ones, do not feel that this is an important aspect of being a parish community.[49]

Sweetser's description suggests that such a parish would be acting contrary to its true context since, as a Christian community, it must join the universal church in proclaiming the justice and reign of God. Because

---

[48] For full-scale approaches to such "local theology" see Robert J. Schreiter, *Constructing Local Theologies* (Maryknoll, NY: Orbis, 1985); Nancy T. Ammerman, et al., eds., *Studying Congregations: A New Handbook* (Nashville: Abingdon, 1998); James D. Whitehead and Evelyn Eaton Whitehead, *Method In Ministry: Theological Reflection and Christian Ministry* (New York: Seabury, 1981).

[49] Sweetser, *Successful Parishes*, 98. See also Place, "Parish Pastoral Councils," 141, who reminds his readers that "the communion of faith is meant to be a reflection of the inner life of the Trinity."

of the immense breadth of the tradition and its implications it is more than likely that each community will have blind spots of the sort Sweetser notes. One of the functions of the universal communion, and the central structures that serve it, is constantly to call communities back to the richness of the tradition out of which they have arisen. Yet it remains crucially true, as Sweetser also implies, that the particular application of Christian faith and tradition within the local community must be a matter of local prayer, discernment, and self-understanding. In this fashion each local community not only respects this element of its context but also enriches it with its own "response to the Lord's call."

Personal Faith. Close observation of parish communities yields many examples of an individualist conception of church as "sanctuary of personal devotion." Even apparently communal images of church such as "helper" or "teacher" can be used to suggest that the church exists solely to serve personal needs, both material and spiritual. The apparent willingness of some parishioners to move in and out of a community based on the provision of these needs reinforces the cautionary note about community that Putnam, Bellah, and other social analysts sound. Community belonging and participation are no longer automatically expected of believers, but instead are based on separate and deliberate personal decision. The network model suggests, however, that this individual choice does not necessarily mean that faith has become a thoroughly privatized commodity. Often enough it is an indication of just the opposite, as a person with options chooses to associate with other people of faith and thus to build community in some intentional way. In any event, a person's Christian faith already in itself indicates at least a peripheral connection to a network of human relationships through which that faith was acquired. The decision to attend church in whatever capacity only underlines that connection. At the same time the strength of the individual members' faith commitments is a crucial factor in the community's overall strength. Without that personal conviction the community will gradually lose meaningful connection to the Christian tradition itself, which is a defining element of its context and meaning.

Relationships Beyond the Community. A survey of lay involvement in parishes at the end of the 1990's pointed out that "community-building, or relationship building, has become a major emphasis in liturgical life, faith formation, and social ministry among other aspects of parish life."

The Notre Dame survey had found indications of similar interest in the 1980's.[50] Even as this is the case, however, it is essential to recognize that the relationships the church community can itself build are only a small part of the human network into which its members are tied. As we have seen, relational bonds that are prior or external to the parish itself can and do contribute enormously to the church's sense of community. Within the sample parishes, ethnicity, nationality, language, neighborhood, friendship, and family connections all play essential roles in determining the composition and shape of the communities. Despite the fact that no one set of factors is usually strong enough by itself to hold people, and movement in and out of the communities is frequent, these are no individualistic collections of persons. The presence of particular persons in the community is virtually always the result of a complex set of relationships that extends far beyond the local church itself.

The existence of these broad networks in the lives of individual Christians creates a series of expectations, both directly religious and broadly social. Because of it people may approach the church community with particular fears and hesitations to be overcome, or they may come with instilled faith and respect for the Christian message that the church experience can build upon. Very likely, whether they arrive seemingly alone or already connected to the parish through friends and family, they come with both fear and faith. Their expectations may range from the quality of specific ritual procedures—the way confessions will be heard or how the scripture readings will sound—to general affirmations of the importance of a friendly and personal atmosphere in church.[51]

Whatever their specific content, it is clear that such expectations, and the way in which the community responds to them, will contribute greatly to the shape of the parish and even to the way in which the authority of its pastors is exercised and received. Published studies as well as observations in the sample parishes, for example, point out that personal relationships with pastors or other staff members are a very significant factor in the hiring of lay parish

---

[50] Murnion and DeLambo, *Parishes and Parish Ministers,* 44. The Notre Dame survey showed that even in the absence of strong social bonds from beyond the parish structures, qualities of personal interaction were highly valued by "core Catholics" in determining their allegiance to a particular parish community. See Castelli and Gremillion, *Emerging Parish,* 55, Table 4.

[51] Castelli and Gremillion, *Emerging Parish,* 55 (Table 4) noted "quality of pastoral care" as an important reason for attendance at a particular parish.

ministers.[52] Castelli and Gremillion describe the familiar situation in which "a formal network of lay leadership was supplemented by an informal network of friends who were present throughout the leadership structure."[53] They also point out how much the character of a given community relies on its relationship to past and present leaders.[54]

Undoubtedly, plain favoritism and cliquishness do play a role in such connections, sometimes a major role. The more important and consistent reality, though, is the influence on the community of the networks to which its members belong. Some types of organizations and communities find it necessary to insulate themselves from such external influence as much as possible. There are rules and policies discouraging husband and wife from working in the same department of a business and laws against public servants hiring relatives. With regard to a local church community, however, the network of human relationships is part of its very core. The discussions of "boundaries" that are now so much a part of public discourse in all sectors are indeed crucial in identifying issues of vital importance to the local church community, particularly given the terrible scandal of clergy sexual abuse. However, uncritical application of general standards, without proper attention to this interrelational feature of the community's context, can also create even further dangers for the church and its members. As a response to Christ's invitation to *life*,[55] the local church community is composed of *whole persons*, with all their relationships and complexities. It is not a sect, seeking to close off its members from the world at large, but rather through these very networks of relationship to which they belong the community seeks to offer Christ's invitation to the world.

Culture and Society. Viewed on the larger scale, the existence of the network of human relationships means that the parish community is enmeshed in the human culture that surrounds it. It follows that, if the parish is part of a cultural experience of the people, then their ideas and understanding of church will necessarily evolve and shift with the evolution of the wider culture. As Castelli and Gremillion have put it,

---

[52] Murnion and DeLambo, *Parishes and Parish Ministers*, 40.
[53] Castelli and Gremillion, *Emerging Parish*, 117.
[54] Ibid. 65.
[55] See John 10:10.

We have often referred to the parish as a community. But while the parish does function as a community, it also exists within a wider community—in a specific city, in a specific state, in a specific country. We have emphasized that parish life is shaped by the personalities of individual leaders, but it is also shaped by geography, economics, ethnicity, population density, and the proportion of Catholics in the general population. The parish is also part of its community, relating to it and serving it in a variety of ways. It becomes involved in community problems, and its members care deeply about local, national, and international issues. Catholic parishes never operated in isolation from their surrounding community, even in the days when they served as a refuge from a society ill disposed towards immigrants. In that period, the parish served to socialize immigrant Catholics into their new home.[56]

Any individualist notion of church has had to yield to the evident importance of the personal connections that individuals carry. Now we must also set aside sectarian models and emphasize the connection of the local community to its cultural milieu. There are struggles involved when contemporary communities seek to balance a sense of mission with the temptation to an inward-looking concern for group maintenance[57] or to honor the unique, lay-centered, and worldly spirituality of the people over against a more traditional clerical and monastic spirituality.[58] Such struggles are nonetheless worthwhile. Understanding the cultural setting in its effects both *outside* and *within* the church community is a necessary part of understanding the local church community itself.

As the three sample parishes show in their own particular ways, one cultural element that can exercise major influences on the shape of a church community is language. Saint Matthew's became a center of Haitian Creole language use in the 1980's. Its Haitian population was encouraged to grow even more as people sought a comfortable atmosphere in which to worship and socialize in their native tongue. At the same time both tensions and opportunities for cooperation increased between this growing linguistic group and the English speakers who had dominated previously. For a short time something similar looked to be happening with a Spanish-language group, but this phenomenon was too

[56] Castelli and Gremillion, *Emerging Parish*, 176.
[57] Murnion and DeLambo, *Parishes and Parish Ministers*, 67.
[58] Sweetser, *Successful Parishes*, 119.

dependent on a few key people who did not remain active in the parish. At Aquinas small efforts to accommodate the unofficial but genuine English dialect of the lower classes routinely raise objections from better-educated parishioners and highlight class tensions. (Similar tensions are not unknown among St. Matthew's Haitians.) At St. Joseph, almost entirely English-speaking for most practical purposes, the use of French in certain liturgies and other pastoral situations signifies a reverence for the roots of the culture and for the faith itself. This acknowledgment resonates in the entire community, even with non-Franco-American members, but most especially with older parishioners.

Another cultural feature of significant impact on the church community is the approach to law and authority. This includes very basic beliefs and attitudes. I have already described some of the vexing problems such questions can raise among the class groups at Aquinas. At St. Joseph's several years ago, as well, a number of older parishioners were quite seriously disturbed when the pastor of a neighboring parish declared, during a daily Mass shared with St. Joseph parishioners, that "Adam and Eve never existed." Calling the biblical narrative into question seemed to rock the whole foundation of faith for some who look on authority and law as fundamental structures that may not be compromised. This is quite the opposite response from those who, seeing law as a social construction, give themselves great latitude to assent to or dissent from official teachings of the church.[59] Clearly the functioning of the community looks very different from these two perspectives, and the blending of them in a single community brings about a complexity that must be carefully attended to by anyone wanting to understand the church in this location.

Specific legal structures and statutes also, of course, have important impacts, such as the general removal of special legal status for the Sunday Sabbath. At St. Matthew's very many parishioners must juggle work schedules in order to attend weekly Mass. Saint Joseph's faced a controversy recently regarding the city's scheduling of children's football games during traditional worship hours. In both cases attendance and attitudes toward Mass on the part of both children and adults are inevitably affected. The development of professional standards and practices in various fields also affects local communities. Licensing requirements, accreditation procedures, and general expectations of

---

[59] See Castelli and Gremillion, *Emerging Parish*, 4.

clientele change a church community's ability to respond to a variety of social needs, from marriage counseling to primary education. Parishioners are accordingly encouraged in or discouraged from turning to the church for help with particular problems.[60]

Perhaps even more influential than specific legal structures are the more general mores and norms of society that members necessarily carry with them into the local church community. These shape the community in direct and profound ways, both positive and negative. However, they can be so pervasive in the general culture that most parishioners are apt to take them for granted. The "practical ecclesiology of voluntary association,"—the power of individual choice discussed earlier—is a case in point.[61] Unexamined adaptation of this attitude encourages thinking that could overlook the depth and commitment of the Gospel call and put the church on a par with service organizations like the Rotary Club. At the same time it is an attractive way of thinking because it also tends to further the practical involvement of at least some lay people. Another example is the growth of a kind of indifferent pluralism among church members. Again there is a legitimate attractiveness to the openness and ecumenical value of an attitude like that of the St. Matthew's parishioner who had "nothing [negative] to say about their religion" to fellow believers in Jesus. Yet there is also the potential for losing track of the distinctiveness of various spiritual and religious traditions, and thereby undermining commitment to any community at all. These are merely simple contemporary examples of the interaction of culture and the understanding of church. This interaction is a permanent feature of church history, but one particularly noticeable in a society in which the church no longer has the effective control of the culture it once seemed to have.

The general challenge and demand that traditional Christian values justify themselves, issued by a powerful segment of contemporary American culture, underlines the close interaction of church communities and society at large. New Jersey pastor William Bausch's pessimistic notes on secularism in *The Parish of the Next Millennium* are a good example of the discomfort this awareness causes some members of the church. In one part of a long list of cultural temptations for today's

[60] Ibid. 72–73 (Table 9) found that parishioners accept certain parish social services much more readily than others.

[61] See Searle, "The Notre Dame Study," 332.

Christian community Bausch includes narcissism, pragmatism, restlessness and compulsion, loss of numinous vocabulary and tradition, and relativism as the legacies of secular culture to the church.[62] In less discouraged tones Thomas Sweetser also describes the cultural situation of the Christian community:

> The parish, because it is itself a social organization, is shaped and influenced by the culture within which it functions. It is influenced, but hopefully not swallowed up, by the surrounding culture. If the parish is to remain faithful to its transcendent purpose and origins, though, it must maintain an autonomy. In this way, it can become a challenge to and critic of the culture.[63]

That the culture influences the shape and function of local Christian communities will never be in question. Whether this influence will enhance or detract from our ability to live out a commitment to the Gospel is in large part the contemporary challenge for the church.

The Larger Church. I have focused on particular church communities throughout this discussion. I have tried to maintain, however, at least a tacit assumption of a worldwide church as an essential part of the local communities' context. Particularly with reference to Roman Catholic communities, a congregational model of church would be just as inadequate as any individualist or sectarian model. Yet catholicity contains an unavoidable paradox. This particular "mark" of the church signifies a worldwide unity, making of the church a meeting ground for people from many different nations. By the same token it names a gathering of diversity rather than uniformity, interrelating and christening cultural riches in a way that gives the universal church an extraordinary breadth and strength. As the cases demonstrate, the interplay of these two aspects is more obvious in some local communities than in others and is often underscored by the struggle it entails. Nonetheless, the dynamic itself of unity and diversity is evident at the very roots of the church. The Pentecostal opening of the apostolic ministry in Jerusalem is marked by a miracle not so much of "tongues" (as is sometimes claimed in comments on Acts 2:4)[64] but of "ears," if you will: in an exact reversal of

---

[62] See Bausch, *Parish of the Next Millennium*, 25–34.

[63] Sweetser, *Successful Parishes*, 179.

[64] The various ways of interpreting the relationship of "the gift of tongues" to the Pentecost phenomenon are discussed in Richard J. Dillon, "Acts of the

the Tower of Babel story in Genesis, the apostles and their hearers would have been endowed with the common language that is said to have been lost through pride. In Acts 2, however, all in the vast crowd of visitors hear the one message in their *own* languages.

The awareness of a broader "belonging" within Roman Catholicism, beyond the local community alone, is also an integral part of the experience of the parishes. I have contended that the Christian faith tradition is the most basic element of a local community's context. Because of this the community as a whole is constantly aware of an objective body of belief to which it seeks to conform. The question, "What does the church teach?" still comes readily to parishioners' lips. They expect to receive direction and guidance about the faith from an external source that represents the broad Catholic world. As Paul VI and John Paul II both have reminded the universal church, "No one can arrive at the whole truth on the basis solely of some simple private experience, that is to say, without an adequate explanation of the message of Christ, who is 'the way, the truth, and the life' (John 14:16)."[65] The Christian tradition and the Gospel message themselves, then, are a constant reminder of the breadth of the community's context.

In addition, increasingly large numbers of parishioners have direct experience of other parts of the wider church, and they are aware that others in the community also have such experience. This is particularly true in a parish such as St. Matthew's, where immigration is the norm and experiences contrast widely even within a given ethnic community such as the Haitian. Saint Joseph's in Biddeford, though still racially and economically quite homogeneous, now includes many families who come from different roots, have moved frequently, or have traveled widely. Aquinas, in addition to its built-in social mix, has through most of its history been staffed by non-Jamaican clergy and because of its university connections has always included many non-Jamaican members.

There are also ongoing direct contacts between local communities. At one point St. Matthew's received nearly $50,000 toward the operating

---

Apostles," in Raymond E. Brown, et al., eds., *The New Jerome Biblical Commentary* (Englewood Cliffs, NJ: Prentice Hall, 1990) 730–31.

[65] Pope Paul VI, "Concluding Address to the Synod of Bishops on Catechesis," *Actae Apostolicae Sedis* 69 (1977), quoted in Pope John Paul II, *Catechesi Tradendae: Apostolic Exhortation on Catechesis in Our Time* (Boston: St. Paul Editions, 1979) 19–20 (#22).

budgets of both school and church from contributions originating in other parishes. Saint Joseph's has for some years been in a cooperative arrangement with two other Biddeford parishes, involving administration, parochial schooling, faith formation, and even daily Mass. Aquinas still has a living memory of being a "chapel" of the original Sts. Peter and Paul parish. It has since given rise itself to another parish community, in a more remote section of its own original territory, with which it continues to cooperate.

Pastors and certain other local leaders receive yet another reminder of the wider church through their own identification with the diocesan church, generally stronger than the identification with the local community itself.[66] This connection seems to be much more tenuous on the part of lay ministers and parish members in general. As far back as the mid-1980's the Notre Dame study noted a lack of knowledge about diocesan structures and activities among active parish volunteers.[67] At about the same time a "disturbing" sense of independence from the diocese, and even from local pastors, was noted on the part of parish pastoral councils.[68] A study in the 1990's found that the rapid development of lay ministry at the time originated locally, in the parishes, rather than at the diocesan level, and that lay ministers felt closest to the church at the parish level. The same study, however, noted a growing feeling of connection to the church as a whole on the part of lay ministers and an increasing commitment to lay ministry on the part of dioceses.[69] The most likely moments of contact between parishes and diocesan officials, however, do not yet seem sufficient to provide a sense of communion rather than one of distance. Large dioceses and crowded episcopal schedules limit the ordinary parish visits of most bishops to unusually formal affairs with little opportunity for ordinary parishioners, or even entire parish staffs, to engage in personal exchange with the bishop. Various types of diocesan gatherings usually do no better in this regard, although they may foster valuable inter-parish connections and in that way further communion with the diocese.

[66] Castelli and Gremillion, *Emerging Parish*, 111.

[67] Ibid.

[68] Bishop Victor H. Balke, "The Parish Pastoral Council," *Origins* 16:47 (1987) 821. Balke has been the bishop of the Diocese of Crookston, Minnesota, since 1976.

[69] On these respective points see Murnion and DeLambo, *Parishes and Parish Ministers*, iii, 31, 23, 66.

Because of this lack of connection with diocesan officials, diocesan involvement conceived as service to local communities is often experienced instead as an intrusive burden by local pastors and their communities.[70] Saint Matthew's, for example, has for many years received far more in assistance from the Archdiocese of Boston than it returns in contributions. (One year the figures were $165,000 and $3,200 respectively!) Yet ordinary parishioners at St. Matthew's have experienced diocesan involvement in their community in what they take to be less benevolent ways. They have faced the archdiocese's non-communication about their pastor's sudden removal, the poorly prepared parish merger, and recently the listing of the parish with scores of other "closeable" churches. In such confrontations parishioners have demonstrated their first loyalty to the *community as Catholic,* then to the local leaders whom they know, and only quite grudgingly to the diocesan structures, over which they have no control in any event. Certainly the legacy of tension between St. Joseph's Franco-American community and the Irish-dominated chancery in Maine has underscored similar loyalties. In Kingston, interestingly, a long tradition of archdiocesan synods with elected parish representation, coupled with very active recruitment of parish involvement in archdiocesan projects, has softened this sort of tension.

Discussing the case of a rural parish cluster in which they were involved, Srs. Myra Lambert and Linda Hatton remark:

> In rural faith communities there is an identity with the local community as well as with the faith community. They share a history and a common heritage. When the diocese began to talk of merging parishes or of closing parishes, there was no respect for this history or heritage, and it caused more feelings of abandonment and misunderstanding.[71]

Respect for local history and conditions is, in the end, the pivotal point in the discussion of the relationship between larger church structures and the local community. The local community cannot, without doing violence to itself and the spiritual roots of its members, deny its connection to

---

[70] NCCB Committee on the Parish, *Parish Life in the United States: Final Report to the Bishops of the United States by the Parish Project* (Washington: United States Catholic Conference, 1983) 47–54, provides a series of suggestions for service-oriented diocesan programs for local communities. David K. O'Rourke, "The Priest Proof Parish," *Church* 15:1 (1999), on the other hand, articulates a complaint about diocesan intrusiveness.

[71] Lambert and Hatton, "Women Religious as Pastoral Leaders," 138.

the larger church. For Roman Catholic communities this connection (which exists in some form for all Christian communities) is a vital part of their very definition. Neither, however, does it do justice to the relationship between them for a diocese or other broad authority to act as if the specific historical, social, and spiritual context of a local community is of no consequence to grander schemes of organization or development.

The struggle to gain the balance of unity and diversity has relevance not only within the Roman Catholic Church but also within the wider Christian church. The inability to come to mutual agreement about the balance of the two meanings of catholicity has led to a millennium of formal Christian division. This thousand-year-old fracture itself proves that the work of understanding the church as the community of Christ's followers is far from complete. True as it may be, it is not enough ecclesiologically to say that "the diversity that is the result of the Spirit working through the charisms of individuals and groups is ordered for the sake of mission by the authoritative pastoral leadership that has been entrusted to the college of bishops, along with and under the Bishop of Rome."[72] A reverence for and understanding of the diversity itself, whether within or beyond the boundaries of Roman Catholicism, must precede the attempt to order it. Developments and implications of this theme can be found in Vatican II's *Unitatis Redintegratio* (on Christian unity) and *Ad Gentes* (on the missionary apostolate) and are further elaborated in Pope John Paul II's encyclical *Ut Unum Sint*.[73] The Congregation for the Doctrine of the Faith echoes these sources in its "Reflections on the Primacy of Peter": "Listening to what the churches are saying is, in fact, an earmark of the ministry of unity, a consequence also of the unity of the episcopal body and of the *sensus fidei* of the entire people of God."[74]

In this area the pluralist cultural milieu of American local church communities may already have helped them develop a broader understanding of themselves as church. The Notre Dame study found "broad

[72] Searle, "The Notre Dame Study," 141.

[73] Second Vatican Council, *Unitatis Redintegratio,* in Walter Abbot, ed., *The Documents of Vatican II* (New York: Herder and Herder, 1966) 341–66 (especially #4 and #9); *Ad Gentes,* in ibid. 584–630 (#15, for example); John Paul II, *Ut Unum Sint,* in *Origins* 25:4 (1995) (especially #28–30).

[74] Congregation for the Doctrine of the Faith, "Reflections on the Primacy of Peter," *Origins* 28:32 (1998) 562 (#10) (hereafter cited as "CDF, 'Primacy of Peter'").

support for ecumenical contact" in the mid-1980's.[75] More recently questions of unity and cohesion within Catholicism itself have come more to the fore, as the drift toward a "traditionalist" identity at St. Joseph's suggests. These two developments in fact may influence each other. As one popular work on the spirituality of lay ministers puts it, there are moments when "we might find ourselves in closer *koinōnia*, or spiritual union, with people from other denominations than we do with people from our own pews."[76] Such a spiritual connection is as likely to be experienced between traditionalist Catholics and evangelical Protestants as it is between progressivist Catholics and "mainline" Protestants. This has been true for even longer in the predominantly Protestant cultural setting of Aquinas in Jamaica. Despite the strong Catholic loyalties elicited by the sometimes quite virulent and open anti-Catholicism of certain groups in Jamaica, there is a quite widespread expectation of inter-congregational cooperation among mainline Christian groups. Especially among the poor, whose primary identification tends to be with their religiously mixed physical neighborhoods, there is often little hesitation about blending participation in the activities and worship of both Catholic and Protestant, or even syncretist, congregations. Such apparently "divided" loyalties rarely discourage people from considering themselves, and being considered by others, to be active members of the Aquinas congregation. Altogether, the close daily contact that many Catholics in such situations now have with members of other faith communities extends their network of relationships beyond denominational boundaries. At the same time it may possibly even enhance their connection to the local community that claims them as members.

Local Community and Authority

Despite its limitations, and largely because of the unique features of its particular context, the local church community enjoys a certain authority among its members and in its particular place. For some this church is a protector: a community of concern to which members and strangers both can turn in particular need. The shape of this reliance

---

[75] Castelli and Gremillion, *Emerging Parish*, 179.

[76] Greg Dues and Barbara Walkley, *Called to Parish Ministry: Identity, Challenges, and Spirituality of Lay Ministers* (Mystic, CT: Twenty-Third Publications, 1995) 58.

depends a great deal on the particular church community in question. Parishioners of St. Matthew's, St. Joseph's, and Aquinas rely on the church community in many ways for protection from material hardship, from the immigrant's uncertainty, from the fear of lost identity. It may be true that, in those places where there is greater development of social institutions, contemporary generations seek less assistance from the parish than previous ones did,[77] and that for certain kinds of need members are much less apt to turn to the church at all. Nonetheless, many parish communities are still significantly involved in social assistance in ways that tend to raise their relevance and standing among their own members and within the wider society.[78]

Congregations that readily understand themselves as community appear to be more likely to reach out to those in need.[79] This connection between community sensibility and Christian praxis suggests that the intimacy of community has an authority of its own that arises in its encouragement of the concrete practice of Christian life. This could also be referred to as an "authority of belonging." The complex process of building and maintaining the network of human relationships gives an authority to the community that both comes from and extends over the lives of its members. While cherished statements of orthodoxy and tradition may come from the wider church, they are apt to remain dead letters unless they are animated within a community of solidarity, whether that be parish, small group, or family.

We are led, then, by a kind of practical logic, to consider the *teaching* authority of local community. Among traditional parishioners there are some who profess their loyalty to the church by declaring that they recognize as true religion "only what the nuns taught me." Yet this, curiously, is also an affirmation of the authority of the local community. In the past the teaching sisters were such an important part of the network of relationships in a parish that their word took on the authority of "The Church." Many teachers of the post-Vatican II era have had the

---

[77] Castelli and Gremillion, *Emerging Parish*, 74.

[78] See Putnam, *Bowling Alone*, 68.

[79] Alan K. Mock, et al., "Threading the Needle: Faith and Works in Affluent Churches," in Carl S. Dudley, et al., eds., *Carriers of Faith: Lessons from Congregational Studies* (Louisville: Westminster John Knox, 1991) 99. Philip J. Murnion, "The Community Called Parish," in Lawrence Cunningham, ed., *The Catholic Faith: A Reader* (New York and Mahwah, NJ: Paulist, 1988) 188–90, discusses this link under the rubric of "Community as Solidarity."

experience of hearing the words of councils and popes countered, in full confidence, with the simple explanations once offered to children in a parish school. Fortunately for a more growth-oriented Christian praxis, contemporary Catholics are no longer so apt to look to parish staffs for the answers to "all of life's problems."[80] The Notre Dame study found core Catholics matching levels of authority with the perceived scope of the issue at hand and not looking for higher authority to deal with what are perceived as local or personal problems.[81] Therefore, while no one would claim that the authority of the local community surpasses that of the hierarchy, indications are that the local level of church is beginning to recognize and exercise, as a Christian community, its own influence over the teaching and policies of the church as they affect the local community directly. In light of this influence it is understandable that Bishop Robert Carlson should have referred to the parish as "the active expression of [the] local Church," which actually "shapes the priest's ministry by its needs,"[82] and that Philip Murnion and David DeLambo should have remarked that "it appears that the practice of pastoral ministry that led to engaging more and more lay people in parish ministry outstrips the theology and church policy regarding lay ministry."[83]

It would be easy to misconceive this authority of the local community as just a species of hierarchical authority, exercised through the local pastor. To go beyond this simplification, the community must begin to experience itself as a family of disciples within the universal church, with its own type of inherent authority. Because it is rooted in interrelationship and not in office, this authority is genuine and effective not as a political counterweight to hierarchy but as exercised in relationships of generosity and mutuality. In light of the Notre Dame parish study, Castelli and Gremillion described the parish "as an integrated, life-giving community" that "with its own history, self-awareness, and future . . . animates lay participation and communal purposes throughout the People of God and similarly enlivens

[80] Castelli and Gremillion, *Emerging Parish*, 74.

[81] Ibid.

[82] Robert J. Carlson, "The Parish According to the Revised Law," *Studia Canonica* 19 (1985) 6, 7. At the time of this article Carlson served as auxiliary bishop in St. Paul/Minneapolis. He later served as the Bishop of Sioux Falls, South Dakota, and was appointed to the Diocese of Saginaw, Michigan, in 2005.

[83] Murnion and DeLambo, *Parishes and Parish Ministers*, 74.

society."[84] This affirms the practical authority of the local community to shape the way in which the universal mission of the church is expressed in a particular area. Murnion and DeLambo note that this very thing is an expression of the pastoral style of the U.S. church—parishes originate the attitudes and programs they require in order to accomplish the universal mission.[85]

In exercising this practical authority the local community may indeed develop a certain resistance to interference by what it perceives as external sources, even if the interference comes from other sectors of the church itself. This is evident in the histories of the sample parishes' relationships to diocesan structures. At the same time there is a level at which the diocese is also recognized as "family." Bausch quotes the Conference for Pastoral Planning and Council Development, in their document on the reorganization of parishes:

> A tension exists in parish reorganization efforts because the Catholic Church is a communion that is hierarchically constituted. In the practical order, this tension can be either creative or destructive. Were Catholics simply congregationalists . . . this would not be the issue, but the collegiality of families related as body to the pastor as head, of parishes related as body to the local ordinary as head, and of dioceses related to the bishop of Rome as head, significantly affects the decision making process. This is not to say that those in headship merely dictate the process of outcomes without regard for the body. Rather, there is a potentially creative and life-giving struggle between the rights and responsibilities of each parish and the rights and responsibilities of the diocesan church.[86]

This concept of creative struggle might address the tensions between parish and diocese by placing them in a more meaningful and hopeful context, and help ensure a certain respect for local heritage. The reasonable expectation that this could occur requires clear recognition in ecclesiology of an inherent local authority that is based not only on the relationship of a pastor to a bishop, but on the contextualized reality of the whole local community of Christians.

To make this claim for authority on an ecclesiological and not a merely sociological basis, of course, one must see the local community as a

---

[84] Castelli and Gremillion, *Emerging Parish*, 210.

[85] Murnion and DeLambo, *Parishes and Parish Ministers*, 67.

[86] Bausch, *Parish of the Next Millennium*, 113.

place in which Christ's Spirit dwells and is at work. The Spirit alone is the source of genuine authority throughout the church.[87] Now, it is a commonplace in ecclesiology that "where two or three are gathered" in Christ's name, his Spirit is present in their midst.[88] Bishop Victor Balke, for example, urged the pastors of his diocese "to listen carefully to the ideas and insights expressed by the [parish pastoral] council in the conviction that the Holy Spirit speaks in and through them."[89] John Paul II described a parish as "the community in which and with which Jesus Christ reconfirms the presence of God."[90] Bishop Thomas Murphy affirmed that "each parish must respond in its own unique way to the needs of its people in order to reveal the presence of God."[91] The common thread in all of these statements is the confidence that the Spirit of God is at work also in this local level of church. Thomas Sweetser outlines a pattern in church history by which "new models become accepted and incorporated into the main body of Church life and operation" after beginning in particular—even marginalized—local communities.[92] If this confidence is well founded, we must learn to listen carefully even when what we hear is unexpected. The Spirit in our local communities will forge not only practical policy but also modes of faith, prayer, and mission.

To sum up, the very idea of community is beleaguered in the present social circumstances, especially but not exclusively in the U.S. Yet the notion of community is essential to local church bodies and, indeed, to the church as a whole. Contemporary ecclesiology cannot ignore the task of coming to understand the practical meaning of community today,

[87] An interesting statement of this fundamental point is made in reference to the "Holy Spirit, who governs the church" as the ground for papal primacy in CDF, "Primacy of Peter," 562 (#10).

[88] Castelli and Gremillion, *Emerging Parish,* 210, linking this assurance to the parish vitality demonstrated by the Notre Dame study, present it as the central reason for hope in the U.S. church.

[89] Balke, "The Parish Pastoral Council," 824 (#21).

[90] John Paul II, as quoted in Carlson, "The Parish According to the Revised Law," 8.

[91] Thomas Murphy as quoted in Carlson, "The Parish According to the Revised Law," 8. At the time he made this statement Murphy was bishop of Great Falls, Montana; he later served as coadjutor and then archbishop of Seattle, and died in 1997.

[92] Sweetser, *Successful Parishes,* 163–64.

even as it acknowledges its complex and ever-widening context. On the other hand, the Christian community's self-understanding cannot neglect its own tradition. In the following chapter I will underscore that this tradition does not call merely for a binding social institution that could be called "community." Rather, it requires a kind of *intimacy* that is based on the presence of Christ himself within the church.

Chapter Three

Intimacy, Authenticity, and the Foundations of Community

The stories of actual communities, and a close look at the idea of community itself, suggest a perspective on the church as a local phenomenon characterized by personal bonds and face-to-face relationships. This local quality is not just a feature of an individual's encounter with the church, but is embedded in the whole of church history. It cannot be regarded as merely an inconvenient consequence of our limited physical existence unless we are willing to cast doubt on our whole understanding of the church as existing and acting within human history. Localness is more than an accident tolerated within certain boundaries while we wait for perfect unity. In the Christian tradition *koinōnia*—communion—is an essential dimension of living with faith in Christ.

As the preceding chapter has pointed out, the most daunting challenges to this foundational idea at the beginning of the twenty-first century are practical and cultural. Researchers such as Bellah and Putnam underscore a profound cultural ambivalence toward community structures, at least in the U.S. Some of the same research and other studies more specifically aimed at church life help to establish that it is both possible and necessary to challenge this ambivalence. Nonetheless, disagreement remains within the church about the expectations we should place on the actual experience of community. Prominent commentators on church life in the decades since Vatican II have sometimes flatly rejected the notion of "intimacy" as a community ideal. I have mentioned that Canadian theologian Gregory Baum has called such an ideal "illusory" because it asks for too much; the church is only one of many communities to which people belong.[1] Sociologist Andrew Greeley echoes this perspective in warning against "misguided attempts to force highly stylized forms of intimacy on everyone, whether they are ready for it or not." He concludes that "the enthusiasm of some clergy for 'creating community' is simplistic when it is not dangerous."[2] The pastoral researcher Philip Murnion considered the idea of "solidarity" in parish communities more evocative than that of "intimacy," which seemed to neglect outreach beyond a closed circle.[3] The accuracy of such objections is among the reasons why it is so important to see local community in its full context, as one of a series of ever-widening circles of church and society.

Even given these hesitations, however, personal interaction remains foundational in the origins, history, and theology of church. It is this face-to-face community experience that I call "intimacy" in the context of the local community. The church at this concrete and personal level is the way in which most people, whether members of the church or not, encounter the institution. A large part of the most practical work of the church is accomplished here, and much of the institutional support for larger structures flows from it, both directly and indirectly. Even more fundamentally, the local community conceives its own particular perspectives on Christian faith and passes them on to the larger church in a variety of ways. As I have already begun to indicate, therefore, the local community is also a place where the church is extensively *shaped*, and its way of understanding itself and living its mission in the world is deeply affected. The importance of the intimate local community as a part of the overall structure of the church is not just practical, but authoritative.

In the church, then, "intimacy" and "authority" are concepts that help to explain each other. Rather than a mere imposition, authority as I will present it here flows from the history and ongoing function of a society and acts to bind a community together. It therefore requires a founda-

---

[1] Gregory Baum, "The Church of Tomorrow," in *New Horizon: Theological Essays* (New York: Paulist, 1972) 141.

[2] Andrew Greeley, "The Persistence of Community," in Andrew Greeley and Gregory Baum, eds., *The Persistence of Religion. Concilium: Religion in the Seventies* (New York: Herder and Herder, 1973) 34.

[3] Philip J. Murnion, "The Community Called Parish," in Lawrence Cunningham, ed., *The Catholic Faith: A Reader* (New York and Mahwah, NJ: Paulist, 1988) 188–90.

tion in shared values that all levels of the community can recognize in the life and leadership of the institution. These binding values are kept vital not by official decree, but by concrete acceptance, practice, and transmission—the very fabric of local community life. The Catholic Christian recognizes the source of these values in the tradition of the ministry, death, and resurrection of Jesus Christ, and regards the pope and bishops as essential conservators and preachers of this tradition. Yet it is in the intimate setting of the local community—whatever shape that community may take under a wide variety of circumstances—that Christians receive the tradition as a living thing, put it into practice with other believers, and allow it to unfold in the realities of daily life.

This chapter will look more closely at the relationships among these fundamental concepts. I will begin by considering the word "intimacy" itself, and the way in which I justify its application to local Christian communities. I will then turn to the three interwoven terms "authority," "authoritative," and "authenticity," in order to shed light on the connection between the intimacy of local communities and the authenticity of the church as a whole. This authenticity is a reflection of the ministry of Jesus himself, which passed into the life of the early church and, despite serious challenges, has continued to shape its structures. After tracing some elements of this history I will conclude the chapter with another look at how these concepts are being demonstrated in the community lives of parishes like St. Joseph's, Aquinas, and St. Matthew's.

The Interweaving of Intimacy and Authority

Intimacy and the Local Community. The question of how great a degree of intimacy should be demanded of a church community recalls the distinction between the German terms *Gemeinschaft* and *Gemeinde*, first introduced into ecclesiology in Martin Luther's Large Catechism and employed in the early twentieth century by sociological pioneer Max Weber.[4] Both terms can translate as "community," but the first focuses

---

[4] Martin Luther, "The Large Catechism: Of the Creed," trans. Friedrich Bente and William H. T. Dau, in *Triglot Concordia: The Symbolical Books of the Evangelical Lutheran Church* (St. Louis: Concordia Publishing House, 1921) 565–773, Section 10, Article 3. Max Weber, *Economy and Society: An Outline of Interpretive Sociology*, ed. Guenther Roth and Claus Wittich (New York: Bedminster Press, 1968) 2:452–57.

on a broad "communion" or "association," while the other, used by Luther to designate the *congregation,* is experienced as an immediate, felt bond among people, a "primary group."[5] The standard German translation from Latin of the Nicene Creed's phrase *"communionem sanctorum"* ("communion of saints") was *"Gemeinschaft der Heiligen."* To this Luther objected, saying that the correct phrase in German was *"heilige Gemeinde"* ("holy congregation"), "upon earth a little holy group and congregation of pure saints."[6] Luther's point seems to be that the *communio* of the creed is neither a distant heavenly body nor a vague earthly communion, but a visible assembly "where there is nothing but [continuous, uninterrupted] forgiveness of sin, both in that God forgives us and in that we forgive, bear with, and help each other."[7] Despite the clear interpersonal implications of this description, Luther does speak at the same time of "Christendom," and so understands the visible "holy congregation" also in a broader sense.

Weber's work with the two terms does not dismiss one in favor of the other, but tries to understand how they relate. With regard to religious community in particular, the immediate bond of the "primary group" *(Gemeinde),* while it may be based on deeply shared convictions and experience, is affected by the very structural arrangements that attempt to preserve it as a *lasting* community *(Gemeinschaft).*[8] The structures come to substitute for the felt bond that they were meant to make permanent. Since the "association" relies on a broad communal iden-

---

[5] For the terms "association" and "primary group" see Evelyn Eaton Whitehead, "The Structure of Community: Toward Forming the Parish as a Community of Faith," in eadem, ed., *The Parish in Community and Ministry* (New York: Paulist, 1978) 38. Note that the distinction being made here is somewhat different from the perhaps more familiar distinction between *Gemeinschaft* ("community") and *Gesellschaft* ("society") promoted by the nineteenth-century German sociologist Ferdinand Tönnies. See his *Community and Civil Society,* ed. José Harris; trans. José Harris and Margaret Hollis. Cambridge Texts in the History of Political Thought (Cambridge and New York: Cambridge University Press, 2001). Gregor Siefer, "Ecclesiological Implications of Weber's Definition of 'Community,'" in Gregory Baum and Andrew Greeley, eds., *The Church as Institution. Concilium* 91 (New York: Herder and Herder, 1974) 149, suggests that Weber seeks to distance himself from Tönnies' approach.

[6] Luther, "Large Catechism," Section 10, Article 3.

[7] Ibid.

[8] Siefer, "Ecclesiological Implications," 150.

tity, to reduce the "primary group" to a "mere administrative district" risks making it "a calcified relic" of a community identity *(Gemeinschaft)* that has ceased to exist.[9] Such an assembly would be a parish, but not a true congregational community *(Gemeinde)*.[10] Weber thus stresses the necessity of *active* influence on the part of the laity who make up the parishes, building up a picture of small local communities that deliberately *choose* their association with one another.

> Mere "feeling" for the common position and its consequences no longer produces [communization]. Only when they [people distinguished by a common characteristic] *direct* their behavior *towards* one another on the basis of this feeling, does a social relation arise between them—not only between each one of them and the environment—and "community" comes into being only to the extent that it bears witness to a felt togetherness.[11]

As an observer, Weber is not remarkably optimistic that local congregations are capable of keeping alive the felt community bond of Christianity.

Regardless of the challenges and difficulties sociology may see, ecclesiology is not free to make a purely practical decision about the role of intimacy in local church communities. *Koinōnia,* a basic biblical designation for Christian community, has a root meaning in Greek which "suggests what is common, hence words such as 'fellowship,' 'participation,' 'communion,' and 'solidarity,' always with a personal element."[12] It is this "personal element" that I am underlining by the use of the word "intimacy." In light of the cautions already voiced this term may not seem particularly appropriate, since the most popular uses of "intimacy" and "intimate" rely heavily on ideas of "close familiarity" or even "sexual familiarity." The most basic sense of these words, however, refers to what is inmost, essential, or intrinsic. When "intimate" is used as a verb it refers to making something known or familiar.[13] Despite the more narrow popular usage, these nuances make "intimacy" a meaningful

---

[9] Ibid. 149.

[10] Weber, *Economy and Society* 2:455.

[11] Weber, *Wirtschaft und Gesellschaft,* quoted in Siefer, "Ecclesiological Implications," 158.

[12] Christopher O'Donnell, "Communion—Koinonia," in *Ecclesia: A Theological Encyclopedia of the Church* (Collegeville: Liturgical Press, 1996) 94.

[13] See *Oxford English Dictionary,* 2d ed., s.v. "intimate, *a.*" See also ibid., s.vv. "intimacy" and "intimate, *v.*"

term for a wide variety of situations, from the intimacy between a husband and wife to the intimate feel of a Roosevelt "fireside chat" delivered to the entire nation. In the discussion of local church communities "intimacy" serves to highlight relationships based on face-to-face contact between persons, as opposed to those sustained entirely on an institutional level. It further underscores the essential ("intimate") character of these relationships to the church and their potential for revealing ("intimating") the presence and work of the Spirit more deeply.

There is no denying, of course, that the very flexibility of the word can also give rise to misunderstanding. For reasons that are explored in the social research on community, some situations that might today be described readily as "intimate" might perhaps be better termed "simultaneous individualism." Contemporary American culture has a well-recognized difficulty with personal commitment. The problem has grown alongside a tendency to disconnect the search for intimacy from the formation of a stable personal identity within a community.[14] "Intimacy" can then come to designate a certain rejection of community rather than its inmost reality. We speak of trying to "be alone with someone."

Because of such developments it is crucial for Christians to understand the interpersonal dimension within the institutional and stabilizing elements of their communities. The physical and social structures on the parish level are far from being mere obstacles to intimacy, as easy as it may be to caricature them in that way. The sample parishes demonstrate concretely that formal structures help to create, maintain, and give shape to interpersonal relationships and networks and are, in fact, essential to them. It is difficult to imagine Biddeford's Franco-Americans retaining their distinct spiritual identity, or Dorchester's Haitians cooperating with so many other ethnic groups, or the elite and the poor of the Papine area of Kingston coming together in shared effort, without their respective parish structures. To describe the local church community as "intimate" acknowledges that at this level—most often the parish, but by no means always—Christians encounter one another face to face even while being aware of themselves primarily as church. Here they must somehow come to terms with the personal demands the relationship of Christian community makes upon them.

Robert Bellah's research strongly suggests a felt need for intimacy in this local experience. Catholics, he says, "identify their faith primarily

---

[14] William Kilpatrick, *Identity and Intimacy* (New York: Delacorte, 1975) 14–16.

with what goes on in the family and local parish," and look for "personal and accessible priests" and "warmer, more personal parishes."[15] The dangers of isolation and superficiality in such thinking are clear enough, yet the crucial nature of interpersonal relationships in the local church also stands out in the interaction of subgroups and personalities in the sample parishes. There the intimacy of the local community is evident despite, and even within, the undeniable individualism, tribalism, and disorganization. Each of the three parishes is a different example of the ways in which the demands, struggles, and self-expression of the local community give shape and substance to the church in its particular place. From their very beginnings communities like St. Joseph's, Aquinas, and St. Matthew's have carried a built-in expectation that they would foster face-to-face interaction among their members. This expectation has continued to play a crucial role in shaping the community. It lies behind the identification of the parishes with traditional neighborhood, class, and ethnic groups, but also with the almost instinctive outreach beyond those groups to new neighbors, more recent immigrants, those in particular need. The desire for, search for, and expectation of intimacy is a major life-giving force in local church communities.

Authority, the Authoritative, and Authenticity. Both what the local community identifies with and what it reaches out to can help to define "church" in the minds of the community's members. Living in the intimate connections built up in the local community, people form an idea of the *authenticity* of church—what it must always be in order to remain legitimately *church.* This identity is based on the beliefs and values the community has come to hold as *authoritative.* There can be no genuine *authority* without this shared sense of what is most basically true. These interrelated qualities arise in the rich network of associations that develop among persons within the community. They become foundational for the particular members of the community to the extent that they are intimately a part of that network. In turn, they serve as a measure both for maintenance and for reform of the community. Though they have an organic quality, they are not a transitory or unstable phenomenon, but build up over time and are conveyed to new generations and new arrivals in the community.

[15] Robert Bellah, et al., *Habits of the Heart: Individualism and Commitment in American Life* (updated ed. Berkeley, CA: University of California Press, 1996) 226, 232.

Following the approach of theologian David Stagaman, I understand *authority* as the very bond that creates and maintains communal relationships.[16] As distinct from *domination,* authority is exercised and experienced within a concrete situation that it both acknowledges and responds to. In the church this concrete location is the rich context of Christian community life. In situations such as the sample parishes this community location both shapes and is shaped by the exercise of authority it experiences. This means that the shape of the community and the exercise of authority within it are inseparably related. Authority reveals itself in the customs, practices, and attitudes that foster both initiative and a sense of obligation among the members of a community. Authority "gives a particular identity to a community"[17] and so is analogous to rational free choice in an individual. The rule of conduct and belief that follows when authority is understood in this way has meaning for the Christian community not only because it issues from a respected external office but, most essentially, because it *resonates* with the lived Christian experience of the community.

Stagaman uses the term *"the authoritative"* to describe "foundational beliefs and values of the community that make the group the particular community it is."[18] In the Christian context the authoritative is the particular community's very identity *as* Christian, within which all the rules and norms given by those acting in authority must resonate. Stagaman writes that the authoritative has the same relationship to authority that *character* has to individual *freedom:* it "functions as the reason why the person chooses as she or he does."[19] The exercise of authority within a community shapes its identity—the self-understanding that the community will consider authoritative from then on. On the other hand, the authoritative self-understanding that the community already holds also shapes the way the community can understand and exercise authority to begin with. The relationship between "authority" and "the authoritative" is, then, completely reciprocal. Genuine authority must therefore connect with the community within which it operates at a *depth* that is variously described as the "fundamental law" or the "com-

---

[16] David J. Stagaman, *Authority In the Church* (Collegeville: Liturgical Press, 1999) x.

[17] Ibid.

[18] Ibid. 10.

[19] Ibid.

mon conscience"[20] of a society, the basis for shared forms of reasoning,[21] or the "directions of action" a society takes collectively.[22] This deep authoritative base imparts what one writer calls a "sacrosanct character to everything invested with authority."[23]

The quality of recognizing and owning the authoritative foundation of a community, living and exercising authority in a way that resonates with it, is called *"authenticity"* by Stagaman. For Christians, Jesus is the ultimate exemplar of this quality, which always accompanies authority as the New Testament describes it.

> Jesus himself acted with assurance and decisiveness. . . . But it was the fact that he lived the rule of God the way it should be lived that best exemplified his authority. There was no disparity between what he said and what he did. In both his words and deeds, he was totally consumed with the rule of God, so much so that the message and the works drew attention to the rule of God, and not to him.[24]

Jesus' authenticity, Stagaman goes on to contend, was mirrored by the disciples who proclaimed him with the power of his own Spirit after the Resurrection.

Jesus acted in such a way that he touched the heart of what the community already held dear. He did so not because it was expected of him or imposed on him, but because this authoritative heart was his *own.* For these reasons it was impossible for those who experienced him to be indifferent. Clearly, for many the experience was one of scandal that led to the rejection of his authority to interpret the relationship between God and God's People. For disciples, however—for those who would

[20] Charles W. Hendel, "An Exploration of the Nature of Authority," in Carl J. Friedrich, ed., *Authority. Nomos* I (Cambridge: Harvard University Press, 1958) 11, 17.

[21] Carl J. Friedrich, "Authority, Reason, and Discretion," in Friedrich, ed., *Authority*, 35.

[22] Talcott Parsons, "Authority, Legitimation, and Political Action," in Friedrich, ed., *Authority*, 198.

[23] Hendel, "Exploration of the Nature of Authority," 10. Hendel's statement recalls the analysis of the connection between Roman religion and Roman ideas of authority in Hannah Arendt, "What Is Authority?," in eadem, *Between Past and Future: Eight Exercises in Political Thought* (New York: Viking, 1968) 121ff.

[24] Stagaman, *Authority in the Church*, 67.

become the nucleus of the church—Jesus so enlivened their understanding of this relationship that the template for *authentic* teaching
and action in the church would, from then on, be the life of Jesus himself. Because of his authentic interpretation of the authoritative roots of
his community, Jesus' own authority—his right to shape and transform
what would now be acknowledged as authoritative—was recognized
as the ultimate authority for a new community.

Intimacy and Authenticity. Christian authenticity is, therefore, something that can be recognized and responded to in the personal interactions of members of the community, according to the pattern of Jesus'
relationship with his disciples. Such recognition and mutual understanding require a certain shared history, an authoritative foundation
that is not unlike the *personal* identity that psychologist William Kilpatrick describes:

> [A crucial factor in sustaining identity] is the presence of other people
> who have shared our past or who at least can affirm our memory of the
> past. An identity cannot stand alone—not for long. We need others to
> bear witness to our personal history, others who are willing to take note
> of our passage. They give to us something we cannot always give to
> ourselves: the assurance that our history has been and is being recorded.
> . . . Without others to confirm his self-worth, a man *[sic]* soon comes to
> doubt that he has any.[25]

This relationship is not one of mere receptivity, however. Kilpatrick further points out that "as identity develops, the urge to share it grows
more insistent. Yet by giving ourselves over to the things and people
that matter to us we get back a fuller identity in return."[26] The individual, moreover, is not the only beneficiary. The kind of personal commitment and identity formation Kilpatrick describes lead directly to the
strengthening of the interpersonal ties that form the network that is the
local community.

I have already emphasized that a local church community, by virtue
of its relationship with the whole Christian tradition, does not simply
create its own identity. Both in human history and in its spiritual connection to Christ, the community *receives* its identity. Even the spiritual
bond itself—the *koinōnia*—is gift in this sense. Yet precisely because this

---

[25] Kilpatrick, *Identity and Intimacy*, 4.
[26] Ibid. 6.

identity is that of a living community it does not and cannot remain static, as if it were always and forever imposed from the outside on a more or less uncooperative subject. It is lived and owned by the particular persons who relate to Christ and to one another in this particular community. Having been brought into a *koinōnia* that preceded them, they have claimed it as their own identity by living in it. The structures that seek to institutionalize this bond in Christ among the members can never legitimately substitute for it, but must always serve it. To the extent that these structures are "authentic," therefore, they derive their authenticity from the *koinōnia* and not the other way around. So it is the *koinōnia*, embodied and therefore enlivened in the intimate day-to-day interactions of the local community, that gives the community an authentic voice.

Catholic philosopher Dick Westley argues persuasively that this voice is no mere parrot, but a place to which the whole church can look for authentic revelation. This realization is based, in the first place, on the conviction that human intimacy is itself to be understood by Christians as an embodiment of the love of Christ. Westley calls this "redemptive intimacy."[27] In describing the concept he emphasizes the way in which Christian love is expressed in encounter with the other rather than in purpose-driven confrontation.[28] As Jesus' own ministry demonstrates, it is not indignant defense of the Law but grace-filled invitation to relationship that nurtures the Gospel. To shape lives that embody both this invitation and its acceptance requires surrender and self-sacrifice—again, the qualities of Jesus' own ministry. As Westley puts it, "There is no use our any longer pretending to love everyone in general (Christian charity) if we are not willing to risk being intimate with someone in particular."[29]

For Westley this essentially embodied experience of Christian intimacy is not merely the fulfillment of a duty revealed to us in some other forum, but is in itself a place for encountering the Word of God. As is made most dramatically clear in the story of the Last Judgment in Matthew 25, Christians seek and find Christ in the midst of their relationships with one another: "For I was hungry and you gave me food" (Matt 25:35). Westley adds a further perspective:

[27] Dick Westley, *Redemptive Intimacy: A New Perspective for the Journey to Adult Faith* (Mystic, CT: Twenty-Third Publications, 1991) 103–18.

[28] Ibid. 98.

[29] Ibid. 105.

> Sometimes when we act we affect others in much the same way as the
> Lord did. . . . They are happier just knowing we are there. . . . We
> would never have been able to discern this by ourselves; we learn of
> our gifts from others. Conversely, they learn of their gifts from us. For
> in our smiles, loving glances, joyful songs, and feelings of enhancement
> is revealed to them their truest and most gracious selves.[30]

Learning of our "most gracious selves" necessarily means learning
of God, the Creator and Giver of Grace. As Westley consistently maintains, human experience of this sort profoundly shapes our theological
understanding. In turn, it is this understanding that shapes our desire
to build and maintain the human structures that are necessary to continue sharing these formative experiences. The picture emerges of a
church made up of a complex interaction of intimate experience, reflection on the presence of Christ within that experience, and commitment
to the structures that allow that experience to continue. Westley com-
pletes the picture of this theological view of human intimacy by making the direct link to redemption:

> Only intimate encounter can deliver us from our loneliness, isolation,
> and alienation. Only intimacy heals us by assuaging our doubts about
> God's forgiveness and empowering us to forgive one another. Only in
> intimacy do we "encounter" the one who makes intimacy possible—
> the Great Self in whom all being is rooted and finds redemption. If inti-
> macy is not redemptive, then nothing in this life ever can be.[31]

The Authoritative in the Life of the Local Community: A Social Analysis.
An initial reaction to the concept of "the authoritative" may well be that it
is too broad and deep a reality to look for in a place as restricted as a local
community. The concrete lived experience that we find in the local community is shaped by a variety of deeper influences, rooted as far back as
its most distant origins, which give it meaning and purpose in the minds
of its members. Countless elements of what has weight and influence
come to the community from outside itself. These elements are carried
forward from other generations through tradition, and they are carried
across from other communities through assimilation. On the other hand,
the function of the authoritative, as the foundational aspect of authority,
requires it to have an intimate connection with daily life and interper-

[30] Ibid. 125–26.
[31] Ibid. 109.

sonal relationships. Otherwise it is precisely its essential depth and breadth that will be lost; what does not connect to concrete living comes to be seen as irrelevant. For that reason, regardless of where the various elements of the authoritative come from, their overall sense and direction must be "owned" and lived out by the members of the community if they are to be an actual foundation for genuine authority.

Political theorist Hannah Arendt provides an ancient, pre-Christian example of this essential link between the authoritative and the living community in her description of the ancient Roman sense of authority. In addition to the founding of the city itself Arendt names "the sanctity of house and hearth" as the other essential element of "the deeply political content of Roman religion,"[32] the wellspring of the Roman understanding of authority. Unlike the Greeks, the Romans understood that the gods dwelt permanently in their city with them, and so the ordinary life of the city was *re-ligatus*, "linked back" to the founders and all that had happened to the city since the beginning. To speak of authority in Rome was to speak of the very identity of its people.

By contrast, Johannes-Baptist Metz offers a glimpse of what happens if this connection between the sources of authority and the life of a community is lost. In his commentary on the "crisis of tradition" in the Western world[33] Metz notes that since the eighteenth-century Enlightenment we have tended to view tradition as "an object of historical knowledge or a storehouse of information."[34] This seriously compromises the Christian function of tradition as a living link back to the origins of the faith, in the style of the Romans as depicted by Arendt. Whereas "the most tradition-minded centuries," in the words of theologian Henri de Lubac, "were soaked through with it,"[35] we instead tend to speak of tradition as something to which we *return*. In considering tradition we seem to believe that we face a choice either simply to recreate a past experience or set of conclusions or to reject tradition as obsolete and irrelevant. Either way we lose the ability to see religious tradition as binding together a *living community*. Instead it becomes a mere tool either for a privatized religious devotion or for a sectarian

---

[32] Arendt, "What Is Authority?" 121.

[33] Johannes-Baptist Metz, *Faith in History and Society: Toward a Practical Fundamental Theology*, trans. David Smith (New York: Seabury, 1980) 36–39.

[34] Ibid. 36.

[35] Henri de Lubac, *The Splendour of the Church*, trans. Michael Mason (New York: Sheed and Ward, 1956) 1.

attempt to withdraw from "the world" (that is, from ordinary human history itself). At these extremes we focus either on an ideal based on our notions of the past, apart from the reality of the community as it actually exists, or we focus instead on individual experience, ignoring its true context. In either case the *community's story* is lost; it may not even seem to *have* a particular story. Metz's critique of what he calls "middle-class religion" is particularly relevant here:

> One of the greatest dangers of middle-class life is that everything that does not conform to calculating reason and the laws of profit and success is left to individual and private choice. By making religion a purely service religion to which he turns as a private individual, the middle-class citizen has also made tradition a value of which he makes use as a private individual.[36]

Yet communities such as St. Joseph's, Aquinas, and St. Matthew's know intuitively that they do indeed have a particular story, that the individual experience and understanding of church would be very different in another context. This is the very reason for taking time to consider the particular circumstances and issues within these communities and some of the social factors that exercise an influence on them. Generally community members relate to these factors as "given"—that is, they do not usually analyze them carefully.[37] When they do reflect on them, their apparently simultaneous or even circular operation on the community may defy any imposed timeline or analytical system. Yet it is to these influences that one would have to turn to begin constructing a detailed account of the *content* of the authoritative foundation for any particular local community.

Every local church community comes into existence within a general cultural setting that exists first. In most instances that background culture provides many of the basic attitudes and values for the community itself. At the very least it provides the contrast that makes the differing attitudes and values of the community stand out and so receive a different significance and new meaning. Especially in culturally mixed communities (as all three of the sample parishes are in their own ways), the crosscurrents

---

[36] Metz, *Faith in History and Society*, 37.

[37] Hans-Georg Gadamer, *Truth and Method*, trans. Joel Weinsheimer and Donald G. Marshall (rev. 2d ed. New York: Continuum, 1995) 276: "Long before we understand ourselves through the process of self-examination, we understand ourselves in a self-evident way in the family, society, and state in which we live."

of influence can become extremely complex and difficult to trace. Is St. Joseph's no longer a French-Canadian enclave, now that appreciable numbers of Catholics from other places and backgrounds have found a spiritual home there? Is Aquinas a "university parish" or a "parish of the poor"? How have Haitians at St. Matthew's found themselves changing in response to years of negotiating a place amidst English-speaking neighbors and Irish pastors? It is actually in such situations that the power of these cultural forces—which are the effects over time of the kind of contextual features (language, law, etc.) discussed in Chapter Two—becomes especially evident.

This is why, in looking for the foundations of *authority*, it is preferable *not* to begin specifically with the work of God's Spirit forming the community, even though it is ultimately a theological understanding that we seek. The experiences and concepts by which God's presence and work can be recognized and understood are initially given, or withheld, by the various cultures within which the community exists and by which its members have been nurtured. The most basic determinants of the authoritative, then, will not be theological formulas so much as concrete social structures—family, friendship, work, government, and so forth. These are the factors that underscore the cultural setting, whether of Christian inspiration or otherwise, that the community must negotiate daily. How any particular community will understand—and integrate into their lives and experience—God, the church, and a host of particular values depends on the interaction of these social structures with a great variety of other influences.

The shared values that develop in the cultural, structural, and relational bonds of a community are more than just "a common set of goals or activities."[38] They comprise what one writer refers to as the "wisdom capital" of the community.[39] This is not unlike the way in which sociologist Anthony Giddens defines "common sense," which he sees as "comprising a more-or-less articulated body of theoretical knowledge, drawn upon to explain why things are as they are."[40] The process by which this "body of knowledge" is constructed and utilized, however,

[38] Claire Gaudiani, "Wisdom as Capital in Prosperous Communities," in Frances Hesselbein et al, eds., *The Community of the Future* (San Francisco: Jossey-Bass, 1998) 63.

[39] Ibid. 59–69.

[40] Anthony Giddens, *New Rules of Sociological Method: A Positive Critique of Interpretative Sociologies* (London: Hutchinson, 1976) 121.

is not just a simple accumulation of experiences, facts, and aphorisms rationally applied as necessary. Philosopher Hans-Georg Gadamer contends that since our understanding begins "in a self-evident way in the family, society, and state in which we live," therefore "the prejudices of the individual, far more than his judgments, constitute the historical reality of his being."[41]

Modern human beings tend to want to scrutinize these authoritative prejudices, to see if individual reason will prove their legitimacy. Yet even this process of legitimation itself is complex and bound up in factors that originate not with the individual but with the community. Sociologist Talcott Parsons suggests four such factors: the specific content of common values, the kind of thinking that is used to understand and apply them, the way in which they are learned and appropriated, and the social position of the individual who applies them in a particular circumstance.[42] The depth at which such factors operate within the whole community gives an extraordinary strength (for better and for worse) to the community's particular authoritative foundation, often making of it an apparently "natural" standard of judgment for members of the community.[43]

This, of course, gives rise to a question: do the beliefs of its members shape the community or does the community shape the beliefs of its members? What is more influential in the formation of shared values—the authoritative—and in their legitimation in Christian communities: the content of the Gospel, the choices of individuals, the social context? Though different theoretical approaches may emphasize one part of the process or another, it is clear that all these elements play important roles that are not easy to prioritize. Reflection on this kind of interdependence of elements suggests a similar relationship in the balance between local communities and larger structures of the worldwide church. In every case the local setting receives vast resources from the larger tradition, and in every case these resources go through an intense, relational, and sometimes shadowy process of shaping and appropriation for concrete living.

---

[41] Gadamer, *Truth and Method*, 276.

[42] Parsons, "Authority, Legitimation, and Political Action," 201.

[43] Herbert J. Spiro, "Authority, Values, and Policy," in Friedrich, ed., *Authority*, 57, remarks: "The true values, and the sources of authority which they provide, are more stable than policies, even under totalitarianism."

The Authoritative in the Life of the Local Community: A Theological Analysis. Members of Christian communities, of course, will not be satisfied with a purely social analysis, even if all the obscurities could be clarified. Because of its interpersonal nature, the local community also helps make it possible for the church to recognize God as something other than a social structure or a concept. Dietrich Bonhoeffer, the German pastor who died in his attempt to resist Nazism, remarked that "man's [sic] entire spirituality is interwoven with sociality, and rests upon the basic relation of I and Thou."[44] In a similar vein, the great ecclesiologist Yves Congar found "the kind of life, the fullness of joy which a man [sic] can experience . . . [with] a person whom he loves" to be "a genuine image of that presence of God in the soul which enables us to enter into contact with him . . . ."[45] Because the presence of God becomes a real experience for us in our intimate relationships with others, the network of these relationships within a particular social context becomes "local church community" both through the working of human social forces *and* by the presence of the Holy Spirit. "The unity of the Christian church," insists Bonhoeffer,

> is not based upon the oneness of human spirits, but upon the unity of the divine spirit, and the two are not identical. . . . And yet . . . the objective unity subsisting in Christ is realised in the *persons*, and it is only in being thus realised that it is objective unity.[46]

Our intimate relationships, and the community that both fosters and arises from them, are not, then, merely resources for the church's later use. Rather, they are the actual medium within which the Spirit of God continually creates and shapes the church. Seeing this, we may understand Roger Haight's contention that the Spirit "is not an objective proof of the community's being related to God," but "rather, an existential witness that God is at work in this community as God was at work in the life and ministry of Jesus."[47] In a similar vein Haight contends

---

[44] Dietrich Bonhoeffer, *The Communion of Saints: A Dogmatic Inquiry Into the Sociology of the Church,* trans. R. Gregor Smith (New York: Harper & Row, 1963) 48.

[45] Yves M.-J. Congar, *The Mystery of the Temple, or The Manner of God's Presence to His Creatures from Genesis to the Apocalypse,* trans. Reginald F. Trevett (Westminster, MD: Newman Press, 1962) 239.

[46] Bonhoeffer, *The Communion of Saints,* 138–39 (emphasis added).

[47] Roger Haight, "The Structures of the Church," *Journal of Ecumenical Studies* 30 (1993) 409.

that "the work of God as Spirit in the community [is] prior to all office
and all ministry."[48] It is the authoritative foundation of the community
in all its multiple origins that allows for the creation, acceptance, and
development of these church structures. It is therefore possible to conclude, with Haight, not despite but because of the sociological considerations, that "God as Spirit [is] the ultimate ground of offices in the
church."[49] It is in the gritty realities of day-to-day human community—
so diverse in its details from one place and time to the next—that the
Spirit, often unseen and unacknowledged, forges with us the love that
"is the bond of church unity."[50]

The ecclesiological implications of this divine cooperation in the life
of the local Christian community are deeply appreciated by the Franco-
Canadian ecclesiologist Jean-Marie Roger Tillard. In order to bear its
intended fruit, he insists, the transcendent Word *must* be incarnated in
concrete human living. This bestows upon the local community a crucial importance:

> The local church is also the crossroads of the revealed Word and its au-
> thentic reading in human existence through which God "speaks" to his
> people. This Word wills to give meaning to existence. It can attain this
> goal only if it finds resonance, if it appears as a response to an expecta-
> tion. It comes, certainly, from God—that is, through the complex net-
> works by which it connects the hearers that God wants to give to it.
> But even though its origin is thus in the transcendent mystery of the
> living God, it can only bear its fruit if it encounters another word,
> immanent "in the depths of the collective soul" with "its roots, its mes-
> sage, and its meaning," which finds in it its authentic finality. A "corre-
> spondence" is needed, even "the communion between that which
> teems in the shadowy heart of society and that which is given from be-
> yond or from on high. Not merely a balance, but the living link be-

---

[48] Ibid. 410.

[49] Ibid. 411.

[50] Bonhoeffer, *The Communion of Saints,* 140. At p. 141 Bonhoeffer also notes
the importance of this bond between particular members of the church in the
prospects for church unity: "We must not forget that unification from below is
not the same as unity from above, and that the wish for unification should be
realised, first of all, in the smaller and even the smallest congregation." See also
Aidan Harker, *Commentary on an Agreed Statement on Authority in the Church,
1976* (Enfield: Catholic League, 1977) 20, on charity as the "divine incorruptible
life-force uniting . . . every member with every other member."

tween immanence and transcendence, in the co-incarnation of an existential word."[51]

The balance to which Tillard refers arises from the depths of a community's origin and purpose as a community of believers, shaped by the Word in its midst. It thus becomes a standard for all the members—the authoritative, seen now in its specifically Christian aspect as *sensus fidelium*. Tillard describes this "sense of the faithful" as "the expression by [all the baptized] of the consciousness of the Body of Christ, in relation to their context, to their needs, to their mission, to their struggle for personal fidelity to the Gospel."[52] The joint statement on authority by the Anglican-Roman Catholic International Commission speaks of the concept in this fashion: "Shared commitment and belief create a common mind in determining how the gospel should be interpreted and obeyed. By reference to this common faith each person tests the truth of his own belief."[53] The *sensus fidelium* "actualizes and concretizes" the more elusive *sensus fidei*, "sense of the faith," which Tillard describes in turn as an "instinct" that is the expression of "a Christian life led in the authenticity of the Gospel."[54]

One ancient perspective—that of Plato, as expounded by Hannah Arendt—stresses that the ultimate source of authority is not a human product and is actually beyond the sphere of human power.[55] Christians, recognizing the Holy Spirit as the ultimate foundation of the authoritative, must certainly concur. As Canadian theologian Daniel Donovan writes, "As humanly comprehensible as so much of [the church's] life and growth is, its deepest meaning lies hidden in the divine mystery itself."[56] At the same time, the God who is active in everything

---

[51] J.-M. R. Tillard, *L'église locale: ecclésiologie de communion et catholicité* (Paris: Cerf, 1995) 127 (my translation). Tillard here cites Alphonse Dupront, *Puissances et latences de la religion catholique* (Paris: Gallimard, 1993) 56.

[52] Tillard, *L'église locale*, 315 (my translation).

[53] "Authority in the Church," #2, in Edward J. Yarnold and Henry Chadwick, *Truth and Authority: A Commentary on the Agreed Statement of the Anglican-Roman Catholic International Commission "Authority In the Church," Venice 1976* (London: SPCK / Catholic Truth Society, 1977) 42.

[54] Tillard, *L'église locale*, 314–15 (my translation).

[55] Arendt, "What Is Authority?" 111.

[56] Daniel Donovan, *The Church as Idea and Fact* (Wilmington: Michael Glazier, 1988) 23.

that shapes our understanding and response to authority is clearly not one who "is simply alien to human experience, who simply contradicts it and stands over against it."[57] God's authority is of a peculiar and overarching kind, represented in external standards and in internal processes of growth and development, both personal and communal. It is our faith in this divine presence in the church that ultimately allows us to be responsive to the authoritative history and culture of both the local community and the universal church, for the response also has a distinctive character. John E. Skinner, an Episcopal theologian, describes it in this way:

> All authority is derived from God, derived from his nurturing and liberating presence in nature and in history. Consequently, all authority should express itself as both a nurturing and liberating presence reflecting its ultimate source in the creative and redemptive act of God. The Gospel of Christ, as a result, becomes the criterion for the Christian in order to determine whether authority is present, or only organized power parading as authority.[58]

Skinner gives us here the ultimate criterion for the discernment of the Christian authoritative from amidst the whole tangled mass of foundational elements in the human community—a criterion that is the starting point of the discussion that follows.

The Roots of Christian Intimacy

The Intimate Community of Jesus and His Disciples. Emphasizing the crucial role of the local community in the maintenance of the whole church's authenticity and credibility is not merely a response to a contemporary situation. It is an original quality of the church founded in the relationship between Jesus and his disciples. Those who followed Jesus in the beginning did not respond to an established institutional structure or to new theological ideas *per se.* Rather, Jesus touched the expectation that was already in them, called them to look with new eyes at what they already knew of his Father, and challenged them to live out the truth they had already heard. He could do this because, as a first-

---

[57] Nicholas Lash, *Voices of Authority* (Shepherdstown: Patmos, 1976) 12.

[58] John E. Skinner, *The Meaning of Authority* (Washington, DC: University Press of America, 1983) 4.

century Jew, he himself knew the expectation, the call, and the truth of his people's covenant with God. To this common experience he brought his own unique relationship with the Father, his own mission, his own depth of love and commitment.

Through his ministry Jesus himself establishes human intimacy as the standard by which to judge Christian community. The Hebrew Scriptures already describe Israel's relationship with God as a familial bond between God and specific persons (as the very name "Israel," given by God to Jacob, underscores). Building on this tradition, Jesus calls his own disciples to a familial intimacy. Told that his own family is waiting to see him, he replies: "Who are my mother and [my] brothers? . . . Here are my mother and my brothers. [For] whoever does the will of God is my brother and sister and mother" (Mark 3:33-35). This attitude of the Master is to be mirrored by the disciples: "Whoever loves father or mother more than me is not worthy of me, and whoever loves son or daughter more than me is not worthy of me . . ." (Matt 10:37). To the would-be disciple who asks, "Let me go first and bury my father," he responds, "Let the dead bury their dead. But you, go and proclaim the kingdom of God" (Luke 9:59-60). The command to love "as I have loved you" (John 13:34) and its stunning sacramental expression in Jesus' washing of the disciples' feet (John 13:1-20) locate the very heart of this kingdom in the Lord's intimacy with his disciples. The gospels continually show us the permanent nature of this intimacy within the church, but nowhere more poignantly than in the eucharistic instruction to "do this in memory of me" (Luke 22:19), or in the assurance of the Last Judgment parable that "whatever you did for one of these least brothers of mine, you did for me" (Matt 25:40).

The intimacy Jesus shows toward and calls forth from his disciples is ultimately a mirror of his own relationship with God his Father. The Christian community comes to understand and describe this relationship through an unfolding variety of images,[59] from "son of God" to "one in being with the Father." Even without attempting to trace the intricacies of these theological developments we see clearly from the New Testament not only that Jesus related to God in a remarkably close

[59] Roger Haight, *Jesus Symbol of God* (Maryknoll, NY: Orbis, 1999) 152–84, maps five dominant christological approaches from the New Testament, not merely as "stages of development" toward the classic view, but with an eye toward the contexts that contributed to each and continue to suggest a contemporary relevance for each.

and intimate fashion, but also that this was remembered as an essential characteristic of his teaching. The accounts of Jesus' baptism in the Synoptic Gospels all include the voice of God declaring, "You are my beloved son; with you I am well pleased" (Luke 3:22; see also Matt 3:17 and Mark 1:11). Jesus regularly employs this Father–Son dynamic in his own prayer:

> Jesus rejoiced in the Holy Spirit and said, "I thank you Father, Lord of heaven and earth, because you have hidden these things from the wise and the intelligent and have revealed them to infants; yes, Father, for such was your gracious will. All things have been handed over to me by my Father; and no one knows who the Son is except the Father, or who the Father is except the Son and anyone to whom the Son chooses to reveal him." (Luke 10:21-22, *NRSV*)

He teaches his disciples to think of God in this same fashion:

> Love your enemies, and pray for those who persecute you, that you may be children of your heavenly Father, for he makes his sun rise on the bad and the good, and causes rain to fall on the just and on the unjust. (Matt 5:44-45)

Their prayer is to be like his prayer: "When you pray, say: Father, hallowed be your name" (Luke 11:2).

The Gospel of John develops the realization that the familial intimacy between Jesus and God involves a dimension of *mutual identification*. To a question by Philip, Jesus replies: "How can you say, 'Show us the Father?' Do you not believe that I am in the Father and the Father is in me?" (John 14:9-10). Although John does not fully clarify this identification (a task taken up in the classic christological statements of the early church councils), he does make it clear that it, too, is in some measure to be shared by Jesus' disciples:

> All mine are yours, and yours are mine; and I have been glorified in them. And now I am no longer in the world, but they are in the world, and I am coming to you. Holy Father, protect them in your name that you have given me, so that they may be one, as we are one. (John 17:10-11, *NRSV*)

This sharing by the disciples in the relationship between Jesus and the Father is presented in the same discourse in which the coming of the Spirit is announced: "He will declare to you the things that are to come.

He will glorify me, because he will take what is mine and declare it to you. All that the Father has is mine" (John 16:13-15, *NRSV*). Thus the intimacy with the Father that was the central feature of Jesus' earthly life also becomes the central feature of the life of the church, by the presence of the Spirit with the church after the ascension of Jesus. Moreover, this intimate unity between Father and Son is to bind not only individual disciples of Jesus to God the Father, but also all the members of the church with one another. As Westley sees it, Jesus' words to Philip announce

> that God is not to be found outside of humankind, but *within*, in the intimacy and togetherness of human and divine, promised and foretold in the Covenant, effected and realized in the Lord Jesus, and present in each one of us when we truly walk with him in faith.[60]

It is no accident, then, that the Christian community forms initially not around particular doctrines and structures, but around the person of Jesus. Putting concrete persons ahead of abstract structures is a hallmark of Jesus' ministry, and thus arguably essential to the community that looks to him as its standard of authenticity. He stirs controversy all along with such a preference:

> Hypocrites! Does not each one of you on the sabbath untie his ox or his ass from the manger and lead it out for watering? This daughter of Abraham, whom Satan has bound for eighteen years now, ought she not to have been set free on the sabbath day from this bondage? (Luke 13:15-16)

When he begins to order the community of his disciples he chooses followers capable of making the same option for the concrete and personal over the abstract. The Twelve, by and large, are found "not organizing the synagogues but fishing on Lake Galilee."[61] Suitability for "office" from the structural point of view is not Jesus' concern in choosing and appointing them; neither is it the community's concern later in following them.[62] The point, rather, is the kind of authority that is

---

[60] Westley, *Redemptive Intimacy*, 83.

[61] Teresa Pirola, "Church Professionalism—When Does It Become 'Lay Elitism'?" in Richard Lennan, ed., *Redefining the Church: Vision and Practice* (Alexandria, NSW, Australia: E. J. Dwyer, 1995) 77.

[62] This recalls the insistence of Roger Haight, "The Structures of the Church," 411–12, that the divine inspiration of offices in the church "is not juridical."

displayed in direct human interaction, in the openness and love of Jesus, the image of the Father.[63]

Intimate Community in the Early Development of the Church. All these qualities of Jesus, though very personal, are inherited by the community of his disciples and become the authoritative foundation of the church. The mechanism by which this occurred and continues to occur might be presented sociologically as the "routinization of charisma."[64] Its theological meaning is in the church's reception of the Holy Spirit. Both these approaches allow us to see how Jesus' authenticity (his own particular "ownership" of the authoritative, which itself becomes authoritative) is passed on to the church to become the criterion of its own authenticity.

In Jesus this authenticity was connected to his reverence for persons and for the authoritative foundations of his culture as well as to his own prophetic voice. In the same way, the church that followed him embarked on an ongoing relationship with the people and cultures around it, living in and adapting to local situations even while authentically challenging and evangelizing them. The Acts of the Apostles is filled with examples of personal encounter and local adaptation in the spirit of Jesus. When Matthias joins the Eleven, the criteria used to select this first-ever successor to an apostle underline the preeminence of personal interaction: "One of the men who accompanied us the whole time the Lord Jesus came and went among us . . . [must] become with us a witness to his resurrection" (Acts 1:21-22). The Christian community at Jerusalem continues Temple worship, but supplements it with

---

[63] With regard to the commandment to love (John 15:10-12) as a basis for authority, note Metz, *Faith In History and Society,* 41, regarding the church today: "The type of authority needed is one that is based mainly on religious competence."

[64] This suggestion that structures develop in order to preserve a group's original enthusiasm is a contribution of Max Weber, mentioned by Daniel J. Harrington, "Sociological Concepts and the Early Church: A Decade of Research," *Theological Studies* 41 (1980) 184. Haight, "Structures of the Church," 413, uses the concept in connection with his argument, also relevant to my method here, that "descriptive explanation of how they arose is also a structural explanation of the ground, status, and character of church offices *at any given time*" (emphasis in the original). Turner's ideas of the interdependence of *communitas* and structure, as presented by Carl F. Starkloff, "Church as Structure and Communitas: Victor Turner and Ecclesiology," *Theological Studies* 58 (1997) 664–65, point in a similar direction here.

close personal bonds (Acts 2:46). A split between the Hellenists and the Hebrews, involving both the administration of goods and the very nature of apostolic ministry, is resolved by the creation of a new ministry of service (Acts 6:1-6). The initial reluctance of even Jesus himself to evangelize beyond the Jewish community (Matt 10:5-6, 15:24) is gradually transformed into a full-blown mission to the Gentiles. This broad movement comes about through response to very *local* situations: the appeal of Cornelius to Peter (Acts 10:5-8), the diversity of the Christian community at Antioch (Acts 11:19-25), the rejection of Paul's proclamation by the Jews of Corinth (Acts 18:6). In all of these moments the image of the church is not one of a community striving to maintain authenticity by scrupulous mimicry, but rather one of great confidence that the new ground being broken is yet blessed by the Spirit of the Lord who remains with them. It is this confidence, and fidelity to the proclamation upon which it is based,[65] that is universal and maintained by the universal authority of the apostles as they move out from their original local community at Jerusalem. As regards community forms and the details of Christian life, as Monika Hellwig has succinctly stated it, "There is every indication that the local community shaped itself, so to speak, from below."[66]

Our picture of this specifically local dynamic is further enhanced by attention to what is known of the "house churches" of the earliest Christian centuries. The particular circumstances in which the Gospel was proclaimed in a given locality greatly influenced the structure and exercise of authority within the community that subsequently formed in that place. One of the most common occurrences seems to have been the adoption of family structures as "not only the basic unit of society but also the basic model for ecclesiastical organization."[67] As one commentator puts it, "The 'oikos-formula' is recurrent in Acts: someone is baptized or

---

[65] See Michael Warren, *At This Time, In This Place: The Spirit Embodied In the Local Assembly* (Harrisburg, PA: Trinity Press International, 1999) 84, for discussion of the role of fidelity in maintaining Christian identity in the early church.

[66] Monika Hellwig, "American Culture: Reciprocity with Catholic Vision, Values and Community," in Cassian Yuhaus, ed., *The Catholic Church and American Culture: Reciprocity and Challenge* (New York: Paulist, 1990) 73.

[67] László A. Vaskovics, "Theses on the Interdependence of Religious Organizations and Familial Sub-Systems," in Gregory Baum and Andrew Greeley, eds., *The Church as Institution. Concilium* 91 (New York: Herder and Herder, 1974) 139.

saved with his or her whole household (cf. 18:8, 16:15, 16:32-34). These texts . . . are reports or legends built around the founding of well-known house-churches."[68] The heads of such households (both women and men, according to the passages cited) were the earliest converts in a particular locale, and so its link to the wider Christian world. They would hold a place of special honor and influence as leaders of the community even after it grew to include those from outside their own household.[69] The house-church itself performed, in its own locality, the essential and universal functions of the church: it was a base for mission and a center for catechesis, preaching, and the Lord's Supper.[70] This most intimate of Christian communities, though not the sole model in use, was thus the setting for much of Christian life, and the source of some of the earliest and most fundamental self-understanding of the church. Indeed, the deep human resonance of the image of "family" has

---

[68] Hans-Josef Klauck, "The House-Church as Way of Life," *Theology Digest* 30 (1982) 155. Klauck's inclusion of the story of Lydia, the founding disciple of the church at Philippi, in his citations from Acts underscores that the term *patres familias*, employed in other discussions of the house-churches (see below), represents a narrowing of the original experience of Christian leadership. (The effects of the growth of Roman patriarchy on the church are discussed elsewhere in this chapter.)

[69] Ibid. Klauck links Jesus' mission instruction in Luke 10:7 to "remain in the same house" to a strategy of establishing a community in the first house which received the Gospel. Daniel Donovan, *The Church as Idea and Fact*, 18, points to 1 Cor 16:15-16 as evidence for the authority of the leaders of such households, and Rafael Aguirre, "La Casa Como Estructura Base del Cristianismo Primitivo: Las Iglesias Domesticas," *Estudios Eclesiásticos* 59 (1984) 46–47, suggests that eventually many of these influential *patres familias* were "officially invested with responsibility" ("ordained as bishops"). (This article is also summarized in Rafael Aguirre, "Early Christian House Churches," *Theology Digest* 32 [1985] 151–55.) John Zizioulas, *Being As Communion: Studies in Personhood and the Church* (Crestwood, NY: St. Vladimir's Seminary Press, 1985) 249, suggests a schema for the evolution of such house-churches into the broader local churches of their respective cities, and rejects the suggestion, once made by Bonhoeffer, *The Communion of Saints*, 159, that the house-churches stood for a familial particularization of the church over against the genuine local church, which was "universal" in its inclusion of all the Christians of a given locality. Klauck, "The House-Church as Way of Life," 154, like Bonhoeffer, supports a distinction "between local church and house-churches."

[70] Klauck, "The House-Church as Way of Life," 155.

been seen as one of the key features of Paul's theology of community and of the early development of ecclesiology in general.[71]

The intimate friendship with Jesus seen in the community of the apostles and the familial intimacy within the local communities seen in the house-churches come together in the early understanding of the ministry of bishops. The relatively late Pastoral Epistles of the New Testament underscore the connection between church and household leadership: 1 Tim 3:5 specifically links management of a household to episcopal office, and Titus 1:7 similarly refers to the bishop as "God's steward." The allusion here is not to a mere functionary, but to the head of a family household. Furthermore, even when the local communities had grown beyond the confines of a particular preeminent household, both the bishop-as-steward and his community would have continued to feel their intimate connection. Bruce Malina describes a communally-focused "dyadic personality structure" basic to the ancient worldview (as contrasted with the individualist emphasis of our own time) which ensured that "the person perceives himself or herself as always interrelated to other persons," as "indistinguishable from the image shared and presented to him by his significant others," and "as embedded in some other, in a sequence of embeddedness."[72]

This mutual identification of bishop and community was aided in part in the ancient church by the scale on which bishops generally operated. The size of the ancient diocese, in terms of both numbers of persons and extent of territory, corresponded much more closely to the parishes of today than to the modern diocese.[73] The term *paroikia* originally described the Christian community itself ("one living in a foreign

---

[71] Aguirre, "La Casa Como Estructura Base," 50–51. Regarding the use of other models, Daniel Harrington, "Sociological Concepts and the Early Church," 185, notes Gerd Theissen's focus on the "wandering charismatics" of this era, and their relationship with local communities. Klauck, "The House-Church as Way of Life," 154, notes the evidence for tension between local assemblies and factions based in particular house-churches, and Aguirre, "La Casa Como Estructura Base," 49, hints that such tension and its attendant dangers may have contributed to the eventual abandonment of the house-church system.

[72] Bruce Malina, "The Individual and the Community: Personality in the Social World of Early Christianity," *Biblical Theology Bulletin* 9 (1979) 127–28.

[73] William J. Bausch, *The Parish of the Next Millennium* (Mystic, CT: Twenty-Third Publications, 1997) 134. T. Howland Sanks, "Forms of Ecclesiality: The Analogical Church," *Theological Studies* 49 (1988) 704, links the boundaries of

country with some rights but without citizenship").[74] When applied to a territory it usually meant the bishop's whole jurisdiction rather than an outlying subdivision of it.[75] The heart of this "parish" would have been the urban center of the area, which even in the increasingly aristocratic Roman empire would still have had a core of citizens with a strong corporate identity, and a distinctive social structure.[76] Thus the original focus of the ministry of the bishop and his assisting presbyters was on a small and united community within an urban society that also had a well-defined sense of itself.[77] From a certain point of view the diocese may still be thought of as coming "before" the parish historically, but *local community* is the root of both, with its most visible functions inherited today not by the diocese but by the parish. Furthermore, it was precisely the perceived necessity of maintaining this intimate community that drove the early development of church institutions. Ironically, practical steps taken to maintain it contributed to the growth of more overarching structures that eventually overshadowed it in many ways.

The Growth of Central Structures. The era after the death of the apostles saw an increased anxiety about retaining authenticity in the face of the passing of the original generation of Christians. How could the *charismatic* authority of Jesus, and those disciples he personally called, be trans-

---

the ancient diocese to those of the Roman province in which it was located, but W. Croce, "The History of the Parish," in *The Parish: From Theology to Practice,* ed. Hugo Rahner (Westminster, MD: Newman Press, 1958) 9–10, also points out that all the presbyters would have had the main city of the province for their residence and primary pastoral focus; the first evidence for multiple congregations in a single city (still without resident presbyters until the fourth century) is from the late second century.

[74] Sanks, "Forms of Ecclesiality," 704.

[75] Christopher O'Donnell, "Parish," in *Ecclesia*, 351, mentions that "the district confided to a bishop was called the *paroikia*" in the *Apostolic Constitutions* at the end of the fourth century. Sanks, "Forms of Ecclesiality," 704, mentions that the term was applied "usually to what we today would call a diocese."

[76] See Talcott Parsons, *The Evolution of Societies*, edited and with an introduction by Jackson Toby (Englewood Cliffs, NJ: Prentice-Hall, 1977) 121.

[77] Ibid. 117. The influence of the city's own corporate sense on the self-understanding of the Christian community within the city is briefly discussed by Parsons.

lated into a stable *traditional* authority that endures?[78] The emergence of apostolic writings, the first stirrings of church law in the Pastoral Epistles and documents such as the Didache, and the gradual regularization of offices in the church communities were all part of the answer to that question as it was asked from the end of the first century onward.

The gradual centralization of authority these emerging institutions represented was at first a *local* initiative and, at least in part, a response to various threats against authentic intimate community attendant upon the growth and expansion of the church. These threats included the potential factionalism of the house-church structure,[79] the external disruptions sometimes presented by wandering prophets and preachers,[80] and the appearance of divisive doctrinal controversies.[81] In the face of these difficulties the looser organizational structures of the earliest times evolved in more and more communities into the mono-episcopal structure. This at first meant one bishop for each community, surrounded by his presbyters with whom he acted collegially. The one bishop made it possible for each local community to demonstrate concretely the unity that is necessarily a characteristic of the universal church,[82] given that it draws its authenticity from the one Christ.

Eventually, with the growth of the Christian communities within urban areas and their spread into surrounding rural territory, the bishops took on more and more the role of central administrators over presbyters who each led a separate parish congregation.[83] What came to be

[78] Richard Sennett, *Authority* (New York: Knopf, 1980) 21, discussing categories used by Max Weber, presents the characteristics of "traditional," "legal-rational," and "charismatic" authority. At p. 156 he discusses Weber's view of the process by which "Christ inevitably becomes the Church." Also relevant here are the previous references to the "routinization of charisma."

[79] Bonhoeffer, *The Communion of Saints,* 159. The point is also made by Klauck, "The House-Church as Way of Life," 154.

[80] See "Didache" 11, in James A. Kleist, ed., *Didache, Barnabas, Polycarp, Papias, Diognetus.* Ancient Christian Writers: The Works of the Fathers in Translation (Westminster, MD: Newman Press, 1948) 6:22–23. See also Harrington, "Sociological Concepts and the Early Church," 185.

[81] See Donal Warwick, "The Centralization of Ecclesiastical Authority: An Organizational Perspective," in Baum and Greeley, eds., *The Church As Institution,* 112.

[82] Zizioulas, *Being as Communion,* 153.

[83] Warwick, "Centralization of Ecclesiastical Authority," 112. For the collegial model and its use as a sign of the desired unity see Ignatius of Antioch, "Epistle

called a "diocese," once a local community with a collegial leadership under the bishop, thus became a collection of local communities with individual leaders. The collegial aspect was theoretically still intact but was now much more hidden from day-to-day view. This gradual development of parish congregations without their own bishops suggests that much of this evolution of structures was strictly practical and not worked out theologically. It involved a slow and largely unacknowledged shift in the understanding of church that had been developing. This made it more difficult for communities to see themselves as images of the whole church, since the bishop, acknowledged as authentic pastor of each local community within his territory, was increasingly "an administrator rather than a eucharistic president,"[84] and so absent from the community's gatherings. Thus although it was initiated in the local communities for purposes of guarding their authentic witness to Jesus, centralization eventually muddied their self-understanding instead. A process of distancing began between these same communities and the offices that were supposed to guard Christian authenticity by linking them to the charisma of the apostolic era.

The Survival of Intimacy. Together, the social and psychological constructs I have been describing set the stage very early in church history for the patriarchal authority of bishops, forcefully presented in the letters of Ignatius of Antioch. Ignatius insists, for example, that the bishop "embodies the authority of God the Father" and must be given "every mark of respect," regardless of his chronological age.[85] As it would for an ordinary family in the Greco-Roman world, connection to this paternal figure defines community membership for Ignatius and, when compared to the devotion of Jesus to God as Father, seems to him to be most Christ-like.[86] Three centuries later, Augustine, too, can best be under-

---

to the Magnesians," 6, in James A. Kleist, ed., *The Epistles of St. Clement of Rome and St. Ignatius of Antioch*. Ancient Christian Writers: The Works of the Fathers in Translation (Westminster, MD: Newman Bookshop, 1946) 1:70–71.

[84] Zizioulas, *Being As Communion*, 251. See also Warwick, "Centralization of Ecclesiastical Authority," 111.

[85] Ignatius of Antioch, "Magnesians," 3, in Kleist, ed., *Epistles*, 70.

[86] On community membership see Ignatius, "Epistle to the Trallians," 7, in Kleist, ed., *Epistles*, 77: "Cling inseparably to God, Jesus Christ, to the bishop, and to the precepts of the Apostles. . . . He that is inside the sanctuary is pure; he that is outside the sanctuary is not pure." For the comparison to Jesus and

stood as *pater familias*—the *patron* in a rather full sense of the term—of the Christian community at Hippo. By then, however, the position held much broader social and political responsibilities in proportion to the wider (though not yet predominant) influence of the church in Augustine's time.[87] The paternal authority of the bishop still had roots in a set of social and theological assumptions by which reference to the bishop was implicitly understood as reference also to the community he represented. As Ignatius put it in his letter to the Magnesians, "It has been my privilege to have a glimpse of you all in the person of Damas, your bishop . . . ."[88] Yet we cannot ignore that this whole line of development also represents the beginnings of a profound metamorphosis: from the intimacy between Jesus and God, the church eventually arrived at the patriarchal structure of Roman civic government.

It might appear that this structural outcome is somehow implied in the very starting point—Jesus' favoring of the image of "Father" in his own relationship to God. This, however, is to read Jesus' relationship to God outside of the context in which it is intended to be understood. Roger Haight makes the point well:

> Ironically, fidelity to Jesus' language about God as a personal father includes breaking open that metaphor to other personal images. Jesus cannot be used to justify an ideological use of Jesus' name for God. Indeed, Jesus' conception of the fatherhood of God is critical of human patriarchy.[89]

This critique, however, had powerful cultural rivals. Elisabeth Schüssler Fiorenza follows the idea of "fatherhood" into Roman political theory. She gives a scathing appraisal of the consequences of the emperors' joining of authority (*auctoritas*) and power (*potestas*) (a link that the Roman republic had resisted) into the *patria potestas*—the father's power. In regard to effects of this development on the church, she concludes:

---

the Father see Ignatius, "Epistle to the Smyrnaeans," 8, in Kleist, ed., *Epistles*, 93: "You must all follow the lead of the bishop as Jesus Christ followed that of the Father."

[87] Descriptions of this quality of the episcopacy in Augustine's time can be found in Peter Brown, *Augustine of Hippo: A Biography* (Berkeley, CA: University of California Press, 1967) 133, 194–95.

[88] Ignatius, "Epistle to the Magnesians," 2, in Kleist, ed., *Epistles*, 69.

[89] Haight, *Jesus Symbol of God*, 114.

"This political and legal concept and definition of imperial Rome has decisively influenced Roman Catholic theological tradition and understanding of authority and power as 'father power over.'"[90] In light of Jesus' own ministry, the potential problems of the concentration of authority and "power over" into the hands of one leader in a community are quite clear: "You know that the rulers of the Gentiles lord it over them . . . . But it shall not be so among you" (Matt 20:25-26). Losing sight of this teaching alienates the members of local communities from the source of authentic Christian life—the invitation of Jesus to share in the intimacy of his relationship to the Father. The more this relationship is modeled by the structures of leadership as "father power over," to use Schüssler Fiorenza's phrase, the more difficult it becomes for the life of the community to visibly embody the invitation.

It would appear, however, that the development of this model of leadership in the church was as much a *local* phenomenon as a broad cultural-political one. To think of the local community as having had its authenticity "stolen" by an ambitious, preexisting central hierarchy would be a caricature at best. Moreover, even the patriarchal family structure seems originally to have fostered a culturally appropriate expression of Christian intimacy within the local community. The root of the difficulties that Schüssler Fiorenza underscores lies, rather, in a gradual loss of true and mutual identification between the bishops and their communities. The authenticity Jesus had passed on to the intimate local community of his disciples had begun more and more to be understood as belonging to structures and offices that were somehow "above," rather than identified with, the community.

Despite the growth of this centralizing ecclesiology, however, the influence of local community life remained strong. Orthodox theologian John Zizioulas invokes the names of some of the bishop-theologians most associated with the development of strong central institutions in the church while nonetheless noting their dependence on their communities:

> [T]he bishops of this [patristic] period, pastoral theologians such as St. Ignatius of Antioch and above all St. Irenaeus and later St. Athanasius, approached the being of God through the experience of the ecclesial

[90] Elisabeth Schüssler Fiorenza, "Claiming Our Authority and Power," in Johannes-Baptist Metz and Edward Schillebeeckx, eds., *The Teaching Authority of Believers. Concilium* 180 (Edinburgh: T & T Clark, 1985) 50.

community, of ecclesial being. This experience revealed something very important: the being of God could be known only through personal relationships and personal love. Being means life, and life means communion.[91]

This interpersonal communion would necessarily become a vehicle by which the culture and aspirations of ordinary people became part of the church's reality in the day-to-day lives of its members in local communities. Thus the ideal of authentic Christian life and thought—that which would ring as true to people as Jesus' own life had done, and could thus be "owned" by them—continued to develop with the religious experience and cultural evolution of the church's members.

One concrete example of this process in the early church is the growth of the veneration of martyrs. In the centuries when both local and general persecutions of Christians were not uncommon, those who had died rather than compromise their faith often became well-known local examples of inspiring Christian heroism. Historian Henry Chadwick describes the practice of venerating their memory as "a matter of private devotion which was then taken over by central authority as it became popular."[92] Chadwick also describes what could happen when "central authority" ignored or rejected such popular devotion. A disagreement between the future bishop Caecilian of Carthage and an influential woman in the church community over the veneration of a particular local martyr helped fuel charges of laxity against the leaders. The eventual result was the Donatist schism, which permanently split the Christian community in North Africa.[93]

The same "intense respect" accorded to the martyr-hero was later also given to "the hermit in his solitude," and eventually the monastic movement became another popular phenomenon that bishops simply could not ignore. The rejection of local community life that the movement itself might seem to imply was also, like some of the controversy surrounding the martyrs, a negative commentary on the perceived laxity of the leaders, an effort to assert another standard of authenticity and so an expression of local authority. Eventually, of course, monasticism came to be seen as one of the ultimate expressions of local Christian

[91] Zizioulas, *Being As Communion*, 16.
[92] Henry Chadwick, *The Early Church* (Harmondsworth: Penguin, 1967) 271.
[93] Ibid. 123.

community.[94] Thus both martyrdom and monasticism occasioned major discussions and tensions concerning the shape of authentically Christian life, and in both instances the sensibilities of local communities exerted enormous influence.

Even the gradual establishment of the authority of Rome over the Western church suggests ways in which local community continued to assert itself. Hannah Arendt's description of the ancient Romans' worldview, read in the context of the seemingly relentless centralization of the Roman Catholic Church across the centuries (and even in the last twenty years), raises the ironic question whether this centripetal force might actually trace its remote origins to the sensibilities of a single ancient local community:

> To be engaged in politics meant first and foremost to preserve the founding of the city of Rome. This is why the Romans were unable to repeat the founding of their first *polis* in the settlement of colonies but were capable of adding to the original foundation until the whole of Italy and, eventually, the whole of the Western world were united and administered by Rome, as though the whole world were nothing but Roman hinterland. From beginning to end, the Romans were bound to the specific locality of this one city.[95]

If something about this description sounds oddly familiar to contemporary Roman Catholics, we should perhaps also attend to political scientist Carl Friedrich's description of the ideal administration of this ancient Roman authority:

> The *patrum auctoritas* is . . . more than advice, yet less than a command. While it was not intended to set limits to the free decision of the community, it was intended to prevent violations of what was sacred in the established order of things . . . . It was a matter of adding wisdom to will, a knowledge of values shared and traditions hallowed, to whatever the people wanted to do.[96]

Whether the worldwide church today be compared to "Roman hinterland" or to something rather more analogous to "a federation of city-

[94] For the comment on the respect given to hermits see ibid. 177–78. For the motivations of the movement see ibid. 175–78. For the efforts of ascetic communities and bishops to come to a *modus vivendi* with one another see ibid. 179–80.

[95] Hannah Arendt, "What is Authority?" 120 (emphasis added).

[96] Carl J. Friedrich, "Authority, Reason, and Discretion," in idem, ed., *Authority,* 30.

states"[97] (neither of which truly does justice to Catholic ecclesiology), the authenticity of the founders, properly transmitted, might still secure for local communities a role they can call their own.

Authenticity and the Intimate Local Community Today. There seems little doubt that the kind of immediate connection between the bishop and his community that the early church took for granted is no longer an outstanding feature of most Catholics' experience of church. To the parishioners of St. Joseph's, Aquinas, and St. Matthew's alike the bishops remain the distant overseers who are generally respected, sometimes beloved, always energetically welcomed on their occasional visits, but also feared. At times they are even resented for their power over the community which, because of lack of sufficient mutual contact, usually seems rather arbitrary. Commenting on this state of affairs from the Orthodox point of view, supported by extensive analysis of patristic ecclesiology, Zizioulas laments the consequences of this distance: ". . . one can hope that one day the bishop will find his proper place which is the eucharist, and the rupture in eucharistic ecclesiology caused by the problem 'parish–diocese' will be healed in the right way."[98] The "right way" for Zizioulas "would be the creation of small episcopal dioceses."[99]

As interesting as it might be to speculate on such structural rearranging, my point in concluding this chapter is, rather, to emphasize once again the importance of local intimacy itself, however it might be fostered in the life of the church. The role of intimacy in an authentically Christian way of life—one that evokes for people the life of Jesus himself—is so central that it cannot be abandoned regardless of what happens in the evolution of church structures. In point of fact, it never has been abandoned. For the vast majority of lay persons who make up the local communities the power, distance, and clerical dominance of the central structures have generally meant that there could be little involvement *except* through the structures of the local community. There, where in the person of the parish priest the formal organizing and decision-making of the central structures have met the daily realities of

---

[97] Parsons, *The Evolution of Societies*, 117, in reference to the various *municipia* of the Roman empire.

[98] Zizioulas, *Being As Communion*, 251. A Roman Catholic perspective (that of Karl Rahner) on the role of the Eucharist in understanding the local church will be taken up in Chapter Six of the present book.

[99] Ibid. n. 6.

the local community, the shared lives of ordinary Catholics have quite forcefully shaped the church "from below."

Particularly at the two immigrant parishes of St. Joseph's and St. Matthew's, the reality of the community in the late nineteenth and early twentieth centuries may not have seemed like an exercise in authority. Conceptually the parish community existed at the very bottom of a hierarchical ladder that seemed to be the established nature of things. People moved with their group and attended their church as a matter of course, not exactly under compulsion but without much reflection, because it was part of the identity of the community from which they drew much of their own personal meaning. These very motivations guaranteed the kind of intimacy and authenticity I have been discussing. Though they may not have been able to articulate a crucial role for their community in the structure of "The Church" (by which they invariably meant the hierarchy and central structures), they nonetheless adhered to the Catholic faith and its practice because it was "theirs." They had learned it from, and seen it in action among, one another, even as they listened to the words of the pastors and studied the bishops' catechism. Belonging to one particular parish or another was, though not indifferent, a matter outside their direct control. Their own experience of the community, though, was not one of compulsion but one of a belonging that took forms deeply associated with their ordinary lives.

At the original founding of St. Matthew's the bonds that already existed in shared expressions of Irish culture, family ties, neighbor-to-neighbor relations, common work experiences, local political coalitions, and so forth, were reinforced by the creation of a neighborhood parish. Parishioners and pastors alike relied on all of this, mostly unreflectively, as a source of cohesion for the church community itself. The Caribbean immigrants who later remade St. Matthew's did not have to petition for the creation of a parish where none had existed. Merely by their presence in increasing numbers they reshaped the existing church and the expressions of Catholicism found there into vehicles of support and expression of their own cultural heritage. In the case of St. Joseph's an ethnically distinct group of people struggled both logistically and financially to bring about the creation of a national parish that would, by its very existence, honor and defend the familial, linguistic, and cultural bonds that were already at the center of their lives. At Aquinas the founders were not of a separate ethnic group, but people who identified with each other through their common affiliation with the university. They gathered first as a matter of convenience, but in the group identity they soon developed they found a way of encounter with others in the neighborhood whose very different lives still constantly interfaced with their own. For all of its struggles, the local church community has drawn much of its understanding of church from this encounter. As in all the other cases, the assigned pastors have had to learn how to be leaders of *this* church.

In the time since the intimate bonds among various groups of people brought these communities into existence, enormous changes have taken place both within the groups themselves and in the general social milieus within which they exist. Although certain ties still bind, there is far less "inevitability" about the cohesion of the communities. This change points toward an interesting irony. The church is at a moment in its history in which the importance and power of central structures actually seems to be increasing all the more, fed by the ascendancy of a conservative ecclesiology, ease of communication, and the general climate of globalization. Yet the importance of the intimate bonds within the local community is greater than ever, even as the social forces that once made these groupings seem all but inevitable have weakened drastically. The existence of vibrant local communities now depends on the deliberate, reflective decisions of the individuals and small groups within those communities, and they themselves are coming to understand this. Consequently they look for an awareness of their role that will honor and nurture both their need for genuine intimacy and their growing desire and ability to involve themselves with the larger questions the church is facing. As parish researcher Thomas Sweetser has put it in advising parish staffs about "The Parish as Covenant":

> The covenantal relationship of the diocese with the Vatican, and the parish with the diocese, should be a mutual relationship, as between Yahweh and the Chosen People. Benefits accrue and demands are made by both parties. It is a joint effort at being church. Parish communities, if they are to remain Catholic, will have to endure the struggles and losses that result from the shortages [of clergy and resources]. They will also have to find a voice to make their concerns and issues known, similar to the insistence of the Syro-Phoenician woman pleading her case before Jesus. "Even the dogs under the table eat what the children leave" (Mark 7:28). She expanded Jesus' horizons about the scope of his ministry and what was possible. The local parish may have to do the same with the larger church.[100]

---

[100] Thomas P. Sweetser, s.j., *The Parish as Covenant: A Call to Pastoral Partnership* (Franklin, WI: Sheed and Ward, 2001) 173.

Chapter Four

Authority: Authentic Christian Life Speaks to the Church

Chapter One presented the stories of three parishes whose practical experience of the Christian life remains the backdrop for the entire discussion. Despite all their limitations as local communities—indeed, *within* the restrictions that require them to remain places of intimate contact, cooperation, and struggle—the authority of Christ is at work for the benefit of the whole church. Here at the midpoint of the book, the central terms of this thesis have been introduced and some of their vital interrelationships explored. "Intimacy" takes on powerful Christian meaning within a community of disciples, in connection with that community's authoritative foundations in Jesus' own life and the authentic mission it receives from him. Because the exercise of authority rests on these same foundations, intimacy and authority must inform one another. In the light of this relationship, what can "authority" itself mean, and how can we understand it in a way that preserves the insights emerging from a careful look at the local aspect of church? I will approach these central questions in this chapter by looking first at a variety of ways in which scholars have understood the meaning of "authority" in general. I will then turn again to the witness of Jesus and his ministry as the model for *Christian* authority. The results of these discussions will suggest approaches to the crisis of authority within the church today and its implications for the role of local communities.

The Meaning of "Authority"

Multiple Approaches. The stories of the parishes themselves point out the many ways in which authority can be claimed and exercised. Formal structures and informal expectations, ordained ministers and elected councils, use and abuse have all played their roles. Interpretations of the concept "authority" itself are correspondingly diverse. Authority might be a communal principle, "the everlasting good principle of the social unity in the pursuit of the common good."[1] On the other hand, it might be a psychological and interpersonal principle, "the ability to impose discipline, the capacity to inspire fear,"[2] or, more affirmatively, "enabl[ing] individuals to become truly centered selves or persons."[3] Authority "rests on . . . an act of reason itself which . . . trusts to the better insight of others";[4] on the other hand it may "[come] from God and [have] a right to exist only insofar as it possesses and mediates perfection."[5] Yet again it may be a product precisely of the meaning and value of the human community in which it is exercised.[6] It is a principle of power—"the emotional expression of power"[7] or "power exercised in accordance with a convention"[8] or

---

[1] Yves Simon, *Nature and Functions of Authority* (Milwaukee: Marquette University Press, 1940) 29.

[2] Richard Sennett, *Authority* (New York: Alfred A. Knopf, 1980) 17.

[3] John E. Skinner, *The Meaning of Authority* (Washington, DC: University Press of America, 1983) 6.

[4] Hans-Georg Gadamer, *Truth and Method,* trans. Joel Weinsheimer and Donald G. Marshall (rev. 2d ed. New York: Continuum, 1995) 279.

[5] Waldemar Molinski, "Authority," in Karl Rahner, ed., *Encyclopedia of Theology: A Concise Sacramentum Mundi* (New York: Seabury, 1975) 61. The discussion of Plato's philosopher-king in Hannah Arendt, "What Is Authority?" in eadem, *Between Past and Future: Eight Exercises in Political Thought* (New York: Viking, 1968) 108–10, is also relevant to the idea of authority as a truth external to both the individual and the community.

[6] See the discussion of the Roman understanding of authority in Arendt, "What Is Authority?" 120–28. Norman Jacobson, "Knowledge, Tradition, and Authority," in Carl J. Friedrich, ed., *Authority. Nomos* I (Cambridge, MA: Harvard University Press, 1958) 118, gives an account of authority in American democracy that partakes of a remarkably similar spirit.

[7] Sennett, *Authority,* 4.

[8] George E. Gordon Catlin, "Authority and Its Critics," in Friedrich, ed., *Authority,* 129.

"the right to use power"[9]—or it is to be carefully distinguished from power.[10]

I have already referred to a work by political theorist Hannah Arendt on ancient Rome. The same remarkable essay argues that our question should be "what was—and not what is—authority?"[11] In searching for the roots of the concept, and our confusion over it, she contrasts the Roman approach, based in reverence for the city's founders, with that of Plato, based in a philosophical idea of social relations. For Plato authority belongs to the philosopher who understands the true idea of society and its natural hierarchies. Ideally his authority is established neither by threat of violence nor by rhetorical persuasion but simply by the force of truth, yet his enlightened rule may in fact have to be secured in some other way.[12] For the Romans, on the other hand, the source of authority was not so much an idea as the shared history of the people and their common respect for the founding ancestors, the *auctores* ("those who build up").[13] For the living, this heritage was epitomized in the elders— the Senate—who, as a link to the founders, did not need to wield formal power in order to exercise their enormous authority.[14]

British sociologist Richard Sennett has called authority "a matter of defining and interpreting differences in strength."[15] Both of the ancient approaches described by Arendt seem to understand this as a central issue, yet they differ markedly on whether "differences in strength" within a society should underscore *inequality* (as in Plato's relational

---

[9] Jackson Toby, "Introduction," in Talcott Parsons, *The Evolution of Societies*, trans. and ed. Jackson Toby (Englewood Cliffs, NJ: Prentice-Hall, 1977) 15.

[10] See Arendt, "What Is Authority?"122, on the Roman Senate's lack of formal power, and ibid. 141 for comments on the loss of the power/authority distinction. Elisabeth Schüssler Fiorenza, "Claiming Our Authority and Power," in Johann Baptist Metz and Edward Schillebeeckx, eds., *The Teaching Authority of the Believers. Concilium* 180 (Edinburgh: T & T Clark, 1985) 50, largely echoes this view of the distinction and its significance.

[11] Arendt, "What Is Authority?" 108.

[12] Ibid. 111.

[13] Ibid. 122. Other interpretations of the Latin *auctoritas* can be found in Schüssler Fiorenza, "Claiming Our Authority," 50; in Molinski, "Authority," 61; and in Skinner, *Meaning of Authority*, 6, who cites G. D. Yarnold, *By What Authority* (London: A. R. Mowbray, 1964) 4.

[14] Arendt, "What Is Authority?" 123.

[15] Sennett, *Authority*, 126.

metaphors of the shepherd, the helmsman, the physician, the master)[16] or *solidarity* instead (as in the Romans' sense of shared citizenship). Our modern images still reflect this ancient tension: our images of authority may see it as something of a personal possession or as belonging in some way to the entire community. In the same vein, we continue to debate whether authority is best considered a necessary substitute for the uninformed free choice of certain persons (minors, non-experts, the incapacitated, etc.) or rather as something essential to those who hold it.[17] In this regard the emphasis falls for some on the conventional *procedures* that establish authority within a society,[18] and for others on the status of an authority *figure*.[19]

This array of disagreements tends to resolve, in the literature of the last few decades, into descriptions of two general types of authority, although claims of what the two types actually are vary widely. In each pair of contrasts that is proposed, however, the fundamental distinction is nearly always the one just mentioned between procedures and persons. "Mandated" authority "springs from a delegation . . . given to a person or group,"[20] and so is attached to recognized structures and hierarchies. "Inherent" authority, arising more spontaneously in the nature of the person or community, is "based on *being* authority rather than *having* authority."[21] This is an important distinction, without which it would be easy to over-

---

[16] See Arendt, "What Is Authority?" 109.

[17] Simon, *Nature and Functions of Authority*, 7–12, discusses basic definitions of authority and suggests that authority is "substitutional" particularly when it deals with "judgement of the nature of things" as opposed to rules for conduct. The characterization by Skinner, *Meaning of Authority*, 3, 47, of authority as a "nurturing presence" suggests that *all* authority is basically substitutional.

[18] Catlin, "Authority and Its Critics," 129, and Jacobson, "Knowledge, Tradition, and Authority," 118, both emphasize this procedural viewpoint, the latter specifically in the context of American democracy. Herbert J. Spiro, "Authority, Values, and Policy," in Friedrich, ed., *Authority*, 53, provides a good description of the distinction between "procedural" and "substantive" authority.

[19] See Toby, "Introduction," in Parsons, *The Evolution of Societies*, 15, and Molinski, "Authority," 61.

[20] Edward J. Yarnold and Henry Chadwick, *Truth and Authority: A Commentary on the Agreed Statement of the Anglican–Roman Catholic International Commission "Authority In the Church," Venice 1976* (London: SPCK / Catholic Truth Society, 1977) 8.

[21] Johann Baptist Metz, *Faith In History and Society: Toward a Practical Fundamental Theology*, trans. David Smith (New York: Seabury, 1980) 41. Yves Simon,

look one aspect of authority or to overvalue the other. However, we must also keep in mind that these two general types of authority are clearly dependent on one another. The mandated type must "build on" (*augere*— "augment"—the Latin root of "authority")[22] the authentic foundations of the community. This always presupposes the role of the inherent type which, as we see in the case of Jesus and his disciples, gives rise to and preserves those authentic foundations.[23] On the other hand, inherent authority must be given concrete expression through some "determinate agency."[24] Otherwise the sense of connectedness and relevance is lost, and inherent authority becomes merely rebellion, destructive of unity.

Authority, Authenticity, and Power. These conclusions support the relationships between authority, the authoritative, and authenticity explored in the previous chapter. Authority not backed by authenticity—by genuine response to a community's authoritative foundation—becomes merely formal and external. It must thereafter either rely on inducing fear or become irrelevant, because ordinary people in concrete day-to-day settings are not engaged with it and do not sense a part of themselves in it. "When . . . authority relies too heavily upon compulsion," write Yarnold and Chadwick, "it lapses into what is called authoritarianism."[25] Therefore

---

A General Theory of Authority (Notre Dame: Notre Dame University Press, 1962) 84, sees a "fundamental contrast" in types according to the *matter* in regard to which authority is being exercised, whether in "issues of *action*" or in "issues of *truth*." Molinski, "Authority," 61, designates the types "objective or official" on the one hand, and "subjective or personal" on the other. Spiro, "Authority, Values, and Policy," 53–54, makes virtually the same distinction in using the terms "substantive" and "procedural." David J. Stagaman, *Authority In the Church* (Collegeville: Liturgical Press, 1999) 51, refers to "*an* authority" and "*in* authority."

[22] See Arendt, "What Is Authority?" 122.

[23] Stagaman, *Authority In the Church,* 51, underlines that the two types are notional, rarely occurring alone.

[24] "But only when it is actually issued and effective is it authority; . . . . The nation or the people are the 'source.' The metaphor is significant: a source is like a spring running down a hillside, taking its courses according to the lay of the land. There is power in it, but the power is delivered only through the particular sluices into which it is channeled for purposes of doing work. Authority should thus always be thought of as power vested in a *determinate* agency . . . ." Charles W. Hendel, "Exploration of the Nature of Authority," in Friedrich, ed., *Authority,* 25.

[25] Yarnold and Chadwick, *Truth and Authority,* 8.

the relationship between the authority behind a particular policy or action and the actual power to carry it out needs to be examined. From one approach authority itself could be understood as power, in both a philosophical and practical sense. "Residing in a person and exercised through a command," according to the Thomistic definition used by philosopher Yves Simon,[26] authority may seem to convey the ability to direct the action of another person. Authority exercises a certain regulatory function over the "greatly increased power" available to modern economies and educational systems, Simon argues. This is true even when it is not a question of an authority figure "knowing more" than other persons.[27] Practically speaking, "the power in charge of unifying common action through rules binding for all is what everyone calls authority."[28]

Hannah Arendt is interested, however, in calling our attention to the question of *how* authority goes about unifying action. In explaining the Roman emphasis on the authority of the founders and the lack of practical power on the part of the Roman Senate, she points to the separation of authority, with its connections to the sources of a people's wisdom, from executive responsibility. She emphasizes what she considers the great flaw in Plato's thought in this regard: "Closely connected with [Plato's] choice of examples and analogies is the element of violence, which is so glaringly evident in Plato's utopian republic and actually constantly defeats his great concern for assuring voluntary obedience,"[29] which Arendt considers the only sound foundation for authority.

The problem, however, is not precisely that Plato's "philosopher-king" holds both authority *and* executive power, even though this is the recipe for tyranny that the Roman republic avoided and the emperors later embraced. Rather, it is that Plato imagines the philosopher-king as seeing a realm of truth that is not accessible to ordinary persons and understands this "seeing" as the essence of true humanity. This would mean "that human affairs, the results of speech and action, must not acquire a dignity of their own but be subjected to the domination of something outside their realm."[30] The resulting distance between people's lives and the meaning that is assigned to them would diminish their "ownership"—authenticity—and thus decrease the possibility of volun-

---

[26] Simon, *Nature and Functions of Authority*, 7.

[27] Simon, *A General Theory of Authority*, 45.

[28] Ibid. 48. (Emphasis added.)

[29] Arendt, "What Is Authority?" 111.

[30] Ibid. 115.

tary obedience. Ironically, then, placing the sources of authority beyond the sphere of practical power turns out to be a two-edged sword. It can keep authority *per se* free from political manipulation (as in the Roman location of it among the ancestors), but it can also drive a wedge between supposedly authoritative meaning and daily life. Because what is then *said* to be authoritative becomes distinct from what ordinary people regularly live and respond to, something stronger and more external is required to enforce "authoritative" policy. When more than external compliance is desired in a community, the connection between authority and a people's genuine authoritative foundation is essential.

For the Christian community in particular, therefore, the relationship between authority and power must remain complex. Simply to identify authority and power, as is done when truth is understood to issue only from official sources, may promote an experience of authority "as something endangering, if not actively oppressing, freedom,"[31] (Freedom, remember, is a promised fruit of Truth, for "you will know the truth, and the truth will make you free" [John 8:32]). On the other hand, to completely divorce authority from power is to create the absurd situation in which the supposedly most revered values are those that are least relevant to the actual lives of people. Such a situation cannot be sustained for long and ultimately leads to the same place as its apparent opposite: power wielded without reference to the deepest truths and values of the people over whom it is wielded. [32] For Christians, authority must be

[31] Hans Waldenfels, "Authority and Knowledge," in Metz and Schillebeeckx, eds., *Teaching Authority of Believers*, 32. In a similar vein Hendel, "An Exploration of the Nature of Authority," 14, claims that "power without right lacks not only legality but also authority." For the same point made relative to the ancient context note Arendt, "What Is Authority?" 123, on the Roman senate: "The authoritative character of the 'augmentation' of the elders lies in its being a mere advice, needing neither the form of command nor external coercion to make itself heard." Note also Schüssler Fiorenza, "Claiming Our Authority," 50: "[After Augustus] *auctoritas*, authority, was no longer the power of persuasion and counsel rooted in personal and social integrity, capability and prominence, but now served as legitimization of absolute imperial rule and force."

[32] This is not unlike the situation of the church in the midst of a secular society. One means of coping with the apparent absurdity is suggested by Carl F. Starkloff, "Church as Structure and Communitas: Victor Turner and Ecclesiology," *Theological Studies* 58 (1997) 650, in his discussion of Turner's use of the

experienced neither as an imposition of power nor as a separation from power, but as the *empowerment* that occurs when what is truly authoritative is honored. Michael Downey puts this in terms of Jesus' own power:

> It is a matter of recognizing new ways of perceiving and being more in keeping with the word and the work of the Crucified and Risen One whose power was disclosed in his refusal to lay claim to the power of lords, kings, priests, and patriarchs. To share in this power is to listen to those who speak in a different voice. It is to turn one's ears and eyes from the center to the edge of church and society.[33]

Failure within the church to grasp this uniquely Christian understanding of power and its relationship to authority has deep implications for the genuineness of worship, for Christian art and expression, and ultimately for the religious passion and doctrinal truth these signify.[34]

The Christian Meaning of Authority

The Contemporary Crisis of Authority. Even our being able to recognize all the tensions and complexities involved with authority suggests

---

familiar concept of *liminality,* which is applied to ritual moments in which *communitas* prevails over structure: "a condition of 'secular powerlessness' joined to 'sacred power,'" in which what is not ordinarily given room for expression asserts the depth of its genuine authority.

[33] Michael Downey, "Looking to the Last and the Least: A Spirituality of Empowerment," in idem, ed., *That They Might Live: Power, Empowerment, and Leadership in the Church* (New York: Crossroad, 1991) 191. See also Rebecca S. Chopp, *The Power to Speak: Feminism, Language, God* (New York: Crossroad, 1989): "Power is the ability to take one's place in whatever discourse is essential to action, and the right to have one's part matter."

[34] Michael Warren, *At This Time, In This Place: The Spirit Embodied In the Local Assembly* (Harrisburg, PA: Trinity Press International, 1999) 81: "'Worship' is a word brimming with connotations of agency. When it is used to name a communal activity suppressing the agency of the community, 'worship' helps hide the fact of passive participation. Nothing very deep is questioned by the elite speakers, and nothing spoken of by the elites is questioned by their audience." Note also Jean-Marie Roger Tillard, *L'église locale: ecclésiologie de communion et catholicité* (Paris: Cerf, 1995) 129: "By its essence, authentic artistic creation—which brings together aspects of human reality that are otherwise radically inaccessible—resists the uniformity of an abstract universal" (my translation).

something of the crisis surrounding it through much of the past century. The problem is connected to that regarding community itself, as discussed in Chapter Two. As Arendt puts it, "we can no longer fall back upon authentic and undisputable experiences common to all."[35] This lack of commonality in the midst of an ever more global society would account by itself for problems in agreeing on a model of authority. Further, though, even within the experience of individuals or groups with much in common it has become difficult to acknowledge genuine authority. Palpable in much of the post-World War II writing on this topic is the dilemma one author described this way: "[Modern people] are buoyed up by the past achievements of specialists and recognize that a process of collectivization is at work which needs first-class guidance . . . . But [they] are also distrustful of authority, feeling there a vague threat to their personal life."[36]

The church, far from being immune from this social crisis, has been among the most conflicted institutions. Metz explains the danger with which we have been wrestling: "A continuous insistence on an authority which is no longer universally convincing and has ceased to be socially plausible can easily assume the character of coercion and authoritarianism. When this occurs, criticism inevitably intensifies."[37] Criticism of the church's "authoritarianism" (both real and imagined) flows from the fact that the changing society within which the church exists "is much more inclined to see reality in terms of a sea of influences rather than a structure of orders."[38] This kind of outlook requires wider participation and greater diversity in the institution, but there is ambivalence even toward this popularization and the commitment it demands.

[35] Arendt, "What Is Authority?" 91.

[36] Molinski, "Authority," 60.

[37] Metz, *Faith in History and Society,* 39. Metz's use of the word "authoritarian" is in agreement with the definition of Waldenfels, "Authority and Knowledge," 33: "behaviour opposed to both freedom and reason and often behaviour imposed by force." This is in contrast with Arendt, "What Is Authority?" 97, who insists on a distinction between "authoritarian government," which even in the worst scenario is bound to a source outside itself, and the far more arbitrary "tyranny."

[38] Charles E. Curran, "Responsibility in Moral Theology: Centrality, Foundations, and Implications for Ecclesiology," in James A. Coriden, ed., *Who Decides for the Church? Studies in Co-Reponsibility* (Hartford, CT: The Canon Law Society of America, 1971) 141.

Those who want greater social participation fear it as well, and their drive for inclusion is countered by a drive for avoidance. They fear the time and energy greater involvement will cost. It will surely disrupt patterns of passive entertainment. Religious participation is also afflicted by its own fears of too-great involvement and even of religious transformation that greater participation may call for.[39]

A growing sense of alienation from institutional structures throws their authority into question altogether, and encourages a fiercer stance on the part of certain individuals and small groups in defense of personal and traditional values. The polarization that has become so familiar in church and society ensues.

The sense that "mandated" authority is being used in a way that undermines "inherent" individual or local values can produce, at the least, what might be called a "moral withdrawal" from the authority in question—in other words, alienation increases, and strategies develop for minimizing the impact of the authority's policy on personal or local life. This withdrawal may be silent and noticed only in reduced enthusiasm and participation, or it may become a public questioning of the authority's mandate over a particular issue: "How can a mere priest advocate communion in the hand when the Pope himself opposes it?" or, "What right does the Pope have to interfere in the relationship of a married couple?" On the other hand, in a pluralistic situation values that are authoritative for some will rarely meet with unanimous approval and so will *seek* the legitimation of a mandate. Those seeking to promote a particular point of view in the community may seize on the authority behind one statement or another as the vindication of their position: "The Pope has endorsed Opus Dei!" "The U.S. Bishops have called for compassion in welfare reform!" "The Catechism is against capital punishment!" Thus the dilemma continues: a particular understanding of authority that has long endured in the church no longer addresses the real circumstances of the community, while serious obstacles yet remain to prevent the adoption of a more appropriate approach.

Concrete examples of this contemporary situation can be seen in all three sample parishes. Their complex histories have produced, for different reasons in each of the three, membership with multiple origins, making shared values a serious challenge and tending to promote (especially at St. Matthew's and at Aquinas) more or less autonomous subcommu-

---

[39] Warren, *At This Time, In This Place*, 92.

nities that have to work hard at their mutual interaction. Further, the cultural, linguistic, and psychological distances that can separate parishioners from official church leaders—both local pastors and diocesan officials—underline an experience of alienation that is not limited to recent immigrants or the poor. Nonetheless, the wide variety of personal and group attempts to meet the challenges of being a local church community under such circumstances have fashioned, in the midst of the "sea of influences" in these parishes, a rich experience that is not quite the chaos one might expect. In an institution in which the historically-preferred "structure of orders" cannot provide all that is needed, the networks of relationship within the communities themselves assume an even more crucial position. Yet there is no solid conviction, either in official ecclesiology or in the self-understanding of most ordinary parishioners, that the community has *authority* to shape itself in this way.

Since the work of the eighteenth-century Enlightenment philosophers such as Immanuel Kant, Western thinking has been aware of the danger of a kind of authority to which we submit out of "a lack of decision and courage," and which, in Metz's description, "cannot be tested or questioned with regard to its legal status."[40] In our trying to deepen the church's self-understanding, questions about the proper nature of authority *are* raised in order to understand authority's legitimate role in the Christian context. That Christian setting itself will insist on some of the same elements that made "a lack of decision" anathema to the Enlightenment: conviction, equality, and participation.[41] For Christians these values are expressed as shared *faith* in the God of Jesus Christ whose reign is at the heart of the Gospel; as mutual *love* expressed in the recognition of Christ's Spirit at work in every believer; and as lively *hope* expressed in mutual responsibility and commitment to the Christian community that points toward the Reign of God. An understanding of authority that systematically runs counter to these values cannot

[40] Metz, *Faith In History and Society*, 39.

[41] Ibid. Metz quotes Kant's famous definition of Enlightenment and discusses it in terms of the "principle of equality" and opposition to "an authority which is no longer universally *convincing*," which "can easily assume the character of *coercion*." It should be noted, though, that Metz's primary point in discussing the Enlightenment view of authority is that because of its social and economic setting it ultimately threatened authority's role as "a precondition and inner aspect of critical and liberating reason," a role that is absolutely basic to Catholic theology.

be a *properly Christian* understanding, regardless of what other values it may seem to support and regardless of the fact that just this sort of inadequate understanding can be found at work in much of the history of the church.

Pastorally effective solutions to the divisive situations that exist in many local communities today cannot focus either on stronger insistence on uniformity or on flight from the notion of authority altogether. Rather, they must look for a more careful balance between mandated and inherent forms of authority. Authority that is balanced between these two types is more readily understood as strength for the entire community rather than as a source of burden and suspicion. Mandated authority that acknowledges and works *with* the inherent authority of the local community is less apt to meet the kinds of destructive resistance just described.[42] As German theologian Heinrich Fries has noted, "It is . . . not at all the case that *authority* is universally rejected today. It is accepted and even welcomed when it argues convincingly on the basis of the insights of faith and proves itself competent." Under such circumstances authority as a whole, operating under both its aspects, can be experienced as a constructive, freeing, and properly Christian *process.*[43]

Authority and the Local Community. Given the essential role that intimate local community plays in the church, and in light of the idea of authority emerging here, it is increasingly clear not only that local community possesses its own proper authority in the church, but also that this authority is actually foundational to the church in a variety of ways. Yet I do not propose this argument to set aside the essential connection, already established, between the local community and the broader structures and authorities of the universal church. Nor do I intend precisely to promote what could aptly be called a "democratization" of the church.

---

[42] Heinrich Fries, *Suffering From the Church: Renewal or Restoration?* trans. Arlene Anderson Swidler and Leonard Swidler (Collegeville: Liturgical Press, 1995) 46. Similarly Gadamer, *Truth and Method,* 279: "Authority cannot actually be bestowed but is earned, and must be earned if someone is to lay claim to it. It rests on acknowledgment and hence on an act of reason itself which, aware of its own limitations, trusts to the better insight of others."

[43] Yarnold and Chadwick, *Truth and Authority,* 8: "Even God, from whom all authority is derived, seeks . . . free obedience, not forced servitude." Note also Sennett, *Authority,* 190: "Authority can become a process, a making, breaking, a remaking of meanings. It can be visible and legible."

Because the true source of authority and power in the church is not completely contained within the strictly human sphere but lies in our relationship with God, the Christian authority I am describing still befits what Arendt calls a "specifically authoritarian form of government."[44] Arendt also points out, however, that to impose norms based on fundamental convictions that are assumed but not in fact truly shared is the exercise not of authority but of domination.[45] It is true that the local church community does not simply create itself or invent its own categories *ex nihilo*. Nonetheless, the authority it acknowledges is not the sole possession of any particular class, office, or hierarchical level, however legitimate and necessary these distinctions may be. This authority, instead, arises in the Spirit's gift of shared faith and is exercised in what Metz calls "religious competence"—*being* rather than *having* authority.[46] It is understood not as "power *over*" but rather as "strength *for*" an ongoing community relationship. Authority in the church is not only structural and official, but is also exercised by a community as it forges, through its collective day-to-day experiences and choices, its specific way of living in the Spirit of God.

Local Community as Sacrament:
Finding the Authentic Presence of Christ Today

Michael Downey has commented on the perception of power within the church:

> Views of power that accentuate a separation between divine and human power must give way to other views that recognize the unity and interdependence of divine and human power. This necessitates a fuller appreciation of the nature of God's relationship with the world in and through the work of the Spirit that is the very life, presence, and power of God in, through, and to the world.[47]

The theological theme that Downey thus links to an understanding of power and authority is the concept of *sacramentality*—the presence of

---

[44] Arendt, "What Is Authority?" 110. She here discusses Plato's concept of authority.

[45] Ibid. 119. Arendt here discusses the ancient Roman concept of authority.

[46] Metz, *Faith in History and Society,* 41.

[47] Downey, "Looking to the Last and the Least," 181.

God in and through the concrete realities of the church's day-to-day life. Plato assumed that it is philosophical understanding of transcendent ideas that grasps the true meaning of everyday human life. On the contrary, the church's experience of the Incarnation allows everyday life to point us toward true relationship with the transcendent God. With this sacramentality of the church in mind, I want to explore the possibility of the encounter with God precisely *in* the local community. I will make use of "three foundational principles of the church" presented by Roger Haight: Jesus, the work of God as Spirit in the community, and the mission of the church.[48]

Jesus of Nazareth and the "Body of Christ." Both historically and theologically the church grows out of the intimate community of the disciples with Jesus. Receiving his Spirit, the church is rendered capable of being the Body of Christ in and for the world after the mission of Jesus is complete. But the presence of Christ in the world today is not merely a matter of an abstract theological identification of the church with his Body.[49] This identification is made tangible throughout history in the transformed lives of the real people who have followed and do follow Jesus. The disciples find in Jesus a "nurturing and liberating presence"[50] that exudes the authority of God and is neither distant nor inaccessible. In him "ultimacy is wedded to vivid immediacy."[51] This experience of the disciples is given expression by Jesus himself in an exchange between him and Thomas in the Gospel of John. Thomas, the disciple known for needing firm assurances, asks Jesus, reasonably enough, "We do not know where you are going. How can we know the way?" To this Jesus replies, "*I* am the way and the truth and the life. No one comes to the Father except through me. If you know me, you will know my Father also. From now on you do know him and have seen him" (John 14:5-6). With these words he grounds even truth itself

---

[48] Roger Haight, "The Structures of the Church," *Journal of Ecumenical Studies* 30:3-4 (1993) 414.

[49] The classic expression of this theological doctrine is found, of course, in Rom 12:3-7 and 1 Cor 12:12-31; other Pauline allusions to it are found in Eph 3:6 and 4:1-16, Col 1:18-24; 2:19; and 3:15. These are taken up as the basis for Pius XII's *Mystici Corporis Christi* (1943) and Vatican II's references in the Dogmatic Constitution on the Church *(Lumen Gentium)*, especially at #7.

[50] Skinner, *Meaning of Authority*, 4.

[51] Ibid. 70.

in the personal, intimate relationship that exists between him and his disciples, an image of that between him and the Father himself.

It is not merely "truths" that this relationship conveys, but a complete way of life[52] that becomes the model for the communities founded by the apostles. "If New Testament evidence shows these communities were far from perfect," writes Michael Warren, "it also shows preoccupation with credible ways of living."[53] Perhaps paradoxically, it is precisely because the emphasis in apostolic-era communities did not fall on the structures of authority, but on the quality of Christian life in fidelity to the Christ proclaimed by the apostles, that these communities are able to inherit and display the authenticity of Jesus. Edward Schillebeeckx writes of the *inseparability* of the authority of Jesus from that of those who have witnessed to him:

> Jesus' identity has therefore to be read from and in the salvation that was, thanks to him, made a reality in other people. It is in the conversion and renewal of such people in and through contact with Jesus that who he is and what he does is revealed. This is why the testimony borne by the New Testament and that borne by all people forms an essential part of the answer to the question as to who Jesus was and who he can be for us today. This testimony therefore has a share in the authority of Jesus and cannot be dissociated from that authority.[54]

Thus a strong link is implied from the beginning between the *authority* of the church—its claims to truth—and the network of human relationships established by the ministry of Jesus—the church community. For this reason separation of *authority* from *intimate community* in our thinking about the church runs the risk of falsifying both elements by making them potential adversaries, when initially they are meant to define and authenticate one another. Forgetting this leaves us puzzling over the

---

[52] Roger Haight, "Towards an Ecclesiology From Below," in Jeremy Driscoll, ed., *"Imaginer la Théologie Catholique": Permanence et Transformations de la Foi en Attendant Jésus-Christ. Mélanges Offerts à Ghislain Lafont. Studia Anselmiana* 129 (Rome: Centro Studi S. Anselmo, 2000) 12: "The epistemology of faith is not mere assent to propositional truth, but rests on an existential engagement involving religious experience."

[53] Warren, *At This Time, In This Place*, 78.

[54] Edward Schillebeeckx, "The Teaching Authority of All—A Reflection about the Structure of the New Testament," in Metz and Schillebeeckx, eds., *The Teaching Authority of Believers*, 14.

contrast between Jesus' words in Matt 16:19: "I will give *you* [Peter] the keys of the kingdom of heaven," and his words in Matt 18:20: "Where two or three are gathered in my name, I am there among them" (*NRSV*).[55] To see these statements as natural complements requires us to consider intimate community *and* authority as equally essential traits of the church.[56]

This is reminiscent of Zizioulas' insight into Trinitarian theology, that "God could be known only through personal relationships and personal love."[57] Haight further reminds us that this community of believers is "simultaneously a community of ministry" that "takes as its pattern either the ministry of Jesus or the ideas and values that were entailed in that ministry."[58] In a variety of doctrinal, spiritual, and ministerial ways, then, Jesus Christ is present authoritatively in the real words and actions, the testimony and ministry, of the Christian community. And these words and actions, whatever their ultimate impact, must by their very nature occur locally.

Zizioulas sees what may be taken as the ultimate implication of these insights for an understanding of the church when he defines catholicity as "the presence of Him who sums up in Himself the community and the entire creation."[59] At the dawn of the Christian church in history it was the personal presence of Jesus that was decisive in the formation of

[55] Congregation for the Doctrine of the Faith, "Some Aspects of the Church Understood as Communion," *Origins* 28 (1998) 110 (#11-12), states this contrast quite explicitly by rejecting the notion "that gathering together in the name of Jesus is the same as generating the church," on its way to emphasizing "the identity of the church of every age with the church built by Christ upon Peter and upon the other apostles." Very similar arguments and phrasing can be found in Joseph Cardinal Ratzinger, *Called to Communion: Understanding the Church Today*, trans. Adrian Walker (San Francisco: Ignatius Press, 1996) 80–81, where the unnamed positions with which he contends seem related to those of Zizioulas, Tillard, Bonhoeffer, and Boff, all cited previously.

[56] Franz-Xavier Kaufmann, "The Church as a Religious Organization," in Gregory Baum and Andrew Greeley, eds., *Church as Institution. Concilium* 91 (New York: Herder and Herder, 1974) 71, describes the early church in terms suggesting a coexistence and creative tension of these two traits, in the two principles of presbyteral and episcopal leadership.

[57] John Zizioulas, *Being As Communion: Studies in Personhood and the Church.* Contemporary Greek Theologians (Crestwood, NY: St. Vladimir's Seminary Press, 1985) 16.

[58] Haight, "Structures," 408.

[59] Zizioulas, *Being As Communion*, 159.

the community. Just so now, the local community draws its existence, its purpose, its relation to the universal church, and its own particular authority from that same personal presence of Christ in and through the life of the community. These insights echo Vatican II's Decree on the Apostolate of the Laity, which declares that our participation in Christ's triple role demands an active and responsible share in the church's life for the laity "at the community level," as well as for the clergy:

> As sharers in the role of Christ the Priest, the Prophet and the King, the laity have an active part to play in the life and activity of the Church . . . . The laity should accustom themselves to working in the parish in close union with their priests, bringing to the church community their own and the world's problems as well as questions concerning human salvation, all of which should be examined and resolved by common deliberation.[60]

From the presence of Christ in the lives of believers in community there follows an assurance of the authenticity of both individual and community prayer and discernment. As Christ is present, so he also speaks to the communities in their authentic following of him as disciples. Furthermore, Christ is present in the community's acts of *remembrance*—its proclamation of the Word and celebration of the Eucharist. In the New Testament remembrance is linked to *intimacy observed* and to *service received:* of the woman who anoints his head with perfume, to the scandal of the onlookers, Jesus says, "Truly I tell you, wherever the good news is proclaimed in the whole world, what she has done will be told in remembrance of her" (Mark 14:9, *NRSV*).[61] For the Twelve at the Last Supper, Jesus sums up his entire ministry in the eucharistic offering of bread and wine and the command, "Do this in remembrance of me" (1 Cor 11:24-25).[62] Michael Downey connects such an act of remembrance to the ongoing hope of marginal communities: "Proclaiming and hearing the Word from the edge is an act of memory and of hope—

[60] Vatican II, Decree on the Apostolate of the Laity, *Apostolicam Actuositatem,* #10.

[61] See also Matt 26:13. Elisabeth Schüssler Fiorenza, *In Memory of Her: A Feminist Theological Reconstruction of Christian Origins* (10th Anniversary ed. New York: Crossroad, 1994) xliii–xliv, interprets this story in the context of women's discipleship and service and, ibid. 128–30, interprets the related story in Luke 7:36-50.

[62] See also Luke 22:19.

remembrance, in the fullest sense of the term (from the Greek, *anamnesis*), and trust in the divine promise yet to be realized."[63] The prayer of the local community of believers, inasmuch as it is offered in remembrance of Jesus and of his call to love and service, is thus an expression of intimacy with the Lord that once again assures Christ's presence and the Christian authenticity of the community itself.

The Spirit at Work in the Community. This assurance of Christ's presence through the remembrance of the local community is a crucial instance of the community's sacramental nature. It is, of course, dependent on the larger Christian tradition, which the community has received and continues to receive within the universal church. Yet precisely because Christ is truly present to the community through this sacramentality, we understand that the Spirit is at work *within* the community, not only through the broader structures of the church.[64] The Spirit is "an existential witness that God is at work in this community as God was at work in the life and ministry of Jesus."[65] It was Jesus, furthermore, who declared to the Twelve, "I no longer call you slaves . . . I have called you friends" (John 15:15). The embodiment of this intimate relationship with the Lord in the local community prompts recognition of the authenticity of Jesus and allows it to become authenticity for the church today—claiming and committing to all that he is.

Failure to acknowledge the importance of this local embodiment of intimacy does not immediately, of course, destroy the idea of the Spirit at work in the church, conferring grace through the institution of the sacraments, structures, and offices of the church. Some may hold that the chief work of the Spirit is to inspire the structures of authority that maintain the tradition across centuries and continents and cultures, without direct reference to the local community's role in this process.

---

[63] Downey, "Looking to the Last and the Least," 184.

[64] Ibid. 184: "Remembering is made possible by the activity of the Holy Spirit who, in recalling Jesus to mind, makes us understand and actualize his presence." He cites John 14:26. Note also Zizioulas, *Being As Communion*, 160: "In the celebration of the eucharist, the Church very early realized that in order for the eucharistic community to become or reveal in itself the wholeness of the Body of Christ (a wholeness that would include not only humanity but the entire creation), the descent of the Holy Spirit upon this creation would be necessary."

[65] Haight, "Structures," 409.

Yet the sacramental principle of the Spirit present *in and through* the concrete realities of human life remains essential to this point of view. Furthermore, even such a viewpoint must acknowledge some relationship between individual believers and the Spirit, if for no other reason than that they must receive the faith to recognize the authority of the church's offices and structures. Speaking from a more sociological point of view, because of the necessity of *followers* to go along with *leaders* there is a certain sense in which power *must* come "from below,"[66] even when one wants to put maximum emphasis on the authority of the central structures.

This last point is not merely a sociological one. The way in which the Spirit works through the structures of the church in itself demonstrates the intimate relationship between the Spirit and individual believers. In this relationship the Spirit confers on each believer an essential authority of his or her own, which does not disrupt but makes real and concrete the authority of the church's offices and structures. Christian Duquoc, a French Dominican theologian, explains:

> The ideas which support the view that the laity have authority in the doctrinal expression of the faith are very simple. They derive from the gift of the Spirit in baptism, a gift which confers on every believer a share in the prophetic office of Jesus Christ. All have received the Spirit, as the Pentecost story shows, and this reception by all creates the distinctive character of the Church. True, it does not destroy office, but office has no status except in relation to this primary gift. The authority of believers is thus linked with baptism as the sacrament which confers the Spirit and incorporates into the Church. It follows that what has to be worked out in relation to this primary gift is the role of the hierarchy, not the other way round. There is one mediator, Christ who gives the Spirit. The hierarchy is not a mediator in the sense of determining the gift of the Spirit.[67]

[66] Note Catlin, "Authority and Its Critics," 138: "Authority, as used in political science, is *of its essence social and objective*. Legitimacy is a name for wide, enduring recognition, flowing from the constitutional morality and modifying it, as a basis for law, stable order, and 'habitual obedience.'" (Emphasis added.)

[67] Christian Duquoc, "An Active Role for the People of God in Defining the Church's Faith," in Metz and Schillebeeckx, eds., *The Teaching Authority of the Believers*, 81. Haight, "Structures," 410, concurs with this general assessment, and contends that ministries in the church are "autonomous" with regard to their source or foundation, because all are grounded directly in God as Spirit. Note also the analogy between this view and Zizioulas's definition of catholicity (see

It must be understood that the point here is neither to shatter the unity of the Church into fragments the size of individual Christians nor to eliminate an overseeing authority, but to *derive that authority from the work of the Spirit in the midst of the church.*[68]

There is a natural tension that is neither avoidable nor, in and of itself, destructive, between the informal authority of the church's members (which presents itself in the day-to-day life of the communities) and the structured authority of the institution (which tends toward centralization).[69] This tension has been described as a "dualism,"[70] which gives the impression of two incompatible principles struggling against one another. Yet because the *one Spirit* that indwells the members and enlivens the local community also gives rise to the central structures, these different locations of authority are inseparably united with, not isolated from, one another.[71] So the authority of the local, essential as it is, comes

---

above, n. 59) as the presence of Christ in *each* community. Dietrich Bonhoeffer, *The Communion of Saints: A Dogmatic Inquiry Into the Sociology of the Church,* trans. R. Gregor Smith (New York: Harper & Row, 1963) 156–57, although writing from an evangelical tradition whose tendency is not centralization but individualism, insists that "only in the congregation is the Spirit at work; there he dispenses his *charismata.* The idea of a Christian who does not attach himself to the congregation is unthinkable."

[68] See Haight, "Ecclesiology From Below," 15, for a discussion of the way in which "God as Spirit is behind" the institutional authority of the church. He bases his insights on Ghislain Lafont, *Imaginer l'Église catholique* (Paris: Cerf, 1995).

[69] Paul M. Grammont and Philibert Zobel, "The Authority of the Indwelling Word," in John M. Todd, ed., *Problems of Authority* (Baltimore: Helicon; London: Darton, Longman & Todd, 1962) 87.

[70] Ibid.

[71] A. Pailler, "Considerations on the Authority of the Church," in Todd, ed., *Problems of Authority,* 18: "It seems to me a vital necessity for the Christian community to proclaim that the Holy Spirit is the soul of the Church not merely in the sense that he was sent down upon the infant Christian community on the great day of Pentecost, but also in the sense that he is the soul of *the whole social structure* of the Church permanently and in the Church's eternal present." See also Yves M.-J. Congar, *The Mystery of the Temple, or The Manner of God's Presence to His Creatures from Genesis to the Apocalypse,* trans. Reginald F. Trevett (Westminster, MD: Newman Press) 161: "A collective reality: all Christians as persons are God's temple. Where there is a believer, there also is a temple of God. Yet several believers are not several temples, for One Person dwells in and sanctifies them all."

with and *through* the authority of the universal and vice versa. Through the work of the Spirit it is the task of the universal church to set the Word of God before us, "to train us to recognize it, to remain subject to it, and to keep it within us," and to lead us "to the mysterious threshold where the Spirit comes to seize and transform us."[72] Yet because of its presence in creation and human history the Word is already "set before us" in the very fabric of the communities in which we pursue our Christian vocations. Furthermore, individuals and communities are also constantly offering this Word *back* to the larger church, thereby "training *it*," "leading *it*." They do this in their example and practice of the faith, in their influence on the formation of new Christians, in their shaping of the ministries of particular leaders, and sometimes (as in the case of any number of embattled communities) by their direct preaching and theologizing in witness to the Gospel.

It is this local working of the Spirit in the obvious sharing and negotiating of power and authority that we encounter in all its messy concreteness in communities such as St. Joseph's, Aquinas, and St. Matthew's. The presence and action of the Spirit has long been the stuff of inspirational homilies preached to the people of these, and undoubtedly countless other, parishes. At St. Matthew's the Spirit is seen as holding a diverse and hard-pressed group of members together in community. At Aquinas the Spirit calling the members to love and unity across difficult social boundaries has been a frequent theme. At St. Joseph's the Spirit was understood to sustain a distinctive community under adverse conditions and to give them a rebirth at the right moment. Less emphasized has been the theological truth that follows from these messages. *Knowledge* of the Spirit—not always articulate, but no less real for all that—is present in the community precisely because the Spirit is at work there and the people cannot help but experience it. If these communities are to be included fully in the Body—which, as authentic communities of believers, they must be—the authority that flows from the knowledge they have received through their *own* experience of the Spirit at work in the church must be respected.[73] A genuine respect leads naturally to a give-and-take relationship between the community

[72] Grammont and Zobel, "The Authority of the Indwelling Word," 88.

[73] Gérard Wackenheim, "Ecclesiology and Sociology," in Baum and Greeley, eds., *Church as Institution,* 39, insists that the interrelation of knowledge, power, and participation *must* be acknowledged and honored in order for Vatican II's vision of lay coresponsibility, cooperation, and participation to be realized.

and the officeholders who represent the authority of the universal church when it comes to discerning the movements of the Spirit within the whole church. As the first Anglican-Roman Catholic International Commission stated it in 1976,

> Through this continuing process of discernment and response, in which the faith is expressed and the gospel is pastorally applied, the Holy Spirit declares the authority of the Lord Jesus Christ, and the faithful may live freely under the discipline of the gospel.[74]

The Mission of Jesus in the Spirit. The third of Roger Haight's foundational principles and criteria for discernment of church structures is "mission."[75] Particularly in Luke's descriptions of the commissioning of the first disciples by Jesus[76] the mission is given broadly, to the apostles but also to their many companions, and relies on intimate relationship with Jesus. Based on these Scripture passages, as well as on the repeated insistence of Vatican II,[77] we can say that the entire church is called to a mission of witness that is only possible because Christ remains intimately present to his disciples. The Spirit is sent for the accomplishment of that mission, and it is this same coming of the Spirit that forms the collection of individual disciples into the church community. Mission is therefore not a *task* the church performs so much as it is a *definition* of church itself. Consequently, to be a member of the church is to be identified with its mission, which is revealed as authentic "in the way that the entire people of God encounter human life and behave as God's believing people in the general course of human living."[78] Because the church *is* the mission—the community that is sent for the Lord's purpose—the essence of mission is not defined by one or another ministry or position within the church. Mission is defined, rather, by the flow of Christian living that, as I have repeatedly

[74] ARCIC I, "Truth and Authority," #6, in Yarnold and Chadwick, *Truth and Authority*, 45.

[75] See Haight, "Structures," 414.

[76] See Luke 24:33-49 and Acts 1:4-15.

[77] See, for example, The Dogmatic Constitution on the Church *(Lumen Gentium)* #37-38, The Pastoral Constitution on the Church in the Modern World *(Gaudium et Spes)* #92, The Decree on the Church's Missionary Activity *(Ad Gentes)* #2, 5-6, and The Decree on the Apostolate of the Laity *(Apostolicam Actuositatem)* #2.

[78] Waldenfels, "Authority and Knowledge," 38.

pointed out, unfolds in concrete local situations within the church. The pastor (as a representative of the hierarchy within a local community) receives his mission for the *universal* church; nonetheless, he has received essentially the *same* mission as the other members of the local community he leads, although they carry out their mandates in different ways. (This remains true regardless of how one understands the "difference in essence" between the ministerial priesthood and the priesthood of all believers.)[79]

Zizioulas notes that in the ancient church the local community was understood as the "localization and concretization of the general."[80] Understanding the unity of mission in the church that this implies, and its source in the work of the Holy Spirit, makes it easier to grasp that the central authority of the church relies on a concurrent authority in the local community. This is to say that the accomplishment of the mission at one level is dependent on its accomplishment at the other, and at both levels the presence of the authority of the Spirit is essential to mission. The work of the Spirit in building community at the most local level creates the conditions necessary for acceptance of the wider authority of the church. Whether through the family, a small Christian community, the parish, or some other structure, a socializing process is necessary at the very local level if the larger structures of the church are not to become empty shells. The local community, therefore, functions as a practical school of authority for the church as a whole.

The local community, the community "in place," is the only *concrete* church there is. This is not to say that universal aspects of church are not *real* or that they are less important; I have already noted that local communities could not be viable in the absence of these aspects. At the local level, however, is the opportunity to understand the essence of church not so much in institutional structures as in the interpersonal relationships that make "church as mission" possible. These are essential features of *koinōnia* that remain local even when the social mode of the church has shifted greatly from the small house churches of ancient times. This is why both James and John can be so emphatic about the

---

[79] For the statement of this difference see *Lumen Gentium* #10. For reference to the shared mission see *Apostolicam Actuositatem* #10. John Paul Vandenakker, *Small Christian Communities and the Parish* (Kansas City, MO: Sheed and Ward, 1994) 61, presents instead an analysis that stresses the difference in these "two missions."

[80] Zizioulas, *Being As Communion*, 154.

impossibility of loving and serving God "whom they have not seen" without loving the very visible and tangible neighbor.[81] This conviction gives the authority of the local community a built-in defense—incomplete as it may be—against the chaotic individualism that might seem to call for the authority of the universal *over against* that of the local. That defense is the mere fact that the Christian community, just by existing, already stands against self-serving individualism. In fact, because of its concrete nature, it does so even more effectively than an abstract universal "unity" could do without it, because in such a setting people face the immediate challenge of setting aside concrete individualistic behaviors in favor of concrete communal ones. What would the unity of the universal church be to someone who had never had to offer peace to the odd person seated next to him in a gathering of the local community?[82] Part of the authority of the local community is what might be called an "authority of credibility"—the ability to speak and be heard on the *meaning* of Christian life that flows from the struggle of actually having *lived* it. On the strength of such authority the practice of the community actually shapes the theoretical understanding of Christianity. As Jon Sobrino of El Salvador has put it,

> [The sign of the doctrinal magisterium] lives on the reality of the faith achieved in the people of God, on the doctrine that the same people of God are formulating with a greater or lesser degree of explicitness, and on the need this people has to proclaim its faith. In this sacramental model both authorities contribute in different ways according to the nature of each.[83]

Admittedly such authority cuts two ways, because the values we imbibe and never question in our local communities may be, and are, both positive and negative, faithful and self-serving, freeing and binding.[84] This is one reason why the local community cannot stand alone, but is itself shaped in varying degrees by the authority of other communities.

---

[81] See 1 John 4:20 and Jas 2:14-17.

[82] See Hendel, "Exploration of the Nature of Authority," 9.

[83] Jon Sobrino, "The 'Doctrinal Authority' of the People of God in Latin America," in Metz and Schillebeeckx, eds., *The Teaching Authority of the Believers*, 61.

[84] Warren, *At This Time, In This Place*, 57: "Practice of any kind may encode in our lives values and attitudes we may never wish consciously to admit to ourselves. We are unwilling to see or decode what we ourselves have written into our lives."

But even in the case of the central hierarchical structures, Christian authority must ultimately be based on the lived experience of the church in the concrete, because it is there that the mission is actually carried out. Even the personal associations of clerics and their immediate co-workers, on deanery or diocesan levels, or even within the Vatican itself, despite the wide responsibility of their members, remain "local communities." The personal, concrete church experience of these members, and what they have come to understand through that experience, and what they subsequently pass on through the institutional structures which they affect, is still very much a product of locality. Yet, even these local communities would be meaningless without the universal instructions that call them into being, bind them, and bring them into relation to one another.

With the help of Stagaman's concepts of *authority, the authoritative,* and *authenticity,* and an understanding of the work of the Spirit in the church corroborated by many theologians, I have presented here a groundwork for the claim of authority by the local church community. This authority is inherent in the community, arising from its very existence as both a network of human relationships and a gathering of disciples of Christ. Yet this inherent authority does not create an independent community, but one that is increasingly aware of its *inter*dependence with other communities and with the mandated authority of the central institutions of the church. In the final two chapters I will look for a fuller theological understanding of this authority with the aid of the ecclesiological work of Joseph Ratzinger, Walter Kasper, and Karl Rahner.

Chapter Five

Local Authority and the "Priority of the Universal"

The Ratzinger–Kasper Debate

On April 23, 2001, *America* magazine called attention to an unusually public disagreement within the Vatican by printing on its cover the photographs of two cardinals of the Roman Curia under the heading, "On the Universal Church." Inside was an English translation of the "friendly reply" of Cardinal Walter Kasper, the president of the Pontifical Council for Promoting Christian Unity, to Cardinal Joseph Ratzinger, then the prefect of the Sacred Congregation for the Doctrine of the Faith (CDF), on the question of the relationship between the local and universal church. In 1999 Kasper had published an essay in which he had raised practical pastoral questions about the CDF's position that the universal church "is a reality ontologically and temporally prior to every individual particular church."[1] He rejected this understanding of the universal church as something entirely distinct from particular local churches, something that both in principle and in history comes "before" them. Rather, Kasper had insisted that the very idea of the universal church *includes* the local

---

[1] Congregation for the Doctrine of the Faith, "Letter to the Bishops of the Catholic Church on Some Aspects of the Church Understood as Communion," *Origins* 22 (June 25, 1992) 108–12, #8 (hereafter cited as CDF, "Church as Communion").

churches that exist in particular times and places. Ratzinger (now Pope Benedict XVI), who had devised the CDF's wording and defended the ideas behind it in at least two previous publications of his own,[2] had responded to Kasper's essay in a talk given the following spring that was later excerpted in print. He had underscored the danger of reducing the church to a merely human institution that could be understood through sociological categories alone. He further decried what he saw as a growing tendency to consider pluralism the foremost characteristic of the church and to think of the local church (understood throughout the debate as the church headed by a bishop) as self-sufficient.

In the reply that *America* published, Kasper accepted Ratzinger's objections to all these things, particularly the problem of reducing ecclesiology, the study of the church as a human and *divine* institution, to mere sociology. His own position, he insisted, should not be misrepresented as promoting these perspectives. He stood his ground on the question of priority, however, pointing out that his objection to the CDF formula was not based purely on sociology but on problems in biblical interpretation and systematic theology as well.

Six months later *America* published another response from Ratzinger in which the cardinal stressed that it had never been his or the CDF's intention to identify the "universal church" with the pope and the Roman curia. His only purpose all along, he wrote, had been to emphasize the essential unity of the local churches through the one church "palpably present" in the sacraments, word, and creed. The final element of the exchange came just a week later when *America* published a brief solicited letter from Kasper. In it he acknowledged that if the issue were no longer the "priority of the universal" but rather the "priority of inner unity," then he and Ratzinger had reached an important agreement. He continued to hold, however, that any sacramental experience includes both the universal and the local, and that the effect of various ideas on the actual pastoral practice of the church is highly relevant to the discussion.

This debate was triggered by a disagreement over the meaning of the "communion ecclesiology" that has flourished since Vatican II, was affirmed by the Extraordinary Synod of Bishops in 1985, and was the subject of the CDF commentary of 1992.[3] Because of this setting the exchange

---

[2] See Joseph Ratzinger, *Church, Ecumenism, and Politics: New Essays in Ecclesiology* (New York: Crossroad, 1989) 75 (hereafter cited as *Church, Ecumenism, and Politics*), and *Called to Communion: Understanding the Church Today* (San Francisco: Ignatius Press, 1991) 44 (hereafter cited as *Called to Communion*).

was largely engaged with issues of the relationship of papal primacy to local episcopal ministry rather than with the identity of individual local communities in the sense that I have been discussing them here. Nonetheless, the issues involved are very important to the discussion of the authority of these local communities. If we understand the universal church—however it is embodied—as a reality "over against" the local churches, particular communities can only claim authority of their own at the expense of the universal church and more or less in rebellion against it. If, on the other hand, we can conceive of the universal church and the local churches as mutually present to one another, then the discovery of a genuine authority on the part of local communities does not have to diminish any other authority present in the church under another aspect. In this chapter, I will first consider the approach of the current pope in his work as the theologian Joseph Ratzinger. I will then move on to a description of Kasper's position, and then to the common ground and divergences that the two theologians themselves acknowledge. I will then consider how the relationship between local and universal allows for recognition of the authority of local communities.

The Priority of the Universal:
Cardinal Joseph Ratzinger's Position

The Concrete Reality of the Universal Church. Ratzinger made use of the idea of the priority of the universal church as early as 1987 in an essay on the work of the Anglican-Roman Catholic International Commission (ARCIC), which had released a key report in 1981.[4] The work of the commission had raised high expectations for further movement toward full communion between Anglicans and Roman Catholics, and Ratzinger wrote to offer an explanation for the disappointment that befell these expectations. He lays much of the blame on the commission's failure to go into the concrete details of the authority structures of each communion.[5] "For it is of the essence of authority," he wrote, "to be

---

[3] An outstanding review of the development of communion ecclesiology since Vatican II can be found in Dennis Doyle, *Communion Ecclesiology: Vision and Versions* (Maryknoll, NY: Orbis, 2000).

[4] Joseph Ratzinger, "Anglican-Catholic Dialogue: Its Problems and Hopes," in *Church, Ecumenism, and Politics,* 65–98.

[5] Ibid. 66–67.

concrete; consequently one can only do justice to the theme by naming
the actual authorities and clarifying their relative position on both sides
instead of just theorizing about authority."[6] Ratzinger contrasts what he
considers a swift response to the report by the CDF, "commissioned by
the pope as central organ of ecclesiastical authority," with the confusion
about what would even constitute authoritative Anglican comment.[7]

These observations lead into consideration of "the authority of tradition, and the central organs of unity" as the fundamental problem of
the whole dialogue.[8] Scripture is a "basic standard of Christian faith"
and a "central authority" for both Anglicans and Roman Catholics, yet
"the ultimate value of all is not what is written but the life which our
Lord transmitted to his Church, within which scripture itself lives and
is life."[9] Scripture and the church, he asserts, "are linked together in
constantly alternating relationships, so that neither can be imagined
without the other."[10] This sort of relative relationship, however, "presupposes also the existence of the Universal Church as a concrete and
active reality," since the relationship with scripture pertains to the *whole*
church, not just a part of it.[11] Ratzinger then goes on to make this concreteness explicit in responding to the problem of who is able to make a
decision about the legitimate interpretation of Scripture. In the Catholic
approach, he says, "'apostolic succession' is the sacramental form of
the unifying presence of tradition."[12] For this reason "a bishop is someone who can express the voice of the universal Church in his teaching."[13] This demonstrates, he continues, that "the universal Church is
not a mere external amplification," but a concrete and practical necessity.[14] Although the actual practice of Roman primacy was not known
to the early church, other "living forms of unity" were regularly used,
including letters of communion, demonstrations of collegiality at episcopal ordinations, and the convoking of councils (which, at the level of
general councils, always required a central authority—first the em-

---

6 Ibid. 67.
7 Ibid.
8 Ibid. 68.
9 Ibid. 71. Ratzinger cites *Dei Verbum* #8 here.
10 Ibid.
11 Ibid.
12 Ibid. 74.
13 Ibid.
14 Ibid.

peror, later the pope—to convoke them). "Understood in this sense, *the priority of the universal Church always preceded that of particular Churches.*"[15] Although "the outward ways of putting the office into practice are subject to alteration," loss of the practical authority of the "primatial office" would result in "a tendency to particularize Christianity," ultimately to relativize it to culture and politics.[16]

Against "Ecclesiastical Relativism." Several years later, in his book *Called to Communion: Understanding the Church Today,* Ratzinger wrote of the priority of the universal church in the exact form in which the assertion would appear in the CDF document to which Kasper objected. The context this time was a brief theology course on the relationship between the universal and particular churches, given to a large group of bishops in Brazil.[17] (Brazil, of course, is the homeland of Leonardo Boff, who had been censured by the CDF for his writings on this very topic and whose "ecclesiastical relativism" Ratzinger frequently uses as a negative example.) In explaining the fundamental importance of the term *"ecclēsia,"* Ratzinger goes back to the Hebrew term *qahal,* "assembly," and the Jewish prayer for the reassembly of Israel after the Exile. He finds this prayer fulfilled in the apostolic community, Jesus himself being "the living Sinai," "the New Law," and his followers "the chosen final gathering," who in the Eucharist continue to assemble around Christ himself. Thus the New Testament calls the church not merely "people of God," but *ecclēsia,* "that expression that stood for the spiritual and eschatological center of the concept of 'people.'"[18] *Ecclēsia,* Ratzinger continues:

> signifies not only the cultic gathering but also the local community, the Church in a larger geographical area and, finally, the one Church of Jesus Christ herself. There is a continuous transition from one meaning to another, because all of them hang on the Christological center that is made concrete in the gathering of believers for the Lord's Supper. It is always the Lord who in his one sacrifice gathers his one and only people. In all places it is the gathering of this one.[19]

---

[15] Ibid. 75 (emphasis added).
[16] Ibid. 77.
[17] Ratzinger, *Called to Communion,* 9.
[18] Ibid. 31–32.
[19] Ibid. 32.

In tracing this vision of the church in the Acts of the Apostles, Ratzinger finds the "origin and essence of the Church" portrayed in three images. He writes first of "the disciples' retreat in the cenacle" before Pentecost (Acts 2). Here he finds, in the presence of Mary and 120 other disciples with the Twelve, united in prayer and with Peter as their spokesperson, "a mirror of the entire new people."[20] Second, Ratzinger cites Luke's depiction of the primitive church in adherence to the teaching of the apostles, the community, the breaking of the bread, and prayer.[21] Finally, he turns to the description of the day of Pentecost itself. In the descent of the Holy Spirit upon the apostles God confirms that it is his own action, not that of human beings, that creates the church. The spirit of Babel is reversed. The grasping, dominating human will that leads only to division is replaced by the loving Spirit of God, who "brings about recognition and creates unity in the acceptance of the otherness of the other: the many languages are naturally comprehensible."[22] On Ratzinger's reading of the scene, the Jerusalem church depicted here is *not* the first local church, the seed of a later worldwide federation, but rather "the one Church, the Church that speaks in all tongues—the *ecclesia universalis.*"[23] The local churches this microcosmic Jerusalem community then generates "nonetheless are all always embodiments of the one and only Church. *The temporal and ontological priority lies with the universal Church; a Church that was not catholic would not even have ecclesial reality.*"[24] He ends his exegesis of Acts 2 by emphasizing that, in the table of nations given as the astonished onlookers hear their own languages spoken, an unconventional thirteenth is added: Rome, which is "a symbol for the world of the nations" and thus "has a theological status." For this reason Rome "cannot be separated from the Lukan idea of catholicity."[25]

The immediate concerns of the 1992 "Letter to the Bishops of the Catholic Church on Some Aspects of the Church Understood as Communion" from the CDF were not very different from those Ratzinger had in view when he presented his Brazilian retreat two years earlier.

[20] Ibid. 41.

[21] Ibid. 42.

[22] Ibid. 43.

[23] Ibid. 44.

[24] Ibid.

[25] Ibid. 45. (Ratzinger quotes here another of his works, *Behold the Pierced One*, 73.)

The task of its second section, "Universal Church and Particular Churches," is to counter "the idea of a 'communion of particular Churches' . . . presented in such a way as to weaken the concept of the unity of the Church at the visible and institutional level."[26] The theology it presents is clearly the same as that expounded in Ratzinger's books. The universal church is identified with "the Church of Christ" and "the worldwide community of the disciples of the Lord."[27] It is, as *Lumen Gentium* 23 notes, a "body of Churches," but as Ratzinger had warned in his essay on the Anglican dialogue, such a notion must not be held at the expense of concrete institutions of unity. Particular churches come into being "after the model of the universal Church" (*Lumen Gentium* 23 is again cited), which "becomes present to them with all its essential elements."[28] These particular churches must not seek self-sufficiency or weaken their "real communion with the universal Church and *with its living and visible centre*," lest—just as Ratzinger had warned earlier—they become subject to "the various forces of slavery and exploitation."[29] These churches have "a special relationship of 'mutual interiority' with the whole," and so the universal church cannot be conceived of as the sum of them, nor as a federation of them. In sum, the universal church "is not the result of the communion of the Churches, but, in its essential mystery, it is a reality *ontologically and temporally prior to every individual particular Church*."[30]

To support the claim of *ontological* priority for the universal church (that is, precedence by virtue of what it actually *is*), the CDF cites the second-century Christian writings "The Shepherd of Hermas" and the "Second Letter of Clement to the Corinthians."[31] These are sources associated with the ancient church of Rome that speak unambiguously of the church as having existed with God from before creation itself.[32] Moving quickly to the claim of *temporal* priority, the document reiterates,

[26] CDF, "Church as Communion," #7.

[27] Ibid.

[28] Ibid. #7.

[29] Ibid. #8 (emphasis added).

[30] Ibid. #9 (emphasis in original).

[31] Ibid. n. 42.

[32] See Kilian McDonnell, O.S.B., "The Ratzinger/Kasper Debate: The Universal Church and Local Churches," *Theological Studies* 63 (2002) 244 n. 5 (hereafter cited as "Ratzinger/Kasper").

in abbreviated form, several of the observations about the Pentecost event that Ratzinger had made in *Called to Communion*. With these demonstrations presented, the CDF is confident in saying that local churches arise *"within* and *out of* the universal Church" and "have their ecclesiality in it and from it." In this the congregation echoes a formula of John Paul II. At the same time, however, it must acknowledge that Vatican II's *Lumen Gentium* has declared that "it is in these [local churches] and formed out of them that the one and unique Catholic Church exists."[33] The CDF concludes, therefore, that "clearly the relationship between the universal Church and the particular Churches is a mystery, and cannot be compared to that which exists between the whole and the parts of a purely human group or society."[34] Its final argument about this relationship points out that in baptism one enters *immediately* into the universal church, "even though entry into and life within the universal Church are necessarily brought about *in* a particular Church." Therefore, there are never any strangers among the baptized, and "belonging to the *Communion,* like belonging to the Church, is never simply particular, but by its very nature is always universal."[35]

Response to Kasper's Critique. In response to Kasper's criticism of the CDF document Ratzinger emphasizes the direct relationship between communion ecclesiology and eucharistic ecclesiology, noting in this way that he is defending something that is "entirely concrete and still remains entirely spiritual, transcendent, and eschatological."[36] He laments the tendency, which he apparently discerns in Kasper's essay, to reduce theology to sociology—specifically in this case to focus on the question of the mutual political relationships between local and universal.[37] He is willing to admit, on the practical level, that an overemphasis on central structure does need to be corrected, but not at the expense of the genuinely theological element in ecclesiology. "If one sees the Church only as a human organization, then, in fact, what remains is only desolation."[38]

---

[33] *Lumen Getium,* #23.

[34] CDF, "Church as Communion," #9 and n. 44.

[35] Ibid. #10.

[36] McDonnell, "Ratzinger/Kasper," 233.

[37] Ibid. 234.

[38] Joseph Ratzinger, in *Frankfurter Allgemeine Zeitung* (December 22, 2000) 46, quoted in McDonnell, "Ratzinger/Kasper," 235.

Turning to the defense of specific arguments from the CDF document, Ratzinger amplifies the teaching of the Church Fathers about the preexistence of the church. This teaching continues, he explains, the tradition of ancient Israel in seeing creation as the place *where* God's will operates, and the People of God as the instrument *by which* it operates. Therefore the people, the church, is part of "the inner teleology [that is, the goal] of creation."[39] (This is perhaps the origin of a suggestion Ratzinger makes in his last essay in the series, by which the phrase "teleological precedence" might substitute for the original "ontological priority."[40]) Concerning this argument for the church's preexistence he cites Gal 4:26: "The Jerusalem above is freeborn, and she is our mother."

With regard to the Pentecost event Ratzinger essentially repeats the points made in the earlier writings. He is particularly interested in reemphasizing that Luke's theology requires that the gathering of the 120 disciples in the Upper Room be seen *not* as a simultaneous universal and local community, but before all else as the New Israel, present in the Twelve. He declares further that to identify the local and universal in the one community in this way would itself encourage the mistaken assumption that "universal church" necessarily means "the Roman church in the pope and the curia." He is emphatic that this is not the assumption of the CDF document. Rather, the congregation wanted to adopt Vatican II's approach to the universal church. It is an entity entirely bound up in the relationship of Father and Son in the Trinity and in the mission of Christ to establish the kingdom of God and make the Church his "bride"—of one flesh with him. All this can be seen most clearly in the sacraments. In baptism, a theological and trinitarian event, not merely a sociological one, "the universal church continually precedes and creates the local church."[41] The Eucharist, in turn, always comes to the local community from outside, and always leads the community *into* the one Body of Christ. It requires priestly ministry, and this depends on a bishop who is not an "isolated individual" but, in continuity with the apostles, necessarily comes out of the universal church.[42]

Ratzinger concludes this essay with a direct comparison of his approach to the "ecclesiological relativism" of Leonardo Boff. Ratzinger

---

[39] Ibid.

[40] See Joseph Ratzinger, "The Local Church and the Universal Church," *America* 185:16 (November 19, 2001) 10 (hereafter cited as "Local and Universal").

[41] Ibid. 11.

[42] McDonnell, "Ratzinger/Kasper," 237–38.

sees Boff's starting point as the denial of Christ's foundation of the church and an insistence that, instead, all institutions are the result of sociological processes in historical contexts. Therefore all of them are subject to change, and in fact *must* be changed when circumstances warrant. Consequently, Ratzinger judges, there is no "one Church of Christ" in Boff's ecclesiology. By contrast, the church's faith relies on the Spirit—not a vague and insubstantial promise, but the concrete reality of Pentecost. The institutional church is not, therefore, random and inessential, but part of the incarnate nature of the church. It is this institution against which "the gates of hell will not prevail."[43]

The Simultaneity of Local and Universal: Cardinal Walter Kasper's Position

A Pastoral Crisis. Kasper's initial challenge to Ratzinger's position came in an essay dealing with the theology and practice of the office of bishop.[44] Throughout the ensuing exchange Kasper maintains the local point of view he developed as bishop of Rottenburg-Stuttgart, Germany, where he served for ten years until 1999, the year in which the first essay appeared. As a diocesan bishop Kasper experienced what he describes as "an urgent pastoral problem":[45] the imbalance between the college of bishops and the exercise of papal primacy in the worldwide church. Vatican II clearly desired to increase the understanding and the scope for action of both the individual bishop and the episcopal college within the

---

[43] Ibid. 239.

[44] Walter Kasper, "Zur Theologie und Praxis des bischöflichen Amtes," in idem, *Auf neue Art Kirche Sein: Wirklichkeiten—Herausförderungen—Wandlungen* (Munich: Bernward bei Don Bosco, 1999) 32–48 (hereafter cited as "Theologie und Praxis"). See McDonnell, "Ratzinger/Kasper," 229–32, for a summary of this essay in English.

[45] Walter Kasper, "The Universal Church and the Local Church: A Friendly Rejoinder," in idem, *Leadership in the Church: How Traditional Roles Can Serve the Christian Community Today*, trans. Brian McNeil (New York: Crossroad/Herder and Herder, 2003) 158 (hereafter cited as *Leadership in the Church*). This chapter is an English translation of "Das Verhältnis von Universalkirche und Ortskirche: Freundschaftliche Auseinandersetzung mit der Kritik von Joseph Kardinal Ratzinger," *Stimmen der Zeit* 219 (December 2000) 795–804. A somewhat different version (actually the first English translation) of the same article is printed as Walter Kasper, "On the Church," *America* 184 (April 23, 2001) 8–14.

church. Yet throughout Kasper's decade of episcopal ministry there were numerous indicators of a growing recentralization, with more and more decision-making power being reserved to the Roman Curia.

This phenomenon, he points out, is not the result of mere greed for power on the curia's part, but grows out of a number of contemporary challenges. Some local churches have, indeed, forgotten the New Testament emphasis on unity and turned instead to new forms of "ecclesiastical nationalism." Others have, on the contrary, abdicated their responsibilities and shielded themselves from difficulty by calling on Rome for decisions and actions that should have been undertaken locally. In turn, the forces of globalization and instant communication have made it ever easier for Rome to respond to these internal problems by direct intervention, but not always with appropriate pastoral sensitivity.[46] As a result many bishops feel "pulled in two directions,"[47] and many among both priests and people "can no longer understand universal church regulations and simply ignore them."[48] Kasper goes so far as to call this situation "a mental and practical schism."[49] He makes it clear that he himself is not challenging legal or doctrinal structures—the bishops of the world cannot act in an authoritative manner apart from their communion with the pope. Yet, since this is true, a question of leadership *style* arises. When the exercise of the primacy focuses so much on Roman decision-making and decree, is it not true that "the authority and the initiative of the college [of bishops] is *practically* reduced to a naked fiction"?[50]

This is the context in which Kasper objects to Ratzinger's formula, "the ontological and temporal priority of the universal church," first in its use by the CDF and afterward in its defense by Ratzinger himself. Throughout the debate, however, Kasper maintains several points of common ground with Ratzinger, which he makes explicit in his second article. First, he notes, "Jesus Christ wanted only one single church." This oneness is affirmed in the Creed. It is a present reality, not just a future ideal, and it is not merely fragmentary, but subsists in concrete form in the Roman Catholic Church. Second, "as the universal church consists

---

[46] Kasper, "On the Church," 9–10.
[47] Ibid. 9.
[48] Kasper, *Leadership in the Church*, 159.
[49] Ibid.
[50] Kasper, "Theologie und Praxis," 42, quoted in McDonnell, "Ratzinger/Kasper," 230 (emphasis in original).

'in and from' local churches, so each local church exists 'in and from' the one church of Jesus Christ . . . . The local churches and the universal church mutually include each other." Finally, "just as the local churches are not branches or provinces of the universal church, so the universal church is not the sum or product of a combination of local churches."[51] With these points as foundation, Kasper readily grants the CDF's assertion of the "mutual interiority" of local and universal. He also approves of their employment of both *Lumen Gentium*'s concept of "the universal church in and from the local churches" and John Paul II's corollary, "the local churches in and from the universal church."[52] Kasper seems to take these three formularies together as equivalent to his own assertion of the *simultaneous* presence of the universal and local churches in any given situation. Therefore he joins the CDF in rejecting the idea that local churches could ever be viewed as "self-sufficient." Just as Ratzinger has done, he emphasizes that there is no direct analogy between the church and other human societies. "Ultimately, its unity is a mystery, since its archetype is the Trinity of the one God in three Persons." [53]

Kasper's disagreement with the CDF document is not, then, with the doctrinal errors it names but rather with the particular response it makes to them. The one, holy, catholic, and apostolic church cannot be identified exclusively with the universal church, apart from the concrete local churches.[54] Nonetheless, Kasper judges that the CDF document does make this identification, and he goes on to point out a similar problem in the 1998 *motu proprio* of John Paul II, *Apostolos Suos*, on the authority of episcopal conferences. That document used the Ratzinger priority formula to justify the opinion that only the entire college together could exercise the genuinely authoritative collegiality of the bishops.[55] The basis for national or regional bishops' conferences, on

---

[51] Kasper, "On the Church," 12.

[52] See CDF, "Church as Communion," #9. The first formula can be found in *Lumen Gentium* 23, while the second was proposed by John Paul II in an address to the Roman Curia on December 20, 1990.

[53] Kasper, *Leadership in the Church*, 169.

[54] Ibid. 231.

[55] John Paul II, "On The Theological and Juridical Nature of Episcopal Conferences" (*Apostolos Suos*), Apostolic Letter Issued *"Motu Proprio,"* May 21, 1998, *Origins* 28 (July 30, 1998) 154 (#12). The text as issued makes direct reference to CDF, "Church as Communion" #9, but a very similar phrase ("the ontological and historical priority of the universal Church") was in place as early as a

the other hand, must be seen only as an *"affectus collegialis"*—a "collegial spirit" that does not carry genuine teaching authority.[56] This strikes Kasper as an astounding example of the imbalance he is warning against and, as such, a sign that even the pope's *motu proprio* can only be a provisional statement of the issues involved between universal and local church. Kasper himself hopes for further discussion of the possibility that the national and regional conferences could come to be understood as a new form of the ancient patriarchates, which grouped the churches of the Roman empire into particular regions.[57]

In his second response to Ratzinger, Kasper states his solution to the problem of recentralization quite bluntly: "The bishop must be granted enough vital space to make responsible decisions in the matter of implementing universal law."[58] This practical concern, however, clearly has its roots in more than a mere desire for greater diocesan autonomy. Rather, Kasper is responding to a much more general appreciation for the cultural diversity of the church. The theology of the episcopal office is meant to serve that diversity, an essential characteristic of an embodied church. For this reason "the bishop is not a delegate of the pope, but one commissioned by Jesus Christ with a proper responsibility of his own, which is rooted in the sacramental order."[59] In this regard Kasper is quick to point out that the history of the church offers many examples of tools and structures aimed precisely at the protection of a sphere of local autonomy. "Our people are well aware of the flexibility of laws and regulations," he writes, since "they have experienced a great deal of it over the past decades" following Vatican II.[60] Long before that, however, the church valued the virtues of prudence and *epikeia* (moderation in applying the letter of the law), devised systems of legal exceptions and dispensations, and supported the possibility of remonstration and delay on the part of bishops with regard to universal regulations. "The employment of such principles is the fruit of the ecclesiological doctrine

---

1988 working document of the Vatican Congregation for Bishops on this same topic of episcopal conferences. See T. Howland Sanks, s.j., "Forms of Ecclesiality: The Analogical Church," *Theological Studies* 49 (1988) 702 (hereafter cited as "Forms of Ecclesiality").

[56] Ibid.

[57] McDonnell, "Ratzinger/Kasper," 232.

[58] Kasper, "On the Church," 9.

[59] Kasper, *Leadership in the Church*, 160–61.

[60] Kasper, "On the Church," 9.

that a local church is not a province or department of the world church; rather, it is the church in one particular place."[61]

The Historical Record. How this statement differs from Ratzinger's approach to a doctrine they both hold can be more clearly seen in Kasper's way of dealing with the scriptural and historical record. Ratzinger deliberately focuses on the broad themes he detects in sacred history ("history is . . . interpreted as a love story between God and humanity"; "the basic idea of sacred history is that of gathering together, of uniting").[62] These are then used deductively as interpretive principles for understanding details (such as the difficulties with the Anglican dialogue mentioned earlier). Kasper's method in the debate, on the other hand, is very much the method "from below" that looks to Scripture and church history, in the light of ongoing scholarship, to establish a detailed record of *lived* Christianity. This concrete record then serves as the basis for theological principles. In keeping with this approach he declares: "The relationship between the universal church and the local churches cannot be explained in the abstract . . . because the church is a concrete historical reality."[63] For Kasper the fact that local churches are not mere branches of the universal church requires that the universal church be sought *in* the concrete diversity of these same local churches.

In both of his main contributions to the debate Kasper defends this perspective by taking on Ratzinger's interpretation of the Pentecost church in Acts 2. The gathering of the 120 disciples *can* be identified with universal church, he agrees, so long as the concrete *particular* church, which is also present there, is not lost from view. In this way the universal church itself will be understood as concrete and embodied, rather than as an abstraction. The Jerusalem church is thus "universal and local in its single reality."[64] Giving full rein to his historical method, however, Kasper also adds, "Of course this is a Lukan construction, for, looking at the matter historically, there were supposedly from the beginning a number of communities in Galilee alongside the Jerusalem community."[65] In light of this Kasper prefers to understand Luke's focus

---

[61] Kasper, *Leadership in the Church*, 160.

[62] Ratzinger, "Local and Universal," 10.

[63] Kasper, "On the Church," 10.

[64] Kasper, "Theologie und Praxis," 44, quoted in McDonnell, "Ratzinger/Kasper," 231.

[65] Ibid.

in the description of Pentecost, especially in the listing of nations, as the ingathering of the Jewish Diaspora rather than the universal church *per se*. To understand the Lukan ecclesiology it is necessary to attend to the entire story of the expansion of the early church in Acts, not the Pentecost event alone.[66] In fact, Kasper points out, "In Luke's writings, *ekklēsia* can mean both the house church and the local community. We also find a 'holistic ecclesiological conception' in Luke."[67]

In keeping with the historical approach in his second essay, Kasper finds touchstones for the relationship between the universal and local church throughout church history. He notes that the letters of St. Paul maintain a focus on the local church even while clearly holding the doctrine of a single church. "For Paul, the one church of God comes to life in each local church."[68] It is only in the so-called "captivity letters," which most scholars term "deutero-Pauline" and date much later than the others, that the local idea of church fades in favor of the universal. Historically the church's experience and reflection on itself began with the local communities headed by bishops. "Because the one church was present in each and all [of these communities], they were in communion."[69] It was from this local base that concrete institutions of unity developed: the presence of three other bishops at the ordination of a new bishop, local synods of bishops, and eventually provinces, patriarchates, and administrative systems designed to retain local decision-making about local issues ("subsidiarity").[70] Rome meanwhile developed "a decisive moral authority and a prestige" that was neither complete jurisdiction nor "a mere primacy of honor." The church of the first millennium, then, managed to maintain a balance between the local and universal aspects of the one church.[71]

The second millennium in the West, however, saw the development of a centralizing emphasis on papal authority. As it began to emerge clearly, it was resisted in the thirteenth century by Thomas Aquinas, who was a Dominican, but accepted by Bonaventure, his Franciscan counterpart. This papal emphasis was challenged, but prevailed, in a series of great struggles: against the conciliarists who championed the

[66] Kasper, "On the Church," 13.
[67] Kasper, *Leadership in the Church,* 163.
[68] Kasper, "On the Church," 11.
[69] Ibid.
[70] Kasper, *Leadership in the Church,* 164.
[71] Ibid. 165.

authority of ecumenical councils over popes, against the Protestants in
the Reformation, and against various later forms of state absolutism
and national church movements such as Gallicanism in France and
Josephinism in Austria. In the First Vatican Council of 1870 and the
Code of Canon Law of 1917 papal authority "seemed to have found its
definitive seal."[72] Against this background, however, the Second Vatican Council's teaching on local church, the sacramentality of episcopal
ordination, and episcopal collegiality hearkened back to the earlier era.
This new emphasis was developed as "communion ecclesiology" after
the council and confirmed by the 1985 Extraordinary Synod of Bishops.
It was the use of the "communion" theme following the 1985 Synod
that eventually prompted the CDF's 1992 document and, ultimately,
the exchange between Kasper and Ratzinger.

The Preexistence of the Church. Kasper's historical approach predis-
poses him to see the two aspects of church as manifested together in
every situation. Therefore even in commenting on Ratzinger's focus on
the preexistence of the church he continues to speak about the concrete
and local, and finds it surprising that Ratzinger should try to use this
concept as the basis for the universal church's ontological priority. To
Kasper the notion of the church's preexistence, as pointed out in the
early church sources to which Ratzinger refers, "affirms that the church
is not the outcome of chance constellations, developments, and decisions within history: it has its foundation in God's eternal will to bring
salvation and in his eternal salvific mystery."[73] However, it is not only
the universal church as a separate idea that God wills eternally, but also
its particular concreteness, manifest in the local churches. Kasper contends that a reading of Paul's treatment of the church would support
"the simultaneous preexistence of the universal church and the particular churches."[74] The importance of this simultaneity is underscored
in a sentence Kasper quotes from Henri de Lubac: "A universal church
that exists antecedently to all the individual churches, or that is conceived as existing in itself independently of the local churches, is merely
an abstraction."[75] To Kasper, despite one of the subtitles in his second

[72] Ibid. 166.
[73] Ibid. 171–72.
[74] Kasper, "On the Church," 13.
[75] Henri de Lubac, *Quellen kirchlicher Einheit*, 52–53, quoted in Kasper, "On the Church," 13.

article, this is not just "controversy about a scholastic dispute,"[76] but has real resonance in the church's lived relationship to God. "This is because God loves not bloodless abstractions but concrete human beings of flesh and blood. God's eternal salvific will intends the incarnation of the Logos and envisages the concrete church in the flesh of the world."[77]

Two Irreconcilable Positions?

In his second article Kasper characterizes his own method as "Aristotelian/Thomistic" and that of his opponent as "Platonic."[78] That is to say, Ratzinger thinks of a universal concept, such as the universal church, as having a separate and higher existence than any particular example of it, such as a local church (which reflects the universal, more or less fully). Kasper, on the other hand, prefers to locate universal and particular *within* each other, so that the universal is only ever encountered in a concrete instance and the two aspects always illumine each other. Ratzinger seems to have found the Platonic-Aristotelian categorization somewhat trivial, but he never disagreed with it.[79] Indeed, this way of contrasting the two approaches seems quite useful. Given his emphasis on concreteness, it is not surprising that Kasper found Ratzinger's first response to him "abstract and theoretical."[80] It is also quite predictable that Ratzinger, coming from a more deductive approach, would imply that Kasper lacks depth and reduces the essence of church to empirically separate local communities. In their final contributions to the debate both men seem to step back from the controversy. Each gratefully acknowledges certain concessions on the part of his opponent. Neither lets go of his fundamental perspective.

Ratzinger's Conclusions. Ratzinger picks up on Kasper's use of the phrase "scholastic dispute" and speaks of his counterpart as having dropped his "reproach" of the CDF. He implies that he did so because Ratzinger has successfully shown that "the fears voiced by Kasper [regarding the

---

[76] Kasper, *Leadership in the Church,* 169.
[77] Ibid. 172–73.
[78] Kasper, "On the Church," 13.
[79] Ratzinger, "Local and Universal," 10, 11.
[80] Kasper, "On the Church," 10.

practical recentralization of the church] were groundless."[81] He concedes that Kasper's idea of a "perichoretic" relationship between the local and universal church—that is, the kind of "mutual interiority" to which the CDF document had itself referred—"is valid for the church as it lives in history."[82] This, however, misses the real point, he contends. Rather, Ratzinger sees himself as defending "the basic idea of sacred history . . . that of gathering together, of uniting—uniting human beings in the one body of Christ, the union of human beings and through human beings of all creation with God . . . . Variety becomes richness only through the process of unification."[83] Ratzinger here seems to highlight not so much the priority of the *universal church* as "the inner priority of unity."[84] He describes himself as profoundly puzzled that Kasper should resist "this self-evident biblical view of history." The problem must be, he concludes, that Kasper jumps immediately from mention of the universal church to thoughts of the pope, the Curia, and church politics. Ratzinger responds,

> This linkage, objectively speaking, makes no sense. The church of Rome is a local church and not the universal church . . . . And the assertion of the inner precedence of God's idea of the one church, the one bride, over all its empirical realizations in particular churches has nothing whatsoever to do with the problem of centralism.[85]

Ratzinger offers—as primary examples of the ways in which the universal church itself is embodied *apart* from any particular church—the sacraments, the word of God "above the church, yet in it," and the Creed by which "the church receives and appropriates the word."[86]

Kasper's Conclusions. Kasper's final letter could easily have pointed out that Ratzinger's earlier work with these ideas, especially the essay on Anglican dialogue, was quite explicit in making the link between the universal church and central Roman institutions. These earlier pieces, however, lie outside the immediate concerns of the debate. Instead Kasper points to three shifts in Ratzinger's argument that indicate to him that progress has

---

[81] Ratzinger, "Local and Universal," 8.
[82] Ibid. 11.
[83] Ibid. 10.
[84] Ibid.
[85] Ibid.
[86] Ibid. 11.

been made during the discussion: the dropping of the charge that Kasper reduces the church to a mere sociological entity, the acceptance of Kasper's "perichoretic" formula as it applies to the church in *history,* and the shift to the concept of "priority of inner unity." These three points allow Kasper to retain his focus on the practical theological significance of the church's concrete experience without getting lost in the "rather speculative question" of preexistence.[87] He responds to Ratzinger's discussion of the sacrament of baptism by pointing out that while the sacraments are certainly a manifestation of the universal church, they must take place in "a specific (episcopally structured) local church." "The principle of simultaneity holds true precisely of the sacramental event," because the universal sacrament can only be experienced in a local celebration of it.[88] Kasper's second article had begun with the complaint that Ratzinger had not yet addressed the practical concerns that inspired Kasper's first essay. His final word makes it clear that, far from having given these concerns up as "groundless," he continues to hold them as the primary point of the debate. If the church is not "some sort of Platonic republic, but a historically existing divine-human reality, then it cannot be wholly wrongheaded and be chalked off as mere political reductionism to ask about concrete action, not in political, but in pastoral life."[89]

Intimacy, Authority, and the Interdependence of Local and Universal

Local Communities and the Ratzinger-Kasper Debate. The "creation" of the local church by the universal church in baptism, as described by Ratzinger, is certainly an actual event, but only when the phenomenon of baptism is viewed from a particular perspective. Seen "from below," the same event becomes also the embodiment of the universal church by the local. The actual persons involved in the event must make the effort, in their own historical circumstances, to give themselves to the universal church in this sacramental moment. It is this personal giving, which takes so many different forms in the day-to-day lives of the local communities, that locates the authority of the community within the

[87] Walter Kasper, "From the President of the Council for Promoting Christian Unity," *America* 185 (November 26, 2001) 28–29 (hereafter cited as Kasper, "From the President").

[88] Ibid. 29.

[89] Ibid.

church. If it does not take place, the universal church does indeed remain an abstraction because, as Ratzinger also points out, the will of God needs a people to live it out in creation.

In the local community the "mystery" of the Church, which both Ratzinger and Kasper value in their own ways, cannot be turned to "mystification," to an incomplete admission of how very human the day-to-day workings of the church are at every level. Rather, the wonder of the divine working within the human, of the truly universal and preordained existing in an unending "dance" *(perichoresis)* with the concrete local, shows itself in the raw mundane realities of person-to-person interaction. In fact it is only *when* a community can lose a fight with the bishop to keep open a beloved school (as at St. Joseph's), or experience the discomfort of daily miscommunication between members of different social classes (as at Aquinas), or meet wave after wave of disorienting leadership changes and reorganization (as at St. Matthew's), and yet *still* find in these very experiences the presence of the universal church, that the mystery of the church's divine constitution shines forth.

Local Authoritative and Catholic Normativity. Taken together with the observation of particular local communities, the implication of Kasper's argument must be that the local community, because of its potential to disclose the working of God in everyday life, is a fundamentally necessary experience of Christians. Jean-Marie Roger Tillard also champions this understanding when he speaks of the concrete local community as "a knot of the spiritual and the fleshly, a place for the meeting between God and 'the concrete person.'"[90] Only in this "enriching but complex experience of the community" can we concrete, living human beings fully grasp the Word of God.[91] With Kasper, Tillard laments the temptation to forget this very concrete faith, stemming from what he sees as overemphasis in Western theology on the universal aspect of church. Even the CDF document that triggered Kasper's initial reaction, though explicitly continuing this universal emphasis, notes that "life within the universal church [is] necessarily brought about in a particular church."[92] Christopher O'Donnell formulates the essential relationship

---

[90] Jean-Marie Roger Tillard, *L'église locale: ecclésiologie de communion et catholicité* (Paris: Cerf, 1995) 126–27.

[91] Ibid. 131.

[92] CDF, "Church as Communion," 110 (#10).

this way: "People *know about* the universal Church; they *experience* the local one."[93]

The local, then, is where believers actually encounter the church that is also universal, and the God who animates the whole. Although there may be extremely well-articulated doctrine about both the universal church and the reality of God—doctrine the local church acquires from the broader institution and duly disseminates—it is not merely doctrine and law but the creative use to which they are put in concrete situations that ultimately sustains the church's reality. As theologian Patrick Burns explains, applying the sociology of Peter Berger to the life of the church:

> What matters in the end is the everyday reality of the Christian community and the pervasive "of course" statements that control its operations. In terms of the church's mission as the sacrament of the world's salvation, the criterion of effective Christian ministry must be *what is actually communicated* to the community and to the world for which it mediates Christ's redemptive revelation.[94]

These "of course" statements—a manifestation of the authoritative (in the sense discussed in Chapter Three)—cannot be precisely prefabricated. Even when they are received apparently intact via tradition and institution they must be "configured" by real Christians living in contexts as different as those of St. Joseph's in Maine and Aquinas in Kingston. If they are not, they will *not* flow "of course" into and out of the lives of believers. Yet by virtue of the Christian identity of the community and of its members such authoritative beliefs, once lived and articulated, will become mediating paths to the wider church with its universal teaching and shared structures.[95]

It is further true, however, that these wider realities are themselves the product of the ideas, words, and actions of local communities across

---

[93] Christopher O'Donnell, "Local Church," in *Ecclesia: A Theological Encyclopedia of the Church* (Collegeville: Liturgical Press, 1996) 272 (hereafter cited as "Local Church").

[94] Patrick J. Burns, "Precarious Reality: Ecclesiological Reflections on Peter Berger," *Theology Digest* 21 (1973) 332 (hereafter cited as "Precarious Reality").

[95] See Peter Berger and Richard J. Neuhaus, *To Empower People: The Role of Mediating Structures in Public Policy* (Washington, DC: American Enterprise Institute, 1977) 2–4.

broad swathes of time and space. What central authority presents to the local community challenges and reshapes it; in the same way, though, what the local community produces in its Christian life challenges and reshapes what is presented globally. This process happens through a variety of Christian media, through the formation of future Christian leaders, through the playing out of conflict between the local and the central. Such processes establish agendas, shape vocabularies, encourage or discourage certain styles of leadership and of Christian life in general. All of this profoundly affects what will be understood as "authentically Christian" in other times and places. In this way the "everyday reality" of the local community not only *shapes* what it has received but in another sense effectively *creates* the world of the church.[96]

The tether that keeps this give-and-take process from utterly abandoning the historic root of the Christian community is the witness to the life of Jesus. This is provided within the whole church by the New Testament and the living tradition of its interpretation through the action of the Holy Spirit. The life of Jesus, accessed through this witness, is by definition the normative criterion for evaluating the actual content of whatever claims to be authoritative. As Michael Warren points out, however, within these bounds the community plays a crucial role in maintaining the cogency of Christian symbols, doctrines, and practices: "Practice, understood as the implementation of belief in particular circumstances, enlivens meaning."[97] Warren thus follows the lead of liberation theologians in appreciating the contribution of local groups of Christians as they actively interpret the teaching they have received in the midst of the lives in which they must live it.[98] Tillard specifically connects this "exegetical" function of the local community in the face of the Word of God to the church's *catholicity* because it concretizes the relationship between that unique Word and manifold human reality.[99]

[96] See Burns, "Precarious Reality," 331.

[97] Michael Warren, *At This Time, In This Place: The Spirit Embodied In the Local Assembly* (Harrisburg, PA: Trinity Press International, 1999) 95.

[98] Ibid. 79. See Jon Sobrino, "The 'Doctrinal Authority' of the People of God in Latin America," in Johann Baptist Metz and Edward Schillebeeckx, eds., *The Teaching Authority of the Believers. Concilium* 180 (Edinburgh: T & T Clark, 1985) 56. See also Hans Waldenfels, "Authority and Knowledge," in ibid. 38: "The fundamental authority of the Church is the authority of life, not of teaching."

[99] Tillard, *L'église locale*, 133.

Connecting catholicity to the local community is not by any means an intuitive move for most Roman Catholics, as the arguments of Cardinal Ratzinger and the CDF make plain. Catholicity is more easily attributed to the universal church, at the center of which the Petrine ministry is understood to protect and promote the catholic unity of the local churches and communities. The CDF, however, insists that "the ministry of Peter's successor . . . is not a service that reaches each church from the outside, but is *inscribed in the heart of each particular church.*" Here again they employ the term *"mutual interiority"* to describe the relationship between universal church and particular church.[100] The CDF understands this "mutual interiority" juridically, attributing it to the "episcopal power, not only supreme, full and universal, but also immediate, over all pastors and other faithful" of the papacy.[101] It is even more profoundly true, however, if papal authority is seen as part of what is authoritative, truly "inscribed in the heart," in the local community, where doctrine and law become Christian life. Indeed, it would seem that if this perspective is not taken, papal authority—like episcopal authority in certain instances in the sample parishes—will always be experienced as an external imposition, no matter how carefully the letter of it may be observed.

Here the Orthodox theology of John Zizioulas may offer a helpful view to the struggling Roman Catholic imagination. In Zizioulas' view the community that aspires to be both "local" and "church" has a special challenge, one that would seem to be impossible to any community that did not experience the active presence of God in its midst.

> The Church is local when the saving event of Christ takes root in a particular local situation with all its natural, social, cultural and other characteristics which make up the life and thought of the people living in that place . . . . [I]t must absorb and use all the characteristics of a given local situation and not impose an alien culture on it.[102]

---

[100] Congregation for the Doctrine of the Faith, "Reflections on the Primacy of Peter," *Origins* 28 (January 28, 1999) 561 (#6) (emphasis added). The text of this section is nearly identical to that of CDF, "Church as Communion," 110 (#13), which directly attributes to John Paul II, in an address to U.S. bishops, words very similar to those quoted here. See Pope John Paul II, "On Authentic Renewal," *The Pope Speaks* 32, no. 4 (1987) 380.

[101] CDF, "On the Primacy of Peter," 561 (#6).

[102] John Zizioulas, *Being As Communion: Studies in Personhood and the Church* (Crestwood, NY: St. Vladimir's Seminary Press, 1985) 254.

On the other hand, the goal of the church is not to reflect and promote the culture in which it is imbedded—necessarily part of a "fallen and disintegrated world"—but rather to reflect the *eschata,* the fulfillment of the Kingdom. "If the Church in its localization fails to present an image of the Kingdom in this respect, it is not a Church. Equally if the eucharistic gathering is not such an image, it is not the eucharist in a true sense."[103] Roman Catholic theologians might well object here to the idea that the local Eucharist draws its validity from the quality of the community's witness *(ex opere operantis)* rather than from its valid structural connection to the universal church *(ex opere operato).* It is not necessary, however, to take on this particular approach to sacramental theology in order to benefit from the vision of church Zizioulas offers. Even with a valid Eucharist, a local church community does not *effectively* fulfill the mission of the universal church by seeming to lose its particular identity in imitation of a central pattern, but by presenting in its own context a credible image of fulfillment in the Reign of God. It is the mission of the church's universal structures to preserve and promote this vision, yet the vision must be able both to disturb and to bring hope to real persons in particular times and places.

Christians answer in two ways the question of whether the authoritative foundation of a particular community is healthy and faithful. First, the entire day-to-day process of living, loving, thinking, and valuing, which continually draws from and replenishes the foundations of any human community, is understood by the *Christian* community to be permeated with the Holy Spirit. This presence of the Spirit has its origins in creation itself, but it is recognized and accessed by Christians through the sacrament of baptism. For the Christian community the Spirit gradually and continually reveals and redeems what is sinful, what is not life-giving, what is not according to the pattern of the life of Christ. The authoritative foundation of the community—its origins, meanings, and purposes—is to be judged not so much through a separate, external act as in the ongoing effort at Christian life *within* these local circumstances. The healthy and the unhealthy, the faithful and the unfaithful, the "wheat and the tares" (speaking here not of persons but of socio-cultural elements) are separated not by social engineering but by the ongoing work of the Spirit within human society. For this reason the church at large needs to respect the authoritative

---

[103] Ibid. 255.

foundation of the local Christian community, regardless of its particular content, as a place where the Spirit is at work.

The second approach to evaluating the community's foundational meanings and values is found in the interaction of this authoritative base with the broader self-understanding of the church as represented by the central authorities. These "authorities" include not only the hierarchical structures of the church and those who hold office within them—not recognized by all Christians—but also the history, tradition, and Scripture of the church, which these structures preserve and interpret. These universal institutions must in a sense be validated by local communities, because their *effective* authority is only recognizable through the presence of the Spirit of Christ, demonstrated in authentic Christian living day-to-day. Yet at the same time as local Christian life validates larger church institutions, these in turn validate daily Christian living by casting it in the context of Jesus' ministry and teaching and the universal following of Christ. In this way, they show it to be divine and not *merely* the result of particular human circumstances (although it is that as well). Because the authority of the local and the authority of the universal need each other in this way they function best when they are mutually responsive and share together the task of establishing the normative within the church as a whole.

Authenticity and the Interaction of Universal and Local Authority. If we understand authenticity as an "ownership" of the authoritative foundation by which a community lives, it is clear from the discussion up to this point that the church's authenticity cannot be a responsibility of central authority alone. This was one of the insights of the Anglican-Roman Catholic International Commission (ARCIC). The commissioners wrote: "Sometimes an authoritative expression has to be given to the insights and convictions of the faithful. The community actively responds to the teaching of the ordained ministry, and when, under the guidance of the Spirit, it recognizes the apostolic faith, it assimilates its content into its life."[104] The point is that the local community helps to *authenticate* the teaching of official authority, by recognizing and assimilating it, but further and most especially by living as an authentic

---

[104] ARCIC II (Second Anglican-Roman Catholic International Commission), "Church as Communion," *Origins* 20 (1991) 724 (#32) (hereafter cited as "ARCIC II").

Christian community, "a gathering of the baptized brought together by the apostolic preaching, confessing the one faith, celebrating the one eucharist and led by an apostolic ministry."[105] In describing the relationship between that "apostolic ministry" (the episcopate) and the community it serves, ARCIC goes even further:

> This ministry of oversight has both collegial and primatial dimensions. It is grounded in the life of the community and is open to the community's participation in the discovery of God's will. It is exercised so that unity and communion are expressed, preserved and fostered at every level—locally, regionally, and universally.[106]

In its communion with the church at large, then, the local community seeks *authenticity*, not merely submission to official *authority*.

ARCIC, of course, was the body whose work had prompted some of Cardinal Ratzinger's initial concerns about the priority of the universal church. In describing the "visible" aspects of communion, accordingly, the CDF characteristically avoids emphasizing the role of the local church. The Congregation's document on communion locates these visible aspects only "in the teaching of the apostles, in the sacraments and in the hierarchical order."[107] On the other hand, it stresses "an intimate relationship" between these institutions and the "invisible" aspect of communion, that of "each human being" with God and "with the others who are fellow sharers in the divine nature."[108] While "visible communion" between "fellow sharers" is certainly not exhausted by the institutions the document mentions, the discussion of an interrelationship among these elements is much appreciated. It recalls British sociologist Victor Turner's thesis of a necessary dialectic between structure and *communitas*, or group feeling.[109] Carl Starkloff, in describing the operation of this interaction between the "institutional church" and "liminal *communitas* groups" puts the case very baldly as a choice between "tensive unity or schism," which, negoti-

---

[105] Ibid. 725 (#43).

[106] Ibid. 725 (#45).

[107] CDF, "Church as Communion," 110 (#11).

[108] Ibid.

[109] Victor Turner, *The Ritual Process: Structure and Anti-Structure,* The Lewis Henry Morgan Lectures at the University of Rochester, NY (New York: Aldine Publishing, 1969) 129.

ated properly, could lead the church into "no less than a deeper communion or *koinōnia*."[110]

As Kasper in effect concludes, even holding to the priority of the universal church *"in its essential mystery"* need not be an obstacle to recognizing that, in order to preserve *authenticity* in the church, the universal cannot impose itself on the particular any more than the particular can disown the universal. The CDF's own affirmation of the two formulas, *"ecclesia in et ex ecclesiis"* ("the church in and from the churches") and *"ecclesiae in et ex ecclesia"* ("the churches in and from the church") suggests a relationship not of dominance and submission, but of essential interaction. Tillard describes such a relationship as existing between the *sensus fidei* and the teaching role of bishops:

> The books of the Bible deliver their meaning only if they are plunged back into the totality of "memory." For memory comes from the soul of a people who have expressed their faith in an immense variety of styles, literary genres, memories, and contexts. It is necessary to compare, to "weigh," to date, to evaluate. That could not be done democratically. The *"sensus fidei,"* moreover, does not have the capacity by itself to articulate the truth which it apprehends, to give itself perfectly nuanced verbal form, to put in precise words the content of the collective "memory" while doing justice to the role of the miraculous or the epic. This is the service which, in dialogue with the research of theologians, the episcopal ministry gives to the *"sensus fidei."*[111]

Leonardo Boff, too, emphasizes the interaction—the "dialectical relationship"—of the two aspects of church, saying succinctly, "Without popular Catholicism, official Catholicism does not *live*; without official Catholicism, popular Catholicism is not *legitimized* in its Catholic character."[112]

It should be clear from the concept of *inter*action that the local community, despite its necessary creativity, is not free to symbolize and teach the faith in whatever way it pleases. Not all of the strong influences on the day-to-day life of the communities are readily compatible with the Gospel, nor is the very meaning of the Gospel always obvious

---

[110] Carl F. Starkloff, "Church as Structure and Communitas: Victor Turner and Ecclesiology," *Theological Studies* 58 (1997) 663.

[111] Tillard, *L'église locale*, 320–21 (my translation).

[112] Leonardo Boff, *Church: Charism and Power—Liberation Theology and the Institutional Church*, trans. John W. Diercksmeier (New York: Crossroad, 1992) 87 (hereafter cited as *Church*).

in any given local situation. Communion with the other local communities in and through the universal church is thus necessarily *formative* of the local community. On the other hand, the life of Jesus demonstrates powerfully that authenticity is not always about conformity. As they did in the church's early centuries, local communities continue to find ways of asserting elements of their own authenticity—their own attempts to live true to their authoritative roots—that do not meet with immediate official approval and, often enough, lead to tension and conflict with central structures. Local ancestors, heroes, and saints, venerated long before they have been adopted by the church at large, "represent the example of greatness for each successive generation" without which authority is not educative but dominating.[113] Adapted, reinterpreted, or even syncretistic rituals appear continually, and sometimes give birth to new feasts like Christmas, or new devotions like that to Our Lady of Guadalupe.[114] Reformist communities and sub-groups carry on "an active work of interpretation, of pointing out the distance between the way of living of Jesus himself and of his disciples and those of a particular age."[115] Far more passively, but with perhaps even greater effect, "people perform a selection among what is handed down to them . . . not . . . by rejecting the input of the tradition, but by lack of interest in some of its elements."[116] These are the strategies by which local communities fight for their own authenticity. Anyone who has heard the tales of long-established communities like St. Joseph's, about legendary pastors, long-serving teachers, or beloved "pillars of the community" has seen this dynamic at work. It can operate in simple,

---

[113] Hannah Arendt, "What is Authority?" in eadem, *Between Past and Future: Eight Exercises in Political Thought* (New York: Viking, 1968) 119. Arendt's idea about the authority of ancestors seems to harmonize quite well with John Paul II, *Tertio Millennio Adveniente, Origins* 24 (1994) 411–12 (#37), in his discussion of the value of "updating the martyrologies" with contributions from all over the world during the millennium jubilee celebration.

[114] Boff, *Church,* 89–107, in a chapter entitled, "In Favor of Syncretism: The Catholicity of Catholicism," discusses the value of, and the reaction against, such practices.

[115] Warren, *At This Time,* 79. Christian Duquoc, "An Active Role for the People of God in Defining the Church's Faith," in Metz and Schillebeeckx, eds., *Teaching Authority of Believers,* 79–80 (hereafter cited as "Active Role"), presents a similar defense of what he calls "resistance."

[116] Duquoc, "Active Role," 79.

apparently unimportant details such as the persistent use at St. Matthew's of a locally composed setting for the Lord's Prayer at Mass (during which the *entire* community joins hands). It is at work, often unacknowledged, in groups like the charismatic prayer community at Aquinas, which has been silently challenging class, denomination, and role boundaries for years. Such strategies have been used in all parts of the church and throughout its history, affecting and shaping even the official authority that would seem at times to stand against them.

Ultimately the discussion of the relationship between central authority and local communities is not just an internal issue but affects the credibility of the church in the world.[117] "The gospel authenticity of life," says Tillard, "is what gives [the *sensus fidei*] the seal of truth."[118] In an age already suspicious of large religious institutions our search for this authenticity must take in not just the tradition as preserved by the church's universal teaching authority, but also the genuine and transparent *ownership* of that tradition by the local communities with which ordinary people come in contact. The authentic model for this ownership is Jesus himself. Following that model, local communities need to respond not only to what is specifically and traditionally Christian in their authoritative foundation but to *all* the fundamental values and beliefs of their members, because "in every age and culture authentic faithfulness is expressed in new ways."[119] Recognition of this is behind the desire of some recent writers to emphasize church as "event" rather than merely location, institution, or population.[120] John Zizioulas goes so far as to say that "the eucharist . . . is unthinkable without the gathering of the whole Church in one place, that is, without an event of *communion*."[121] Yet the Eucharist, with its universal character, is also what prevents the local event from claiming autonomy. Gospel authenticity is, then, a creative and theological process. It engages the fullness of a local community's reality, shapes the faith and understanding of its members, and in turn allows them to reach out apostolically to shape

[117] See ARCIC II, 720 (#3).

[118] Tillard, *L'église locale,* 315 (my translation).

[119] ARCIC II, 723 (#27).

[120] See Boff, *Church,* 155; Sanks, "Forms of Ecclesiality," 703; Zizioulas, *Being As Communion,* 22. Karl Rahner's use of this approach will be discussed in detail in Chapter Six.

[121] Zizioulas, *Being As Communion,* 22.

the faith and understanding of others outside the community.[122] In all of this it is a process essential to the universal church because it is the point of contact with concrete human reality and so a vital link in the church's effective exercise of authority.

[122] Warren, *At This Time*, 79, refers to small groups coming to terms with implications of their religious tradition as "hermeneutical communities." O'Donnell, "Local Church," 272, maintains that "theology needs strong confident local Churches if it is to be relevant for our times," and Sanks, "Forms of Ecclesiality," 695, concurs: "Without a certain amount of [the lived] experience [of the community] theological reflection is not possible . . . ." Bernard Cooke, "Obstacles to Lay Involvement," in Metz and Schillebeeckx, eds., *Teaching Authority of Believers*, 67, describes the importance of all this for outreach: "The power to form another person's thinking springs basically from one's own faith and understanding. Faith gives both the power and the responsibility to witness."

Chapter Six

Local Community and the Church's Mission: The Work of Karl Rahner

Pope Benedict and Cardinal Kasper each champion values that have been recognized in the church for centuries—the transcendent unity of the Trinity on the one hand and the intense pastoral presence of Christ "where two or three are gathered" on the other. The balance of these in actual church structures that their debate sought, whether or not they actually achieved it, is an ever more urgent goal in today's church. The task is to successfully blend these characteristics in a way that avoids the extremes of rigid uniformity arising from over-centralization on the one hand and discordant self-absorption arising from over-localization on the other. The task is, indeed, as Pope John Paul II said, to "supply institutional reality with a soul."[1] In an increasingly "instant" and "global" culture this goal requires us to become more aware of and respectful toward the genuine spiritual authority that resides at the level of the local community of Christians, where individuals encounter others face to face and are "able to share their joys and sufferings, to sense their desires and attend to their needs, to offer them deep and genuine

---

[1] John Paul II, Apostolic Letter On the New Millennium (*Novo Millennio Ineunte*), *Origins* 30 (2001) 503.

friendship."[2] To be effectively present in the world today the church must claim this arena of Christian life as an indispensable location for the constant work of the Holy Spirit in creating and maintaining the church.

Karl Rahner was a German Jesuit theologian of the twentieth century whose re-reading of the church's theological inheritance from Thomas Aquinas in the light of contemporary philosophy and experience opened broad new avenues for Catholic theology in the decades just before and just after the Second Vatican Council. It is Rahner's work on christology that has suggested a theological approach "from below." Although his own approach to the church does not always use this method, Rahner's basic theological orientations still make his ecclesiology particularly helpful for understanding the inherent authority of local church communities. Beginning from the basic assumption of radical human openness to grace—God's self-communication[3]—Rahner presents "a theology characterized by its emphasis on identifying God as central to all human experience."[4] This in turn gives Rahner's thought a concrete and pastoral bent. His extensive work on the church emphasizes history, an understanding of the dynamics of change, and a realistic hopefulness about the future.

All of this is gathered in the central theme of Rahner's ecclesiology: church as sacrament, where I will begin this chapter. Rahner develops this theme with an emphasis on the concrete manifestation of the church in the local community, where the church must "become event." After discussing the three clear images by which Rahner establishes the presence of the whole essence of church in the local "part," I will consider the various ways in which the local community plays its role of making the universal church concretely present. It will then be possible to consider the diversity of the church as an actual sign of its unity and to appreciate with Rahner the church's role as pilgrim. Connecting all of this back to the concrete mission of the church in the world, the chapter will conclude with a new look at some of the elements of local context I first presented in Chapter Two.

---

[2] Ibid.

[3] Karl Rahner, "Concerning the Relationship Between Nature and Grace," *Theological Investigations* 1, trans. Cornelius Ernst (Baltimore: Helicon Press; London: Darton, Longman, & Todd, 1961) 312–13.

[4] Richard Lennan, *The Ecclesiology of Karl Rahner* (Oxford: Clarendon Press, 1997) 7.

The Church as Sacrament:
A Pointer Toward the Local Community

"The 'incarnation' of grace, and grace's process of becoming tangibly historical, reaches its climax in the sacraments."[5] This succinct statement can serve as a summary of Rahner's understanding of sacraments and their relationship to the mission of Christ and the church. The mission of Christ is to draw humanity into the divine life; such a relationship between us and God is the ultimate meaning of "grace." But this relationship is not accomplished by abstracting the "spiritual element" from humanity and elevating that alone. Christ's grace has an "incarnational tendency." Rahner continues, "This grace . . . is meant to be rather the sanctifying formative principle of the whole body-soul life of man [sic], coming right down into his concrete, tangible daily life, where it therefore receives its 'expression' and takes on its corporality."[6] Grace is therefore embodied, historical, "externalized."[7] As such it touches far more than the "personal spiritual life" of a believer—it is necessarily a social phenomenon, and this is confirmed by the fact that "those who are being sanctified and he who sanctifies are of one race."[8] It is this social embodiment, this continual availability of Christ's grace throughout history, that is presented in the sacraments. The sacramental signs, then, do not offer saving grace in an arbitrary way, as if any sign would do. Rather, this way into relationship with God is completely bound up with the concrete and social aspects of the sacraments. This is why Rahner insists that "the sacrament effects grace *because* it is a sign," an "externalization of grace."[9]

The issue of authority in the church can be addressed in similar sacramental terms. Rahner argues against an understanding of the church's teaching authority as God's constant intervention from outside, taking place in a miraculous manner in the course of the church's

---

[5] Karl Rahner, "Personal and Sacramental Piety," *Theological Investigations* 2, trans. Karl-Heinz Krüger (Baltimore: Helicon Press; London: Darton, Longman, & Todd, 1963) 125.

[6] Ibid. 120.

[7] Ibid. 121.

[8] Ibid. 122.

[9] Ibid. 123.

history.[10] From such a point of view, he continues, salvation and revelation would not really be *part* of the church's history but would appear as interruptions, made by God "to correct the course of the history of the human spirit and to preserve it from deviations"[11] brought about by historical developments.

The assurance of such direct divine intervention may seem to be an attractive counterweight to the uncertainties of history, particularly in times of change that do not favor the church's social and cultural influence. Yet to cut the essential link between the history of revelation and salvation on the one hand and ordinary human history on the other endangers the very concept of a historical faith embodied within a visible society of believers, the church. Such a development risks making irrelevant those very aspects of the church that draw most people to it. Rahner underlines this in *Foundations of Christian Faith*: "Either history is itself of salvific significance" or salvation is only a subjective, interior experience, "so that the rest of human life does not really have anything to do with it." Rahner judges that only the first option does justice to our God-given nature as human beings in time. The church therefore is "not only . . . some useful religious organization," but the concrete source of salvation and grace for us, "and only this makes church really church."[12]

The church itself, then, is a sacrament that "effects grace" not as the incidental instrument of divine authority that descends on Christian communities from on high, but as a sign, "in the flesh," of God's presence in the concrete world of those very communities. As visibly human and historical it is limiting and particularizing, but as a form of God's presence it transcends these same limitations and points out the goal of human history, not in division and isolation, but in communion. In this way Rahner also sees the church's authority sacramentally and requires us to recognize both the dignity of the concrete local community—the church in its most visible and "incarnate" form—and the way this community is ordered toward genuine and visible unity within the overall communion of the church.

---

[10] Karl Rahner, "The Teaching Office of the Church in the Present-Day Crisis of Authority," *Theological Investigations* 12, trans. David Bourke (New York: Seabury, 1974) 9.

[11] Ibid. 19.

[12] Karl Rahner, *Foundations of Christian Faith: An Introduction to the Idea of Christianity,* ed. William V. Dych (New York: Crossroad, 1990) 345.

The Church as "Event":
Three Images of the Local Community

Whether this local authority can be properly recognized, of course, depends very much on the way we understand local church communities in the first place. In his essay on the "Theology of the Parish," Rahner uses three images of the local church—"remnant," "synagogue," and "altar community"—to set the parish into his larger vision of church.[13] He argues that "the church, as event, is necessarily a local and localized community."[14] Although the church has been traditionally understood as a "complete society" (*societas perfecta*)[15] and so has a continuing legal existence even apart from its concrete actions, "still, one cannot dispute that there, where the church *acts*—that is, teaches, prays, offers the Sacrifice of Christ, etc.—it attains a higher degree of actuality than it does by its mere continuing existence."[16] This is because "the church is a visible society; and, as such, it is ever compelled again and again to realize its historical place-time apprehensibility through the visible actions of men *[sic]*. It must always and again and again become event."[17] Granted, this "becoming event" could possibly be accomplished even by a single person empowered by Christ in the church. Nonetheless, when the church can be seen as a community of people "bound together through a visible event and grace" it "reaches a higher degree of event-fullness than it does where an individual endowed with an office" acts without the active cooperation of other members.[18]

It is at this point that Rahner recalls the Jewish theology of the remnant and of the synagogue, taken up in part by St. Paul with regard to the Christian church.[19] The thinking behind these two images holds local

---

[13] Karl Rahner, "Theology of the Parish," in Hugo Rahner, ed., *The Parish, From Theology to Practice,* trans. Robert Kress (Westminster, MD: Newman Press, 1958) 23–35.

[14] Ibid. 25.

[15] Karl Rahner, "The Presence of the Lord in the Christian Community at Worship," *Theological Investigations* 10, trans. David Bourke (New York: Seabury, 1977) 76, describes this designation for the church as "totally inadequate."

[16] Rahner, "Theology of the Parish," 26.

[17] Ibid.

[18] Ibid. 27.

[19] Ibid. A similar discussion is presented in Karl Rahner, "The Episcopate and the Primacy," in Karl Rahner and Joseph Ratzinger, eds., *The Episcopate and the*

communities less as *parts* or *members* than as "a visible manifestation of the whole nation, which is itself wholly present in this part."[20] In the case of "the remnant," this view is called for by the insistence that "God's promises and faithfulness cannot come to naught," even when the "people in the concrete (according to the 'flesh') remains recalcitrant to God's decree and unbelieving."[21] The synagogue communities that began to form during the Babylonian exile seem to have been founded on a similar principle following the loss of the Temple as the physical unifying point for Israel (note Ezek 11:16-17). For Rahner, that such a principle was able to preserve Israel through the catastrophes of exile and diaspora is very significant for the local church, particularly as it enters an era of *Christian* diaspora:

> A limited administrative district in one community cannot cause the totality of this community to live on, when the totality as such has disappeared, if the part was nothing more than a part, a mere organ, not endowed with the sensibility and the various faculties of the whole organism. On the other hand, if the whole is so present in the part that it can fully consummate itself there according to its nature, and if the whole cannot by any means disappear while the part still lives, then the part is indeed more than a mere part, and rightly bears the name of the whole. This is exactly how pre-Christian Jewish theology conceived the faithful remnant, the individual community of brethren, in which God was truly served in faith according to his law.[22]

Rather than remaining an "emergency" measure, then, the principle of the presence of the whole in the part becomes the basis for a deep understanding of the presence of God for Israel, represented by the proliferation of synagogue communities even after the crisis of the Exile had passed.

Making use of this special understanding of local communities, Rahner now employs his third image, that of "altar community," as he continues the search for that place in which the church becomes event "in

---

Primacy (New York: Herder and Herder, 1962) 23. In neither article does Rahner provide any specific citation of Paul, but his description of the remnant concept clearly relies on Romans 9.

[20] Rahner, "Theology of the Parish," 27.

[21] Rahner, "Episcopate and Primacy," 27.

[22] Ibid. 23.

the most intensive and actual sense of the word."[23] This full intensity, he claims, is found in the celebration of the Eucharist, in which the sacramental presence of Christ shows the church itself to be, then and there, the Body of Christ. In that same moment the origin of the church in Christ's sacrifice is also made real and present, as is the ultimate ("eschatological") goal of the church, the communion of Christ and his members. All of this is present in a sacramental event that by its nature "can be celebrated only by a community which is gathered together in one and the same place"[24]—the altar community. Rahner concludes, therefore, that the church's own inner reality moves it toward becoming this local event. Yet "this in no way harms or lessens its universal destiny and mission to all men [sic]." Therefore "the local church is not only . . . an authorized agency of the one universal church which could just as easily dispense with such an appendage; rather, this local church is the event of this very universal church itself."[25] This conclusion leads Rahner, in another place, to a simple but very significant correction of standard ecclesiological terminology, from "the universal church and the local church" to "the church as she is everywhere, and the same church as she appears in one particular place."[26]

Rahner's emphasis on the eucharistic assembly as the most intense instance of the "church event" was further shaped by the Second Vatican Council's inclusion of a similar idea in the Dogmatic Constitution on the Church *(Lumen Gentium)* 26. As Rahner quotes it in "The New Image of the Church," the relevant passage reads:

> The Church of Christ is truly present *(vere adest)* in all lawfully instituted local communities of the faithful who, united with their pastors, are actually called 'churches' in the New Testament itself . . . . In these communities, however poor and small they may be, and even though they may live in the diaspora, Christ is present, Christ through whose power the one holy Catholic and apostolic church is united.[27]

[23] Rahner, "Theology of the Parish," 27.

[24] Ibid. 28.

[25] Ibid. 28–29.

[26] Ibid. 28.

[27] Second Vatican Council, Dogmatic Constitution on the Church *(Lumen Gentium)* 26, quoted in Karl Rahner, "The New Image of the Church," *Theological Investigations* 10, 7–8.

On Rahner's reading[28] this passage was meant specifically to reach an even more concrete level than the "local church" as diocese, even though it appears in a section of *Lumen Gentium* specifically about the ministry of the bishop. Rahner sees the passage as an explicit admission by the Council of the local community's dignity within the church's structure:

> The [Dogmatic] Constitution [On the Church] recognizes and explicitly states that the local and parish community, so far from being a mere minor administrative subdivision in a major religious organization called the Church, is actually the concrete reality of the Church, the presence of Christ in which she achieves her highest fullness, and that too in the word, in the Eucharistic meal and . . . in the love which unites the hearers and those who celebrate the Eucharist.[29]

Rahner understands this conciliar statement as support for his previous positions regarding the relation of the whole and the parts,

> inasmuch as it is precisely the Church (in contrast to every kind of secular society) that is truly present and achieves her fullness at the level of the word of preaching and of the sacrament, that is, still at the level of the social and sacramental life of the Church in itself. In other words the whole is truly present and achieves its fullness in the part.[30]

In statements such as these, Rahner presents the local community as far more significant than one would gather from simply reading canon law, or even some of Rahner's own preconciliar writings.[31] The point is not to present any particular local structure, such as the parish, as unchangeably given by God, but rather to recognize in the local eucharistic community, whatever its legal status or social makeup, the manifestation of the divinely given essence of the whole church. That essence for Rahner is nothing less than the continued vital presence of Christ in the world, speaking "the word that deepens into the unfathomable mystery of God."[32] The heart of the Christian experience—

---

[28] See Rahner, "New Image," 9.

[29] Ibid. 10.

[30] Ibid.

[31] I have in mind here particularly Karl Rahner, "Peaceful Reflections on the Parochial Principle," *Theological Investigations* 2, 283–318.

[32] Rahner, "New Image," 11–12.

indeed, of the human experience—is thus localized in this community. "The Christian of the new age will experience what happens to him in his community no longer—as formerly—as something that takes place *in* the Church, but rather as the impact of the Church herself considered as a vital force."[33]

In the end, then, Rahner's focus on the church as sacrament leads us further and further away from abstractions. Though far from detached from the human sinfulness and incompleteness that necessarily affects the church at every level, the local community is where the authoritative voice of the church will ultimately be most audible to the great bulk of humanity. Here—where bonds of personal relationship and love can be experienced firsthand, where the concrete demands of justice in the world can be recognized and engaged—the church's own sacrament of Christ's presence is celebrated. Here both the possibility and the struggle of genuine Christian community are "realized" in the truest sense.

The Church as Local Community: Functions and Structures of the Whole in the Part

Once the position of the local community is so emphasized, of course, the question arises: what is the meaning, or even the possibility, of unity for the church? To address this question we can go back again to the very basis of Rahner's theology. The primary relationship of humanity to God is located in the actual offer of grace that God makes in every human life. (This is the "supernatural existential" that Rahner made so famous.)[34] Rahner understands Christ as the full expression of this offer in history.[35] These conceptions taken together mean that the offer of grace—of relationship with God—is part and parcel of human life and will not, cannot be withdrawn. The church, as the sacrament of Christ's presence to the world, thus has its origin in this single reality of God's offer of grace to all humanity.[36] From this point of view it is utterly impossible for the church—the People of God—to be other than fundamentally one. Yet as sacrament, its visible, historical dimension, with its inevitable change and diversity, is also essential.

---

[33] Ibid. 12.
[34] Rahner, *Foundations*, 131–32.
[35] Ibid. 204–05.
[36] Ibid. 412.

For Rahner the resolution of this seeming paradox is not in equating unity with uniformity through an emphasis on central structures. He certainly acknowledges that communion with pastor and bishop, and with the universal church, are essential qualities of a genuine local church community.[37] Yet he also finds in *Lumen Gentium* 26 three other characteristics that, in his descriptions of them, appear to be the very foundation of the unity that is expressed by the hierarchical structures. These characteristics are the preaching of the gospel ("itself the basis for this state of 'being gathered together'"),[38] the celebration of the eucharistic meal ("likewise designated explicitly as the basic cause for this brotherly unity"),[39] and the demonstration of love among the members of the community ("which develops precisely from this [brotherly unity caused by the mystery of the eucharistic meal]").[40] All four of these characteristics, Rahner emphasizes, are brought together into a unity by the Spirit, which is the presence of God underlying all of them. The authority of the Word spoken within the community is linked in the Spirit to the intimacy the community experiences with Christ, and among all its members through the Eucharist and the love it sacramentalizes. In this way the necessary unity of the one church is genuinely present in each local community.

These observations confirm the essential relationships that Rahner describes among the local community, the Eucharist, and the universal church. While sacraments *express* the deepest nature of the community, they also in turn by their explicitness make that nature real for the community. The eucharistic assembly, then, must be an embodiment of the universal church, not merely an agent, in order to celebrate the sacrament authentically. The assembly *is* church, yet, because of the church's universal mission, to recognize this demands that the intention and self-understanding of a congregation be universal, not merely local. Should the local church be taken to be autonomous, it cannot celebrate as "church" in a universal sense. On the other hand, if it is taken only as part of a whole it still cannot celebrate in a universal sense. The Eucha-

---

[37] Karl Rahner, "On the Presence of Christ in the Diaspora Community According to the Teaching of the Second Vatican Council," *Theological Investigations* 10, 89.

[38] Ibid.

[39] Ibid.

[40] Ibid. 90.

rist demands an assembly that is local (*this* assembly that celebrates) *and* universal (the church—the body of believers—that is constituted by the celebration) at the same time. Yet even this will not be an authentic liturgical symbol if the local assembly is only seen as "universal" for purposes of the rite itself. The community's ability to be a liturgical symbol of the universal church implies an ongoing, living response to authoritative Christian values. To be authentic, such a response must be in tune with the daily reality and understanding of the believers who respond. This, in turn, implies a certain interpretive authority within the community that also makes its impact on the universal church.

The presence of Christ in the church, which becomes most fully real in the event of local community,[41] does not "trickle down" to that community from more authoritative realms. Rather, it is essential to the church precisely *in* the local community, in the midst of which "the whole Church is there," Rahner says.[42] Indeed, Rahner points out that the proclamation of the Word itself, as long as this is not "mere handing on of . . . human knowledge" but imparts "the reality itself that is being proclaimed"—is an element of that intimate presence of Christ.[43] This implies a faith that is embodied in daily life and leads inexorably toward deeper communion with the transcendent God even if the local community is not able licitly to celebrate a eucharistic liturgy. Every such genuine Christian community has an inner drive toward the Eucharist, a relationship with God in Christ at the heart of its nature that urges the sacramental expression that would confirm and deepen it. It is true that a community could not genuinely express this inner drive in a way that would damage any of its other constitutive elements (such as communion with the universal church through the hierarchy). Still, the anomaly, seen in various parts of the world, of vital local communities being denied their eucharistic expression largely as the result of externally imposed disciplinary regulations (particularly with regard to the marital and educational status of candidates for ordination) must also be seriously scrutinized.

For all this, Rahner is far from suggesting that the local community could or ought to stand autonomously. His words regarding individual faith can be equally well applied to the interpersonal network that is

---

[41] Rahner, "Presence of the Lord in the Christian Community," 75–76.
[42] Ibid. 76.
[43] Ibid. 78.

the local community: "Christianity is the religion of a demanding God who summons my subjectivity out of itself only if it confronts me in a church which is authoritative."[44] This objective authority is represented by the church's magisterium, which establishes norms for all local communities. Nonetheless, Rahner points out that the apostolic preaching of the church relies on the apostle's "own faith in the Resurrection of Jesus,"[45] which was itself received from and nurtured by the church.

> The preaching of the individual apostle, therefore, is not merely addressed to the believing community, but also proceeds from it. It bears witness to a faith which has already been brought into being by God alone in Jesus Christ, and it is only on this basis . . . that it can also justify its own formal authority.[46]

Moreover, this type of dependence of formal authority on the believing community is not just an abstract notion, but also personal and concrete. The church that nurtures the personal faith of "the bearers of this deposit of faith and the teaching authority that goes with it" is "the concrete Church . . . who in her faith, in the history of her faith, and the development of her dogma, is not simply the passive and obedient object of a teaching authority in the church."[47] So it is the local community, as the preeminent event of the church, that bears much of the responsibility for the formation of the very persons who are later entrusted with the apostolic authority.

Even more significant, however, is the community's role in the reception of that authority. This role always exists, but Rahner finds it particularly evident in the conditions of "diaspora" within which the church lives in contemporary times, "scattered," stripped of much of the social influence it once had. As the sample parishes of Chapter One show, this condition can be experienced as the immigrant's sense of isolation and defensiveness, as confusion in a rapidly changing world, as a constant struggle for internal agreement. "What [the teaching office] lacks now," explains Rahner,

> is any effective influence upon the individual prior to his assent of faith
> . . . . the only real significance which it still has depends almost exclu-

---

[44] Rahner, *Foundations*, 344.
[45] Rahner, "Teaching Authority of the Church," 6.
[46] Ibid. 6.
[47] Ibid. 8.

sively, and in increasing measure today, upon the question of whether and how far it succeeds in making its own spiritual authority credible on the basis of the gospel itself.[48]

This credibility, however, depends precisely on authority's ability to express the Gospel in relation to meanings and values that are already comprehensible and concretely relevant among believers and potential believers. For just the same reasons that the local community bears great responsibility for nurturing the church's officeholders, it also bears responsibility for the application of their authoritative teaching. As we have seen, this interpretive function is carried on in innumerable ways in the communities' practical life.

It is not always easy to appreciate this importance of the local community by examining the church's structures. Even the term "local church" is usually reserved for a level of organization larger than the personal networks I have been focusing on here. Furthermore, the most common official structure of local community, the parish, is sometimes organized or reorganized in such a way as to deemphasize the personal relationships that do so much to shape local communities, and instead reemphasize official and hierarchical structures. Rahner's own frequent attention to the episcopal office (in response to the attention of the council itself) might be thought to deflect attention from the more intimate local community. A closer look, however, reveals a number of avenues by which the local community can be highlighted even within Rahner's treatment of church structures *per se*.

In his article on "The Episcopal Office," written during the Council, Rahner discusses the development of office in the church. In a way similar to his approach to the teaching authority, he notes that official functions arise in the essence of the church itself, from the heart of its one mission and one divine authority. These functions are therefore essentially one, as the church is one, and "must therefore never be simply enumerated . . . but grasped in their unity."[49] In applying this unity principle to the relationship between bishops and priests, Rahner makes a series of observations that are relevant to the authority of local

---

[48] Ibid. 27.

[49] Rahner, "The Episcopal Office," *Theological Investigations* 6, trans. Karl-Heinz Krüger and Boniface Krüger (Baltimore: Helicon; London: Darton, Longman, & Todd, 1969) 344–45.

communities. He notes the parallel between the college of bishops with the Pope on the one hand, and the presbyterium—the local body of priests—with its diocesan bishop on the other. Both demonstrate "a monarchical and a collegial element inseparably related to one another."[50] Surely the one can "serve as a guide" to the other, and this leads Rahner to declare that the presbyterium should be thought of as instituted by God *(iure divino)* as "a college for the bishop."[51] He supports this approach with the impression that "the New Testament and the primitive church do not actually show any knowledge of the single priest but only of the presbyterium."[52] On this basis Rahner describes the bishop's relationship to his priests:

> [H]e does not ordain a priest because he cannot be everywhere, but as a helper in his office where he actually is. He does not ordain an individual, but surrounds himself with a college. He does not act without the presbyterium. This does not mean that he is dependent upon his presbyterium juridically and in a way subject to legal action, but that he knows himself to be no lonely, autocratic monarch who could say, or would want to say: "The diocese, *c'est moi!*"[53]

If the singular pastoral office of the church is exercised within a diocese by the bishop *together* with his presbyterium, with its functions distributed in various ways at different times and places,[54] this suggests three further conclusions. First, the original local community setting of the episcopal office is recalled by the image of the bishop surrounded by and working together with his presbyterium, the elders of the community.[55] Second, and following from this, the local pastoral function—including presidency of the Eucharist—is not a lesser function corresponding to a less significant portion of the church, but in fact an episcopal function itself corresponding to the absolutely essential importance of the local community's eucharistic gathering. For this reason, finally, much of what is held ecclesiologically about the "local

[50] Ibid. 340.

[51] Ibid. 341.

[52] Ibid.

[53] Ibid.

[54] Ibid. 343–44.

[55] See Second Vatican Council, Constitution on the Sacred Liturgy *(Sacrosanctum Concilium)* 41.

church" as diocese (as in the discussions in Chapter Five of this book) is relevant to the single local community as well.

The Church as One:
⊂⊃ *Local Diversity as a Sign and Source of Unity* ⊂⊃

Rahner pays great attention in his ecclesiology to the central institutions that serve the church's unity, but he refuses to understand those institutions as the earthly font of that unity and the truth on which it is based. Rahner sees truth itself as demonstrated in "the real life—together in all dimensions, the common celebration, cult, personal love and other active fulfillments of human and inter-human existence,"[56] all of which point us back toward "the mystery which governs everything in unspeakable nearness."[57] This, of course, returns us to the very starting point of Rahner's theology in the personal encounter with God's grace. Ultimately it is this encounter—which binds us together in its universality even while it unfolds in the most private core of our being—that gives the only secure basis for unity.

Because of this, Rahner imagines a church in which, even in the face of continual uncertainty and conflict, the diversity of human life and the commitment to faith and love continually interact to strengthen the community. Without the continual encounter with God in personal freedom not even the most loyal and apparently "faithful" adherence to the official church can guarantee unity.[58] On the other hand, the Spirit at work in the church brings about its purposes even out of seemingly irreconcilable differences among the members. Rahner addresses the plight of one whose spiritual gift is not recognized by the church at large. Genuine charisma, he writes, is given for the church and cannot operate independently of it. Therefore the gift is shown to be authentic if, when rejected or censured (as Rahner himself was at points during his career), the charismatic individual

> bears humbly and patiently this inevitable sorrow of his charismatic endowment, builds no little chapel for himself inside the Church in order

---

[56] Karl Rahner, "A Small Fragment 'On the Collective Finding of Truth,'" *Theological Investigations* 6, 87.

[57] Ibid.

[58] Karl Rahner, "What Is Heresy?" *Theological Investigations* 5, trans. Karl-Heinz Krüger (Baltimore: Helicon; London: Darton, Longman, & Todd, 1966) 502.

to make things more tolerable, does not become embittered but knows that it is the one Lord who creates a force and resistance to it, the wine of enthusiasm and the water of sobriety in his Church, and has given to none of his servants singly the task of representing him.[59]

Rahner is secure in the faith that the ultimate harmonization of differences is in the hands of a God who can and continually does attend to it, with and in the church. He is able, therefore, to accept two notions that might otherwise appear to be at odds with each other. In discussing the possibility of the historical development of church doctrine he reminds his readers that "applications [of doctrine and law] made by individual Christians and theologians are never more than appeals to the Church herself."[60] Yet, considering the relationship between personal faith and church doctrine, he later declares that both individuals and local communities can and must be engaged in the developing "forms of faith" for themselves that respond directly to the particular circumstances and tensions that most affect them in the increasingly complex contemporary world.[61] Further still, considering changeable and unchangeable elements in church teaching, Rahner emphasizes the extent to which even "the Church herself" must dwell in faith with the uncertainties of human existence. Even "the identity and historical continuity" between formulations of the Council of Trent and contemporary faith "is, in the last analysis, itself in turn a statement of faith and hope," he writes.[62]

As is evident in the sample parish stories, the tensions and ambiguities of inclusivity and diversity in the church come from many sources. Among them are the shape of a particular community and its personalities, the pressures and contradictions of a given cultural situation, the modern experiences of globalization, multiculturalism, urbanization, and advancing technology, and the continually shifting relationship between the church and the world. Whatever their specific source, these tensions are built into the call of the church to take up the all-embracing

[59] Karl Rahner, *The Dynamic Element in the Church*, ed. W. J. O'Hara (New York: Herder and Herder, 1964) 78.

[60] Karl Rahner, "The Development of Dogma," *Theological Investigations* 1, 42.

[61] Karl Rahner, "The Faith of the Christian and the Doctrine of the Church," *Theological Investigations* 14, trans. David Bourke (New York: Seabury/Crossroad, 1976) 40.

[62] Karl Rahner, "Basic Observations on the Subject of Changeable and Unchangeable Factors in the Church," *Theological Investigations* 14, 13.

mission of Christ in the Spirit. Though called to embody the universal church, every local community will, by definition, experience a certain separation from other such communities, and by the same token a certain set of tensions within itself. To try to avoid these potentially destructive conflicts by simply deemphasizing local communities in favor of uniformity and increasingly stronger central structures would, strangely enough, fashion a special-interest community out of the once all-embracing worldwide church. It is local difference that, in addition to enriching the church and strengthening its authenticity in a particular place, is the very sign of the catholicity of the church's mission. A better approach might see the tensions and limitations not so much as dangers to be eliminated as goads toward greater openness. They can become the instruments of the Spirit to build up the authentic love and unity within a community as well as among communities that recognize the limited nature of their witness and seek to join it in tangible ways to the witness of others. Real adherence to institutional structures and doctrine is also strengthened in this way, for communities can more readily recognize these institutions as genuine service toward their own catholicity. The universality of the church is fully embodied not by any earthly structure or superficial agreement but by communities that are constantly challenged to see their own visible reality within the unity of the Spirit, which is both its ground and its goal.

The Church as Pilgrim: The Local and the Changeable

Despite the defense of diversity in the church, Rahner is no relativist. He writes about truth, truth that matters to salvation, truth "which can be missed only in a culpable manner."[63] Fundamentally, however, revelation is in Rahner's understanding the open-ended self-communication of God.[64] Traditionally it is described as "closed," Rahner understands, not because there is nothing more to be understood, nor because God has simply decided to reveal nothing more, but because God in Christ opens to us his very self, and there is no greater gift

---

[63] Rahner, "What Is Heresy?" 472.

[64] Karl Rahner, "Considerations on the Development of Dogma," *Theological Investigations* 4, trans. Kevin Smyth (Baltimore: Helicon; London: Darton, Longman, & Todd, 1966) 9.

to give.[65] This self-giving calls the church into being—not by creating a community that possesses correct doctrine but simply by being addressed to human beings who respond in freedom. The church is indefectible not based on its own grasp and defense of particular truths, but because of the permanence and irrevocability of God's self-gift.[66] By this self-gift, moreover, God confirms a relationship in which God will continue to speak throughout the church's history. Rahner thus opens the way to reaffirming God's love for the created and changeable world, which is shown by this relationship to be of enduring value and not something "merely provisional."[67]

Historical conditions profoundly shape and limit individual Christians and their local communities, however pure and complete the truths of church teaching are taken to be. Given these influences, it is impossible in the ordinary life of a community simply to mirror the universal teaching[68] or to capture it completely in their way of life.[69] The concrete exercise of the church's life, therefore, always incorporates the changing and differing elements of its various local and historical contexts. "Man [sic] works out his salvation or damnation in everything he does and in everything which impels him."[70] Moreover, the concrete situation of Christians shapes and forms Christian teaching and belief about morality and doctrine and does so amidst ambiguity, even though there are clearly binding norms and timeless principles. It is concrete Christian living that has to reveal the nature of humanity in its current position "on the journey" and the way in which that nature must respond to the steadfast love of God.[71] On the other hand, it is also through this concrete Christian living that the church has its true

---

[65] Rahner, "Development of Dogma," *Theological Investigations* 1, 48.

[66] Rahner, "Considerations on the Development of Dogma," *Theological Investigations* 4, 9.

[67] Karl Rahner, "The Eternal Significance of the Humanity of Jesus for Our Relationship with God," *Theological Investigations* 3, trans. Karl-Heinz Krüger and Boniface Krüger (Baltimore: Helicon; London: Darton, Longman, & Todd, 1967) 40–41.

[68] Rahner, "The Faith of the Christian," 34.

[69] Ibid. 30.

[70] Karl Rahner, "History of the World and Salvation History," *Theological Investigations* 5, 99.

[71] Rahner, "Basic Observations," 15–16.

impact on the world, so that we can understand adaptation itself as an integral part of the church's mission.

The "changeable factor" Rahner thus presents as central to the church's reality does not, of course, affect only individual local communities. The church's central structures and institutions have their concrete aspects too, and these also illustrate the point very well. Yet even change and development in these areas is most clearly experienced in its effects on the local community. It is here that most Christians encounter the church's historical nature not merely in titles, names, concepts, and headlines, but in flesh-and-blood human beings with their full range of strengths and weaknesses. Here in the local community, too, it becomes clear that it is impossible to understand the church solely according to its own institutional structures. At the local level the shaping of the church by its historical context can best be seen for just what it is: the unavoidable and total immersion of the church's members in all the complexity of the contemporary world. The relation of this local community to the unchanging essence of the universal church is the same as the relation of particular, historical belief to the unchanging truth of the Gospel. In both cases the struggle is to hold the particular, awash in the plural demands of the world, in a strong relationship with the universal. In both cases this negotiation is accomplished by keeping the particular (the lived faith, the local church) bound to a kind of "anchor" (Christian tradition, universal communion) that it may not leave behind. The Christian tradition to which the local community is bound by its communion with the universal church must constantly be incorporated back into what the church is in this particular time and place. All the while, however, it is within the particular and constantly evolving conditions of time and place that the believing community must embody and live its faith.

Global Vision and Local Sensitivity

The church has no choice but to constantly live in the tension—sometimes quite sharp—that is required to balance a more remote and universal ideal with the concrete particulars of the local community. To give in to the temptation to ease the tension by diminishing one of its elements is to fail to recognize the complete interdependence of these two aspects of church. To break the tension denies the church a way of witnessing to the possibility of profound unity. In order to be the universal witness and sacrament of Christ in the world, the church must

be embodied in countless and diverse local communities whose particular contexts shape the specific forms they take. By virtue of being
parts that contain and manifest the essence of the whole, the communities so shaped are also themselves *church*. Thus the contexts out of
which local church communities develop are important elements for
the universal church itself. To examine the contexts of the communities,
therefore, is to come to know the whole church more deeply. Further, to
know these contexts is to know more intimately the challenge and the
mission that the church faces.

Recall that among the various elements of context I first presented in
Chapter Two, *Christian belief and faith* logically come at the head of the
list, since without their presence from the outset there could be, by definition, no community of believers. Since belief precedes (or better, brings
about) the individual Christian community itself, the community must
in a way receive it from outside, through a tradition that is much older
and broader. It has been spread by the seemingly secular struggles of
politicians and soldiers as well as by the spiritual dedication of saints,
through both careful planning and historical accident, for many centuries. For this reason it has been easy in some Christian theologies to
misconceive the local community as the purely passive recipient of a
"faith" viewed as some sort of commodity. However, the Christian faith
that holds a local community together truly as church neither drops
from the sky nor is the product of executive decisions made within a
central institutional structure. The work of maintenance and growth, by
which beliefs may give rise to faith in a theological sense, is always accomplished concretely. This is underscored both by ordinary observation of the life of the parishes and by Rahner's focus on the personal
encounter with God in freedom. Rahner further reminds us that

> it is a basic conviction of the gospel that love of God can be effectively
> realized . . . only in the act of love of neighbour, and that love of neigh-
> bour achieves its radical depths and its absolute significance only when
> . . . it itself constitutes love of God as the innermost reality of man.[72]

When asked about the origin of their own faith, parishioners of St.
Joseph's or Aquinas or St. Matthew's do not ordinarily speak of the history of the Roman Catholic Church in Canada, the United States, Ja-

---

[72] Karl Rahner, "The Function of the Church as a Critic of Society," *Theological
Investigations* 12, 240.

maica, or Haiti. Nor do they speak of the function of the papal office in preserving the integrity and unity of the church. They speak of their parents and grandparents, of the rituals of their childhood, of influential mentors, companions, and friends in their lives. Through all these things they speak of their own experiences of love and of God. The complication of understanding belief and faith as elements of the local community's *context*, the background against which the community exists, is that through these intimate relationships faith also *constitutes* the community as church. In this way the foundation of each community is unique in the relationships that characterize it and yet identical to the foundation of every other local community. Each community is thus church, and a new community is both a unique event and an outgrowth of the same unified church. Conversely, as Rahner has already reminded us, if only one of many communities remains faithful—a remnant—it is yet the foundation of the whole church that survives in this one community.

Another element of the local community's context to which I have referred throughout this book is the *network of human relationships* of which its members are a part. Like belief and faith, this complex set of personal connections is both part of the context and part of the essence of the community. It is based on everything from close friendship to client-provider relationships and includes the range of cliques, factions, marginal groups, and so forth that are peculiar to each community. The images of remnant and synagogue, in that they emphasize no particular size or shape or structure for the local community, allow us to appreciate the relational network itself as a concrete expression of the People of God. The presence of church can thereby be seen in this network, and its multiple features can be understood as contributing to the church's structure and meaning.

Examining these features in the concrete—where and how they actually operate to affect the practice and understanding of faith—brings us face to face with the complexity and downright messiness of day-to-day human life, as we have seen. Such examination requires a serious realism about the presence in these relationships of varying expectations, tensions, conflicts, sin. This acknowledged, it is also clear that within any particular community these limitations themselves continually shape the response that genuine love makes. They affect the understanding of pastoral authority and its modes of implementation, and even the very concept and practical shape of unity itself, including such delicate questions as which official teachings are and are not understood, emphasized, and embraced. In all of this the church comes to an ever-growing concrete realization of what love and unity, intimacy and authority can and cannot mean for it.

The personal networks through which the local community is thoroughly embedded in its social context thus have a profound effect on the local community's relationship with *the larger church*. With Rahner's work in view we are able to see both the worldwide and the local as indispensable aspects of the church's catholicity: it is through the concrete realities of its local communities that the church catholic is a real and unavoidable part of the world to which it witnesses. These communities, therefore, do not drag the church down, as it were, into a realm of instability and sin it would be better off avoiding, but rather they make possible the church's very mission. Through the communities and *because* of their multiplicity the catholic church offers a stunning witness of continuity and unity amidst the change and diversity that the whole human world also experiences. Embodied in the local, it is as if the universal church were saying to the world, "In all our difference and separation, with all our richness, despite all our misunderstanding and sinfulness, it is yet possible for us to believe and love and hope *together*." Making such a witness possible for the universal church, the local communities may then benefit from it. The communities themselves, becoming aware by this very witness of the church's participatory role in the struggles and hopes of humanity, gain confidence for the possibilities of patience and of reconciliation within local communities.[73]

All of this takes for granted one further set of influences in the local community's context: *cultural and social elements* such as language, ideas of law and authority, and general mores. Attention paid to the enormous power of these cultural factors within any given community provides an indication of their importance throughout the entire church. In turn, this importance underlines the fact that the church is a participant in the general historical development of humanity. It shares inescapably in both the regular renewal and reshaping of human life and the effects of human sinfulness that always attend the process. The church has the unique gift of the Gospel to offer the world as its own "critical perspective."[74] Nonetheless, each community makes this offer

[73] These ideas are important themes in Karl Rahner, "The Church's Limits: Against Clerical Triumphalists and Lay Defeatists," in *The Christian of the Future*, trans. W. J. O'Hara. QD 18 (London: Burns & Oates, 1967) 49–76.

[74] Rahner, "The Function of the Church as Critic," 235.

in the same way that the community itself has come to hold the Gospel: it is both an external and an internal reality. On the one hand both church and Gospel are transcendent gifts that come from outside the community, ultimately from God through the workings of history, tradition, and institution. On the other hand they are maintained and shaped and transmitted only within the community to which the Gospel is offered. This dual character is more than reminiscent of the divinity and humanity of Christ. Here is the ultimate source of the conviction that the church's enmeshment in the cultural and social context is of its very essence, and that reverent attention to the interpersonal communities that embody these contexts is key to both the understanding and the success of the church's mission in the world today.

The local community necessarily participates in the church's Christ-given authority. Its role in the church's sacramental mission is not by remote agency, but rather by direct participation in the Holy Spirit. This might be concluded from Rahner's preconciliar work on the church as sacrament, but it is made explicit in his somewhat later works on the presence of Christ and the work of the Spirit in the church. What he understands from *Lumen Gentium* 26 to be the specific constitutive elements of the local community—the preaching of the Gospel, the eucharistic meal, and the love and unity of the community—are elements brought about and unified by the work of the Holy Spirit.[75] The Spirit itself and its fruits—especially Love—are constitutive of the church, not merely present "as though in a container."[76] This fact gives Rahner confidence, despite the obvious obstacles, about the unity of the church[77] and about the guidance of the hierarchy.[78] Yet this confidence is not complacency with a clerical and centralized church, but lies also at the root of his clear conviction that the laity and local communities have essential roles, not merely subordinate ones. If the Spirit and its fruits are constitutive, then they must characterize all aspects of the church, so that the same Spirit that is understood to guarantee the work of the hierarchy is also acknowledged at work directly within the local community. And if the Spirit is at work in the local community, it is necessarily at work in all the contextual elements and human

---

[75] Rahner, "On the Presence of Christ in the Diaspora Community," 90.

[76] Rahner, *The Dynamic Element in the Church*, 74.

[77] Ibid.

[78] Ibid. 76.

relationships that constitute that community and its setting. That being so, the church's mission of witness—whether in locales familiar or unfamiliar—cannot proceed authentically without developing the capacity called for by St. Paulinus: "Let us listen to what all the faithful say, because in every one of them the Spirit of God breathes."

Chapter Seven

Local Community and the Exercise of Authority: A Summary and a Look Ahead

I have aimed to make only one basic claim in this book—that local church communities possess a proper type of authority that makes an essential contribution to the life of the universal church. In the course of six chapters I have tested this statement in a variety of ways, looking at ideas of community, intimacy, and authority from both sociological and theological points of view. I have drawn on the insights of social scientists such as Robert Putnam and Robert Bellah, theorists such as Hannah Arendt, and many theologians, including Jean-Marie Roger Tillard, John Zizioulas, and particularly Joseph Ratzinger, Walter Kasper, and Karl Rahner in the previous two chapters. In the midst of more abstract thinking I have also sought to keep in view the stories of the three parish communities I presented in Chapter One.

The method I have employed with regard to the parish stories might be called "juxtaposition"—placing the stories of the actual struggles for foundation, survival, and identity in these parishes next to sociological and theological ideas that suggest ways of seeing these stories as exercises of authority. I intended references to the parishes in the subsequent chapters to keep this juxtaposition in play throughout the theoretical discussion. This approach served the purpose of giving the theoretical discussion a constant practical reference point while making it clear that the particular stories were not just descriptions of remarkable local circumstances, but glimpses of the universal church itself.

This method, however, still casts the parishes primarily in the role of "occasions for theological reflection." Focusing on recognized sources that could help me establish my primary point as central within Catholic theology, I have not developed here the theological potential within each of the parishes itself. The particular nuances and combinations of belief about faith, salvation, sacraments, prayer, etc., that lie behind the practical activities of these particular communities are certain to be more startling, edifying, disturbing, and instructive than our usual ignoring of them would suggest. Breaking these open within particular communities, using methods already developed by a variety of "contextual theologians,"[1] would itself demonstrate the authority I have tried to establish here. So far the specifically theological voices of these three parishes—and many others like them—have not been heard; this is work for the future. For now I content myself with having allowed a small slice of the lives of these churches to help me better appreciate the role of all such communities in the church.

The Living Authority of the Local Communities

After everything I have said about concreteness and context it is appropriate to observe, as I conclude, that the authority of the local church community is encountered much more in the "lived" and "felt" experience than in the theory that might be used to discuss it. My own encounters with these parishes launched my thinking about their inherent authority *as* communities. All three, like their counterparts everywhere, must be "learned"—particular procedures and customs, the influence of the "pillars" and of the "characters," well-loved stories of the past that situate persons and events in a coherent picture. More to the point, but much more difficult to pin down and express, each community has its own characteristic "tone" with which one comes to resonate only gradually. These identities are instinctively understood, guarded, and carefully shared. By complicated combinations of uneasy resistance and enthusiastic welcome newcomers are initiated into and, sooner or later,

---

[1] Robert J. Schreiter, *Constructing Local Theologies* (Maryknoll, NY: Orbis, 1985) has become a classic in this regard. The method of observation and interview (similar to my approach in some phases of my study of the three parishes) was used theologically by Ada María Isasi-Díaz, *En La Lucha (In the Struggle): A Hispanic Women's Liberation Theology* (Minneapolis: Fortress, 1993).

adopted by the community and given an honorary identity: "When are you coming home?" I hear from time to time in all three locations.

Each community is very much aware of its distinctiveness among church communities in its area. Many St. Joseph's parishioners make clear their preference for their own church building and community over nearby alternatives. Aquinas members identify themselves enthusiastically alongside Kingstonians from other parishes in the frequent archdiocesan meetings and rallies. Saint Matthew's proudly showcases its multiple cultures when archdiocesan visitors are on hand. Whatever their struggles and uncertainties, the parishes see themselves as contributors within their dioceses and not merely receivers. At the same time they realize that they need particular kinds of leadership and that, whether or not it will be noticed when assignments are made, not "just any pastor" will do. Because of all these characteristics, these communities *teach* visitors, newcomers, and pastors about nuances of Christian faith and living that are scarcely met elsewhere.

The conclusions about the importance of local communities to which such experiences have led do not always match the habits and assumptions of a clerical and administrative point of view. Acquiring the appropriate background knowledge (history, language, social setting, etc.) for getting to know the people is too often an optional exercise, although in all three cases the lack of at least some such information is a serious liability. The "knight-in-shining-armor" syndrome—the cleric who suddenly appears to "rescue" the community from some situation or other—is, in my experience, still a very familiar scenario. (I participated in it myself on several occasions in these parishes, with very mixed results.) Dioceses and religious communities alike have made pastoral appointments to these communities with their own larger strategies more immediately in view than the perceptions and desires of the local members themselves. Most dramatically, at one time or another each of the three communities has seen even its continued existence opened to question in the "parish reorganization" efforts of their respective dioceses (about which I will say more shortly).

Challenges to Local Authority

The contradiction between the community as authoritative and the community as expendable originally encouraged me to consider the theological basis for the authority I had personally met. The inadequacy of certain administrative approaches, however, is only one of several important obstacles in the way of a clear recognition and embrace of local authority within the larger church. Some of the reasons for these have already figured in the arguments of preceding chapters. Before moving on to a final consideration of what an "authentic Christian community" might look like, I will reprise some of these problems.

Centralist Ecclesiological Assumptions. The arguments I have posed in these chapters are not intended to promote a "congregational ecclesiology." They do, however, try to join Walter Kasper in moving beyond a theory of the universal church that exalts its central structures and authority (of their nature basically clerical) *over against* local communities and *their* inherent authority (of their nature fundamentally lay). Ideas of the church that fail to see the profound interdependence of these two aspects can make it difficult, particularly for Roman Catholic Christians, even to imagine the real importance of the local community.

In *Called to Communion*, Cardinal Ratzinger described one aspect of the importance of the role of bishop:

> [The Pauline epistles] show us the apostle as the bearer of a Christ-given authority vis-à-vis the community. The apostle's position vis-à-vis the community continues that of Christ vis-à-vis the world and the Church. In other words, it carries forward that dialogical structure that pertains to the essence of revelation. Faith is not something we excogitate ourselves; man [sic] does not make himself a Christian by reflection or ethical achievement. He always becomes a Christian from outside . . . . A community that is its own author is no longer an image of the dialogical mystery of revelation and of the gift of grace that always comes from without and can be attained only in receiving.[2]

Ratzinger spoke here of a fact I have alluded to several times in previous chapters: no local church community has come to its faith—and so to its very existence as local church community—by its own efforts. Rather, it has them as gift from God, in a historical setting prepared by a variety of social structures and relationships. Scripture, of course, warrants Ratzinger's underlining of the apostle's role in this process of reception. The difficulty comes in an oft-encountered inference that the transmission of the gift of faith follows a process as simple and direct as the clear sign of it in the apostolic office might suggest. The "gift of

---

[2] Joseph Cardinal Ratzinger, *Called to Communion: Understanding the Church Today*, ed. Adrian Walker (San Francisco: Ignatius Press, 1996) 120.

faith" can come to be conceived quite literally as a package that is handed from Christ to the apostles and on through their successors. What is often lost in the metaphor is appreciation for the indispensable role of innumerable "ordinary" Christians in and through their local communities. The work of the Spirit is already ongoing in the profound interaction of psychological and social processes in the communities and individuals who receive the faith.

Yet blindness to local authority is not just a "clerical" phenomenon. It is evident in popular and media definitions of the church that seem to begin and end with the hierarchy (and sometimes even with the Vatican or the papacy alone), in reports and histories that present whole communities as the creation of one or another church official, and in certain remarks to pastors, both supportive and critical. Richard Sennett describes the sort of authority that is presumed to operate here: "If a general, a party leader, or an industrialist can deal in universals, he wins a kind of omnipotence. Not that he controls everything in the smallest detail, but everything is ultimately under his control because his will is reproduced as accurately as possible down the chain of command."[3]

Observation of the parishes suggests that the clerically-centered view of church can sometimes cause the progress and dynamism of the community—or its absence—to be credited to the gifts or shortcomings of the particular pastor. The parish stories do indeed seem, at points, to lend credibility to the idea, given the deep shifts in mood that can occur with each change in the pastorate. On closer inspection, though, it is clear that the actions and reactions that shape the parishes come out of the *interaction* of the pastors and the communities, with their various strengths and weaknesses. It is the theological implication of this inevitable interaction that is often missed: the Spirit at work within the processes of the community as a whole, and the influence of this work on the larger church beyond this one community.

An elderly Euro-American parishioner at St. Matthew's once spoke of the days before the arrival of the Haitians as the time when St. Matthew's was "a regular parish." This illustrates one other effect of centralist assumptions about the church. Though clearly the remark bespeaks more than just a faulty ecclesiology, it does suggest that a certain uniformity of experience by parishes was expected. St. Matthew's is not "regular" because it is responding to an ethnic mix and social problems that make

---

[3] Richard Sennett, *Authority* (New York: Alfred A. Knopf, 1980) 174.

different demands on the parish community than those of an earlier time or those of another part of the archdiocese. Urgent need forced the St. Matthew's community to engage its own reality and find distinctive ways of living Christianity. In this way it has realized to some extent its own authority to interpret and shape Christian life. Yet it is also possible for members of a community to experience such an effort as a *burden*. If a community's distinctive response to its particular circumstances makes it "irregular," then its "real" business must be to observe a generic Christianity to which the details of its members' real lives are at least nonessential and perhaps irrelevant. Clearly, this is far from the deep personal and social engagement Jesus preached and practiced, and from which his authenticity shone.

The Difficulty of Community and Intimacy. Hesitation about the effort necessary to respond *as* church community to the specific situation of a given time and place reflects the contemporary problems surrounding community commitment that were discussed in Chapter Two. Part of a standard defense against the increasing complexity, and often faceless-ness, of modern social arrangements is a greater emphasis on personal choice and self-definition. The "communities" that arise from an unex-amined preoccupation with such individualism seem often to rest not on real intimacy and the recognition of a common authoritative foun-dation but on a single shared interest or characteristic ("the community of Ford owners," for example). Individuals are free to "mix and match" these various compartmentalized involvements as suits their situation. Under these conditions church membership, too, becomes a compart-ment in the lives of many people, and intimacy within the local church community ceases to be a recognized value or goal. Members seek their personal spiritual enrichment, become more detached from one an-other, and lose sight of their shared Christian history and of their shared situation as members of *this* Christian community. What is authorita-tive begins to appear to be a matter of personal choice, even when in fact its communal roots run deep.

Such circumstances greatly diminish the possibility of recognizing the authority of the local church community and of engaging that au-thority in shaping the Christian response to *this* time and place. The community's authority is based on what is held in common: the Christian tradition, the encounter with the Spirit of Christ in word and sacrament, the history and circumstances of *this* community that give Christianity its *particular* meaning and purpose. The members of the local community cannot consistently ignore or deny this communal story if they hope for either personal or community integrity. Therefore, if local authority is to have real meaning, the context within which the community and its members have come to believe and continue to exist as a believing community must be fully acknowledged both by official leaders and by the members of the community itself. Paradoxically, this context in our time includes the very fears, confusions, and hesitations that encourage individualism and factionalism in the first place.[4] These cannot be ignored more safely than any other part of the community's reality. Mere exhortation to communal values in the face of them will simply produce greater resentment and lower morale. So addressing these fears is actually one of the important reasons for emphasizing the authority of the local community at all. In the end, however, they must be set with all the rest of the community's context into the even larger context of the Christian hope for a community of love, held together by the Spirit, as a sign of Christ's presence and action in the world.

The Crisis of Authority. The difficulty local communities have in recognizing and owning their own authority is also largely defined, of course, by the uneasy relationship of the contemporary world to authority in general, as was discussed in Chapter Four. On the one hand we need the strength of the universal church, able to maintain, in the world of rapid change, the voice of a faith that has always been global in its import. On the other hand, as many old certainties fade or are suddenly wiped away we need the identity and support of a concrete and intimate local community in the midst of the confusion and immensity of the world. Actually, the local community has *always* performed its authorizing function within the universal church, has always been the place where what was too large to grasp somehow became comfortable daily reality. Yet this local role often went unnoticed in eras when the general culture, or Catholic subculture, was so well integrated that accepting the teaching and decisions of central authorities

---

[4] "The theological turn I argue for envisions the purpose and nature of the church as a community constituted through and for its proclamation to the world. Such a revisioning of the church, a reconstructed logic of the *ecclēsia*, is an exceedingly difficult task, since despite the desires for community in modern theology, it is quite clear that conditions for any substantive sense of community are far from us." Rebecca Chopp, *The Power to Speak: Feminism, Language, and God* (New York: Crossroad, 1989) 8.

seemed a matter of course. Now we seem faced with a choice between two elements that were once all of a piece.

The challenge, then, is to let the identity of local church communities flow from the actual Christian lives of their members rather than from an inauthentic stereotype or caricature. At the same time, the central authority must still perform its mission of guiding and unifying the many communities facing this same dilemma. Yet this balance is made extremely difficult by the alienation from church structures that was easily observable in the U.S. church even before the sexual abuse crisis of 2002 and can now be seen almost everywhere. The evidence is manifold: the now mundane-seeming decrease in Mass attendance or financial support, the more dramatic appearance of lay organizations such as "Voice of the Faithful" or ad hoc "Save Our Parish" committees to resist closure and merger plans, the proliferation of conservative websites engaging in a sort of "doctrinal vigilantism." In each case, regardless of what the particular issue is or whether the slant is "traditional" or "progressive," the message is the same: official structures of authority are not seen as performing the ministry of unity that is theirs by definition. In some cases, in fact, they are seen as themselves being the very obstacles to unity.

These perceptions of alienation are features of local communities that carry an important message and ought not to be neglected, whether or not they appear to be reasonable reactions to the *intentions* of official leadership. Even now it would seem that they do not represent rejection of the very notion of central authority. Were that the case, the committees, groups, and individuals in question would have departed long ago, and we might expect many more than the few reports of breakaway parishes becoming independent congregations "in the catholic tradition."[5] Rather, the message is one of frustration at lack of proper local empowerment.

The frustration arises from attitudes that have been operating among both local community members and official church leaders for a long time, opposition to which has been catalyzed by the more openly contentious atmosphere in the wake of the abuse crisis. It may be assumed, uncritically, that more general levels of the hierarchical structure are

---

[5] The best-known instance of this phenomenon was the "Spiritus Christi" (originally Corpus Christi) parish of Rochester, New York, which was established as an independent church in 1999, well before the national abuse crisis. See http://www.spirituschristi.org/history.html.

able to get a broader, and therefore more accurate, picture of the church's needs. But diocesan programs can then be urged on parishes without much care for flexibility and adaptation to particular situations or respect for effective "homegrown" efforts. Notions of authority as synonymous with power, and of power as a personal possession,[6] may go unchallenged. A new pastor, through personal preference or inclination as much as pastoral motivation, may then discontinue well-developed efforts that flourished under a predecessor. Local leadership may be understood too exclusively as clerical representation of a bishop, a means of central control over a local community, without an accompanying view of the need for representation of the *community's* distinctiveness to the wider church. Then the possible distortions of various measures to deal with the "priest shortage" may go unchallenged: pastors appointed without necessary skills for and sensitivities to their new communities; the neglect of careful development of truly local leadership; administrative parish mergers and closures unresponsive to actual local conditions.

One of the most dramatic crescendos of such attitudes in recent years has taken place in the parish reorganization effort of the Archdiocese of Boston, in which upwards of eighty parishes were originally slated for closure within less than a year of one another. Recommended for closure at one point in the decision-making, St. Matthew's parish barely emerged intact from this process, and it now shares a pastor with another largely Haitian parish in the vicinity. A full and accurate assessment of the motives, criteria, and procedures of this huge undertaking will likely not be possible for a long time to come, but certain features of its impact on local communities became clear very quickly. From the local perspective, particularly that of parishes that were ordered to close, unclear bureaucratic and administrative agendas were being imposed on communities that might otherwise have been viable, even vibrant. The very loyalties that brought these parishes into being at the ground level and sustained them for over a century in some cases, when they brought people into the open to object, were at first dismissed as irrelevant stubbornness. The result in a significant number of cases was not only a rift between parishioners and

---

[6] Michael Downey, "Looking to the Last and the Least: A Spirituality of Empowerment," in idem, ed., *That They Might Live: Power, Empowerment, and Leadership in the Church* (New York: Crossroad, 1991) 181–82, describes this understanding of power as "asymmetrical dualism."

archdiocesan officials but a kind of "sorting" within the parish communities themselves. On the eve of the decision that ultimately "spared" St. Matthew's, various groups could be identified: those who are personally tied to the parish and could not imagine its closure, those who are part of the dominant Haitian community and saw closure as another storm to be weathered, those who are personally comfortable at St. Matthew's but had "contingency plans" ready.

In cases like this the focus on the authority of central structures that are meant to protect the local communities ironically can actually encourage notions of the "church from below" in just the sense that Joseph Ratzinger feared—the idea that the local community constitutes *itself* as church.[7] Since, in Rahner's terms, the local community finds its purpose as the *event* of the universal church, such "independence" would be an absurdity. It is crucial, therefore, that the general cultural suspicion of authority be challenged by a contextualized understanding of authority within the church that includes the place of the local community as an indispensable and authoritative aspect of church.

A Portrait of the Authentic Local Community

The authentic local church community is willing and able to recognize and grapple with these contemporary dilemmas of community and authority. Authenticity, it will be recalled, was defined in Chapter Three, on the basis of David Stagaman's work, as the quality of recognizing and owning the authoritative in a community, living and exercising authority in a way that resonates with the local authoritative. Further, I have assumed throughout the book that the universal church can be discovered in an "ascending" fashion, beginning with an understanding of the church in the concrete, as "event"—the local church community. I will now close the entire discussion with some general observations about the shape of a community that recognizes its own authority and is able to exercise it within the broader church, thus helping to shape the church far beyond local boundaries.[8]

---

[7] See Ratzinger, *Called to Communion*, 81–82.

[8] Available as touchstones for the observations that follow are the qualities of vital local communities presented by three separate studies I have already referenced elsewhere in the book. NCCB Committee on the Parish, *Parish Life in*

The authentic local community must be engaged in a creative dialogue with the various sources of its own authoritative foundation. These sources, I have pointed out, run wide and deep, from the roots of Christianity, to the ethnic histories of the various subgroups of the community, to the community's own shared history, to the cultural context of today. Such sources not only complement one another but are often in conflict. They are certainly not under the *control* of the community, nor can they ever be perfectly discovered and known. An ever-deepening familiarity and mutuality with them, however, are the marks of a community that is coming to understand itself, to accept itself in all its many facets. Thus it comes to a growing appreciation of its own authority and the place from which it can speak to the universal church.

I have spoken often of the *network of human relationships* as the backbone of the local community, the most concrete and obvious aspect of the church for most of its members. These relationships are the first place to look for the values that ground the community. When they are

the United States: Final Report to the Bishops of the United States by the Parish Project* (Washington, DC: United States Catholic Conference, 1983) 29, includes a prioritized list of responses to a question on the Notre Dame Parish Survey about "what most accounts for their vitality as a parish." William J. Bausch, *The Parish of the Next Millennium* (Mystic, CT: Twenty-Third Publications, 1997) 276–79, summarizes his work with twelve statements about the shape of the parish of the future. Michael Warren, *At This Time, In This Place: The Spirit Embodied In the Local Assembly* (Harrisburg, PA: Trinity Press International, 1999) 138, presents a variety of "Characteristics of a Local Church of Vital Practice." The similarity and cohesion of these three lists of characteristics is quite remarkable. Many of their common conclusions are also reflected here: (1) The laity play a paramount role in the local community; their distinctive gifts and those of all their various subgroups are to be recognized and valued; collaboration between them and the clerical leadership is of tremendous importance. (Bausch and Warren would press further toward a new understanding of the function and makeup of clerical leadership.) (2) A shared sense of the community's distinctiveness is crucial; planning and vision flow from this mutual understanding. (3) The *relational* basis of the community is to be noticed and strengthened. (4) The spiritual and wisdom traditions of the church are to be encouraged as the basis of ongoing formation. (5) Bausch and Warren also look forward to communities that are able to recognize the work of the Spirit in a pluralistic society, without relying on positions of social power.

noticed and observed, pointed out and cultivated through various forms of meeting, sharing, cooperation, reflection, and prayer, they provide deep insights about the motivation and inspiration of the church in this place. This type of attention also, of course, points directly back to the origins of the universal church in the intimate relationship of Christ with his disciples and in his command of love, and so puts us in the presence of the Lord in a most tangible way.

Close attention to the workings of personal interrelationships, particularly but not exclusively in multicultural situations, also puts members of the community in touch with important *cultural* features that not merely surround but *saturate* the community with the values of its component groups and of society at large. Attention here will reveal strengths and weaknesses, hidden resources as well as traps, and opportunities for solidarity. The community will explore ways of sharing and cultivating insights and practices offered by other communities or subgroups. It will mobilize to safeguard values that are under threat and it will challenge itself and others in standing against pervasive cultural evils. Such tasks, of course, necessarily imply a breadth of vision that takes in the authoritative sources of its members' lives *beyond* the merely "religious" sphere: various age groups, personality types, occupations, nationalities, races, etc. Further, recognizing the basis for local authority in the action of the Spirit should contribute to a greater awareness of the same Spirit at work in other communities, even outside the Roman Catholic—or even explicitly Christian—communion. The local community seeks to understand itself thoroughly, with an openness to *all* that constitutes its particular world.

This openness, however, does not weaken but rather strengthens the bond between the local community and the universal church. From the universal, the local has inherited not just a mystical but a historical relationship with Christ in the Spirit through the Scriptures, offices, rites, and other structures of the church. For authenticity, however, the local community will know that it must not continue to perceive these things as *external* to itself, but must literally embody them. The shared tradition of the universal church becomes an integral part of this community's story as well. The rites of the universal church, celebrated by countless millions through history, punctuate the lives of *these* Christians, too, and give them common ground with all the others. The "bishop's representative" sent to preside at Eucharist at *this* altar is brought into the network of personal interrelationships and is gradually bound to it by a more and more genuine love.[9] In all such processes the local community learns how to turn the simple fact of its dependence on the universal church into a true and effective communion with local communities across the world and across the ages.

The local community that in these various ways engages its own authoritative sources and becomes increasingly aware of what it really *is* will by the same token increase the involvement and responsibility of its lay members. This engagement issues an open and clear invitation to both members and onlookers to explore and to come to understand how this community touches *their* values and sources of authenticity. Such an invitation requires an ongoing and keen alertness of the community—on the part of leaders first and increasingly on the part of more and more members—to the needs and perspectives of all its members. But this attentiveness promises rich returns in a deep self-understanding, in a strong sense of belonging, and in a genuine desire to gather and to be involved. Such a community *owns* its celebration, its sacramental signifying of the presence of Christ in the world, and so can genuinely embody the church in this time and place. Out of this authenticity, the local community can be a voice that makes itself heard among the communities of the universal church, not only in crisis or in controversy, but in ongoing contributions to the church's understanding of itself and its mission.

The local community, embodying the church in a particular place, teaches the universal church about its own authority by becoming a tangible model of that authority in a concrete location.[10] Once this is grasped, the church's self-understanding can be continually deepened by attention to local communities. What can be said immediately is that the authority of the church is founded on the presence of Christ among his people and not, as Ratzinger warned, on the community's self-actualization. It is *as* the sacrament of Christ that the community realizes its authority.

[9] On the absolute necessity of this for authentic eucharistic celebration, see John Zizioulas, *Being As Communion: Studies in Personhood and the Church* (Crestwood, NY: St. Vladimir's Seminary Press, 1985) 164–65.

[10] Sennett, *Authority,* 179, proposes a similar notion with his concept of "authority *en abyme*" (a term from heraldry, utilized by André Gide, signifying the placing of a second shield within the main shield in a coat of arms), which Sennett describes as "a reflection which is not quite the original," because it is conformed to the special circumstances of its location. In the present case, however, because of the way in which the local church *is* the universal church *in the concrete,* we can say that the "original" comes to be known in the "reflection."

Therefore it is authentic only when its use of authority reflects that of Christ himself. As Michael Downey has put it:

> It is not a matter of giving those at the margins a share in the power of those at the center of church and society. It is a matter of recognizing new ways of perceiving and being more in keeping with the word and the work of the Crucified and Risen One whose power was disclosed in his refusal to lay claim to the power of lords, kings, priests, and patriarchs. To share in this power is to listen to those who speak in a different voice. It is to turn one's ears and eyes from the center to the edge of church and society. It is to live from and for fidelity, nurture, attraction, self-sacrifice, passion, responsibility, care, affection, respect, and mutuality . . . . The spirituality of empowerment is one of surrender to the Spirit, the breath of God anointing to speech and bringing to voice, blessing difference, specificity, solidarity, transformation, and anticipation.[11]

In thus conforming to the authority of Christ the local community demonstrates to the church and the world how authority can be expressed not merely as universal pronouncements that enter from outside the boundaries of a community, but rather *intimately,* in innumerable details of human life together. Neither the local community nor its authority thus understood is a neat and simple package that can be "wielded" like a weapon or a tool.[12] They are relationship and growth and pilgrimage, images the universal church itself can own. Clearly the local community's embodiment of Christ's own authority is limited by the serious shortcomings of human fidelity. These shortcomings are always very evident in the ordinary parish or small community. Yet, continuing to become aware of the endless ways in which Christ is present at its very roots, the community is filled with the hope that arises in the concrete proclamation of the reign of God in word, sacrament, and mission.

---

[11] Downey, "Looking to the Last and the Least," 191–92. Note also Aidan Harker, *Commentary on an Agreed Statement on Authority in the Church, 1976* (Enfield: Catholic League, 1977) 19: "[W]e, who share the common life in the Body of Christ, have to commend the authority of Christ since to us is entrusted the mission of uniting all men *[sic]* in Christ."

[12] Sennett, *Authority,* 165, noting that "the work of authority has a goal: to convert power into images of strength," warns against the tendency to prefer images of strength that are too "clear and simple," since they do not take full account of social reality.

Bibliography

Aguirre, Rafael. "La Casa Como Estructura Base del Cristianismo Primitivo: Las Iglesias Domesticas." *Estudios Eclesiásticos* 59, no. 28 (1984) 27–51.

———. "Early Christian House Churches." *Theology Digest* 32 (1985) 151–55.

Ammerman, Nancy T., et al. *Studying Congregations: A New Handbook*. Nashville: Abingdon, 1998.

ARCIC I (First Anglican-Roman Catholic International Commission). "Truth and Authority." In Edward J. Yarnold and Henry Chadwick, eds., *Truth and Authority: A Commentary on the Agreed Statement of the Anglican-Roman Catholic International Commission, "Authority in the Church," Venice 1976*. London: SPCK and Catholic Truth Society, 1977.

ARCIC II (Second Anglican-Roman Catholic International Commission). "Church as Communion." *Origins* 20, no. 44 (1991) 719–27.

Arendt, Hannah. "What Is Authority?" In eadem, *Between Past and Future: Eight Exercises in Political Thought*. New York: Viking, 1968.

Balke, Victor H. "The Parish Pastoral Council." *Origins* 16, no. 47 (1987) 821–25.

Baum, Gregory. "The Church of Tomorrow." In idem, *New Horizon. Theological Essays*. New York: Paulist, 1972, 152.

Bausch, William J. *The Parish of the Next Millennium*. Mystic, CT: Twenty-Third Publications, 1997.

Bellah, Robert, et al. *Habits of the Heart: Individualism and Commitment in American Life*. Updated ed. Berkeley: University of California Press, 1996.

Bellarmine, Robert. "Controversiarum de Conciliis, Liber III: Qui est de ecclesia militante toto orbe terrarium diffusa." In *Roberti Bellarmini Opera Omnia*. Vol. II. Ed. Justin Fevre. Paris: Louis Vivès, 1870.

Berger, Peter. *The Sacred Canopy*. Garden City, NY: Doubleday, 1967.

Bevans, Stephen B. *Models of Contextual Theology*. Maryknoll, NY: Orbis, 1992.

Berger, Peter, and Richard J. Neuhaus. *To Empower People: The Role of Mediating Structures in Public Policy*. Washington, DC: American Enterprise Institute, 1977.

Boff, Leonardo. *Church: Charism and Power. Liberation Theology and the Institutional Church.* Trans., John W. Diercksmeier. New York: Crossroad, 1992.

Bonhoeffer, Dietrich. *The Communion of Saints: A Dogmatic Inquiry Into the Sociology of the Church.* Trans., R. Gregor Smith. New York: Harper & Row, 1963.

Brown, Raymond E. *The Community of the Beloved Disciple.* New York: Paulist, 1979.

Burns, Patrick J. "Precarious Reality: Ecclesiological Reflections on Peter Berger." *Theology Digest* 21 (1973) 322–33.

Cardenal, Ernesto. *The Gospel in Solentiname.* 4 vols. Maryknoll, NY: Orbis, 1976–1982.

Carlson, R. J. "The Parish According to the Revised Law." *Studia Canonica* 19 (1985) 5–14.

Castelli, Jim, and Joseph Gremillion. *The Emerging Parish: The Notre Dame Study of Catholic Life Since Vatican II.* San Francisco: Harper & Row, 1987.

Catlin, George E. Gordon. "Authority and Its Critics." In Carl J. Friedrich, ed., *Authority. Nomos* 1. Cambridge, MA: Harvard University Press, 1958, 1:126–44.

Chadwick, Henry. *The Early Church.* The Pelican History of the Church. Ed. Owen Chadwick. Harmondsworth: Penguin, 1967.

Chopp, Rebecca. *The Power to Speak: Feminism, Language, and God.* New York: Crossroad, 1989.

Coccopalmerio, Francesco. "De Paroecia ut Communitate Christifidelium." *Periodica* 80 (1991) 19–44.

Congar, Yves M.-J. *The Mystery of the Temple, or The Manner of God's Presence to His Creatures from Genesis to the Apocalypse.* Trans., Reginald F. Trevett. Westminster, MD: Newman Press, 1962.

Congregation for the Doctrine of the Faith. "Letter to the Bishops of the Catholic Church Concerning Some Aspects of the Church Understood as Communion." *Origins* 22, no. 7 (1992) 108–12.

———. "Reflections on the Primacy of Peter." *Origins* 28, no. 32 (1998) 560–63.

Cooke, Bernard. "Obstacles to Lay Involvement." In Johann Baptist Metz and Edward Schillebeeckx, eds., *The Teaching Authority of the Believers. Concilium* 180. Edinburgh: T & T Clark, 1985, 63–70.

Coriden, James A., Thomas J. Green, and Donald E. Heintschel, eds. *The Code of Canon Law: A Text and Commentary.* New York: Paulist, 1985.

Croce, W. "The History of the Parish." In *The Parish: From Theology to Practice,* ed. Hugo Rahner, 9–22. Trans., Robert Kress. Westminster, MD: The Newman Press, 1958.

Curran, Charles E. "Responsibility in Moral Theology: Centrality, Foundations, and Implications for Ecclesiology." In James A. Coriden, ed., *Who Decides for the Church? Studies in Co-Responsibility.* Hartford, CT: The Canon Law Society of America, 1971, 113–42.

"Didache." In James A. Kleist, ed., *Didache, Barnabas, Polycarp, Papias, Diogne-tus.* ACW 6. Westminster, MD: Newman Press, 1948, 15–26.

Dillon, Richard J. "Acts of the Apostles." In Raymond E. Brown, Joseph A. Fitzmyer, and Roland E. Murphy, eds., *The New Jerome Biblical Commentary.* Englewood Cliffs, NJ: Prentice Hall, 1990, 722–67.

Dolan, Jay P. *In Search of an American Catholicism: A History of Religion and Culture in Tension.* New York: Oxford University Press, 2002.

Donovan, Daniel. *The Church as Idea and Fact.* Wilmington: Michael Glazier, 1988.

Downey, Michael. "Looking to the Last and the Least: A Spirituality of Empowerment." In idem, ed., *That They Might Live: Power, Empowerment, and Leadership in the Church.* New York: Crossroad, 1991, 176–92.

Doyle, Dennis. *Communion Ecclesiology: Vision and Versions.* Maryknoll, NY: Orbis, 2000.

Dues, Greg, and Barbara Walkley. *Called to Parish Ministry: Identity, Challenges, and Spirituality of Lay Ministers.* Mystic, CT: Twenty-Third Publications, 1995.

Duquoc, Christian. "An Active Role for the People of God in Defining the Church's Faith." In Metz and Schillebeeckx, eds., *The Teaching Authority of the Believers. Concilium* 180, 73–81.

Foley, Albert S., s.j. *Bishop Healy: Beloved Outcaste.* New York: Farrar, Straus and Young, 1954.

Friedrich, Carl J. "Authority, Reason, and Discretion." In idem, ed., *Authority. Nomos* 1. Cambridge, MA: Harvard University Press, 1958, 28–48.

Fries, Heinrich. *Suffering From the Church: Renewal or Restoration?* Trans., Arlene Anderson Swidler and Leonard Swidler. Collegeville: Liturgical Press, 1995.

Gadamer, Hans-Georg. *Truth and Method.* Trans., Joel Weinsheimer and Donald G. Marshall. 2d rev. ed. New York: Continuum, 1995.

Gaillardetz, Richard. "The Reception of Doctrine: New Perspectives." In Bernard Hoose, ed., *Authority in the Roman Catholic Church.* London: Ashgate, 2002, 95–114.

Gaudiani, Claire. "Wisdom as Capital in Prosperous Communities." In Frances Hesselbein, et al., eds., *The Community of the Future.* San Francisco: Jossey–Bass, 1998, 59–69.

Giddens, Anthony. *New Rules of Sociological Method: A Positive Critique of Interpretative Sociologies.* London: Hutchinson, 1976.

Grammont, Paul M., and Philibert Zobel. "The Authority of the Indwelling Word." In John M. Todd, ed., *Problems of Authority.* Baltimore: Helicon; London: Darton, Longman and Todd, 1962, 79–103.

Greeley, Andrew. "The Persistence of Community." In Andrew Greeley and Gregory Baum, eds., *The Persistence of Religion. Concilium: Religion in the Seventies.* New York: Herder and Herder, 1973.

Haight, Roger. "The Structures of the Church." *Journal of Ecumenical Studies* 30 (1993) 403–14.

———. *Jesus Symbol of God.* Maryknoll, NY: Orbis, 1999.

————. "Towards an Ecclesiology From Below." In Jeremy Driscoll, ed., *"Imaginer la Théologie Catholique": Permanence et Transformations de la Foi en Attendant Jésus-Christ. Mélanges Offerts à Ghislain Lafont.* Studia Anselmiana 129. Rome: Centro Studi S. Anselmo, 2000, 413–36.

————. *Christian Community in History. Vol. I: Historical Ecclesiology.* New York and London: Continuum, 2004.

Harker, Aidan. *Commentary on an Agreed Statement on Authority in the Church, 1976.* Enfield: Catholic League, 1977.

Harrington, Daniel J. "Sociological Concepts and the Early Church: A Decade of Research." *Theological Studies* 41 (1980) 181–90.

Hellwig, Monika. "American Culture: Reciprocity with Catholic Vision, Values and Community." In Cassian Yuhaus, ed., *The Catholic Church and American Culture: Reciprocity and Challenge.* New York: Paulist, 1990, 62–89.

Hendel, Charles W. "An Exploration of the Nature of Authority." In Carl J. Friedrich, ed., *Authority. Nomos* 1. Cambridge, MA: Harvard University Press, 1958, 3–27.

Hesselbein, Frances, et al., eds. *The Community of the Future.* San Francisco: Jossey–Bass, 1998.

Ignatius of Antioch. "Epistle to the Magnesians." In James A. Kleist, ed., *The Epistles of St. Clement of Rome and St. Ignatius of Antioch.* ACW 1. Westminster, MD: Newman Bookshop, 1946, 69–74.

————. "Epistle to the Trallians." In James A. Kleist, ed., *The Epistles of St. Clement of Rome and St. Ignatius of Antioch,* 75–79.

————. "Epistle to the Smyrnaeans." In James A. Kleist, ed., *The Epistles of St. Clement of Rome and St. Ignatius of Antioch,* 90–95.

Jacobson, Norman. "Knowledge, Tradition, and Authority." In Carl J. Friedrich, ed., *Authority. Nomos* 1. Cambridge, MA: Harvard University Press, 1958.

John Paul II. *Apostolic Exhortation on Catechesis in Our Time (Catechesi Tradendae).* Boston: St. Paul Editions, 1979.

————. "On Authentic Renewal." *The Pope Speaks* 32 (1987) 378–88.

————. "Tertio Millennio Adveniente." *Origins* 24, no. 24 (1994) 401–16.

————. "Encyclical on Commitment to Ecumenism *(Ut Unum Sint)*." *Origins* 25, no. 4 (1995) 49–72.

————. "On the Theological and Juridical Nature of Episcopal Conferences *(Apostolos Suos)*." *Origins* 28, no. 9 (1998) 152–57.

————. "Apostolic Letter on the New Millennium *(Novo Millennio Ineunte)*." *Origins* 30 (2001).

Kasper, Walter. "On the Church." *America* 184 (April 23, 2001) 8–14.

————. "From the President of the Council for Promoting Christian Unity." *America* 185 (November 26, 2001) 28–29.

————. "The Universal Church and the Local Church: A Friendly Rejoinder." In idem, *Leadership in the Church: How Traditional Roles Can Serve the Chris-*

tian Community Today. Translated by Brian McNeil. New York: Crossroad/
Herder and Herder, 2003.

Kaufmann, Franz-Xavier. "The Church as a Religious Organization." In Gregory Baum and Andrew Greeley, eds., *The Church as Institution. Concilium*
91. New York: Herder and Herder, 1974, 70–82.

Kilpatrick, William. *Identity and Intimacy.* New York: Delacorte Press, 1975.

Klauck, Hans-Josef. "The House-Church as Way of Life." *Theology Digest* 30
(1982) 153–57.

Komonchak, Joseph A. "Ecclesiology and Social Theory: A Methodological
Essay." *The Thomist* 45 (1981) 262–83.

Lambert, Myra, s.s.c.m., and Linda Hatton, s.s.c.m. "Women Religious as Pastoral Leaders." *Chicago Studies* 37 (1998) 129–38.

Lash, Nicholas. *Voices of Authority.* Shepherdstown: Patmos, 1976.

Lee, Bernard, s.m., et al. *The Catholic Experience of Small Christian Communities.*
New York and Mahwah, NJ: Paulist, 2000.

Lennan, Richard. *The Ecclesiology of Karl Rahner.* Oxford: Clarendon, 1997.

Lubac, Henri de. *The Splendour of the Church.* Trans., Michael Mason. New York:
Sheed and Ward, 1956.

Luther, Martin. "The Large Catechism: Of the Creed." In *Triglot Concordia: The
Symbolical Books of the Evangelical Lutheran Church.* Trans., Friedrich Bente
and William H. T. Dau. St. Louis: Concordia Publishing House, 1921.

Malina, Bruce. "The Individual and the Community: Personality in the Social
World of Early Christianity." *Biblical Theology Bulletin* 9 (1979) 126–38.

Marins, Jose, Teolide Maria Trevisan, and Carolee Chanona. *The Church from the
Roots: Basic Ecclesial Communities.* Quezon City, Philippines: Claretian Publications, 1983. Reprint London: Catholic Fund for Overseas Development, 1989.

McDonnell, Kilian, o.s.b. "The Ratzinger/Kasper Debate: The Universal Church
and Local Churches." *Theological Studies* 63 (2002) 227–50.

———. "Walter Kasper on the Theology and the Praxis of the Bishop's Office."
Theological Studies 63 (2002) 711–29.

Metz, Johann Baptist. *Faith in History and Society: Toward a Practical Fundamental
Theology.* Trans., David Smith. New York: Seabury, 1980.

Mock, Alan K., et al. "Threading the Needle: Faith and Works in Affluent
Churches." In Carl S. Dudley, Jackson W. Carroll, and James P. Wind, eds.,
Carriers of Faith: Lessons from Congregational Studies. Louisville: Westmin-
ster John Knox, 1991, 86–103.

Molinski, Walter. "Authority." In Karl Rahner, ed., *Encyclopedia of Theology: A
Concise Sacramentum Mundi.* New York: Seabury, 1975.

Morris, Charles R. *American Catholic: The Saints and Sinners Who Built America's
Most Powerful Church.* New York: Vintage Books, 1997.

Murnion, Philip J. "The Community Called Parish." In Lawrence Cunningham,
ed., *The Catholic Faith: A Reader.* New York and Mahwah, NJ: Paulist, 1988,
179–94.

Murnion, Philip J., and David DeLambo. *Parishes and Parish Ministers: A Study of Parish Lay Ministry.* New York: National Pastoral Life Center, 1999.

NCCB Committee on the Parish. *Parish Life in the United States: Final Report to the Bishops of the United States by the Parish Project.* Washington, DC: United States Catholic Conference, 1983.

O'Donnell, Christopher. *Ecclesia: A Theological Encyclopedia of the Church.* Collegeville: Liturgical Press, 1996.

O'Rourke, David K. "The Priest Proof Parish." *Church* 15 (1999) 18–19.

Osborne, Francis J., S.J. *History of the Catholic Church in Jamaica.* Chicago: Loyola University Press, 1988.

Pailler, A. "Considerations on the Authority of the Church." In John M. Todd, ed., *Problems of Authority.* Baltimore: Helicon, 1962, 13–26.

Parsons, Talcott. "Authority, Legitimation, and Political Action." In Carl J. Friedrich, ed., *Authority. Nomos* 1. Cambridge: Harvard, 1958, 197–221.

———. *The Evolution of Societies.* Edited by Jackson Toby. Foundations of Modern Sociology, ed. Alex Inkeles. Englewood Cliffs, NJ: Prentice-Hall, 1977.

Paul VI. "Concluding Address to the Synod of Bishops on Catechesis." *Actae Apostolicae Sedis* 69 (1977) 634.

Pirola, Teresa. "Church Professionalism—When Does It Become 'Lay Elitism'?" In Richard Lennan, ed., *Redefining the Church: Vision and Practice.* Alexandria, NSW, Australia: E. J. Dwyer, 1995, 71–87.

Place, Michael. "Parish Pastoral Councils." *Chicago Studies* 37 (1998) 139–48.

Putnam, Robert. *Bowling Alone: The Collapse and Revival of American Community.* New York: Simon and Schuster, 2000.

Rahner, Karl. "Theology of the Parish." In *The Parish, From Theology to Practice,* ed. Hugo Rahner, 23–35. Trans. Robert Kress. Westminster, MD: Newman, 1958.

———. "Concerning the Relationship Between Nature and Grace." *Theological Investigations* 1. Translated by Cornelius Ernst. Baltimore: Helicon; London: Darton, Longman & Todd, 1961, 297–317.

———. "The Development of Dogma." *Theological Investigations* 1, 39–77.

———. "The Episcopate and the Primacy." In Karl Rahner and Joseph Ratzinger, eds., *The Episcopate and the Primacy.* QD 4. Trans., Kenneth Barker et al. New York: Herder and Herder, 1962, 11–36.

———. "Notes on the Lay Apostolate." *Theological Investigations* 2. Translated by Karl-Heinz Krüger. Baltimore: Helicon; London: Darton, Longman & Todd, 1963, 319–52.

———. "Peaceful Reflections on the Parochial Principle." *Theological Investigations* 2, 283–318.

———. "Personal and Sacramental Piety." *Theological Investigations* 2, 109–133.

———. *The Dynamic Element in the Church.* Trans., W. J. O'Hara. New York: Herder and Herder, 1964.

————. "Considerations on the Development of Dogma." *Theological Investigations* 4. Trans., Kevin Smyth. Baltimore: Helicon; London: Darton, Longman & Todd, 1966, 3–35.

————. "History of the World and Salvation History." In *Theological Investigations* 5. Trans., Karl-Heinz Krüger. Baltimore: Helicon; London: Darton, Longman & Todd, 1966, 97–114.

————. "What Is Heresy?" *Theological Investigations* 5, 468–512.

————. "The Church's Limits: Against Clerical Triumphalists and Lay Defeatists." In idem, *The Christian of the Future*. Trans., W. J. O'Hara. QD 18. London: Burns & Oates, 1967, 49–76.

————. "The Eternal Significance of the Humanity of Jesus for Our Relationship With God." *Theological Investigations* 3. Trans., Karl-Heinz Krüger and Boniface Krüger. Baltimore: Helicon; London: Darton, Longman & Todd, 1967, 35–46.

————. "The Episcopal Office." *Theological Investigations* 6. Trans., Karl-Heinz Krüger and Boniface Krüger. Baltimore: Helicon; London: Darton, Longman & Todd, 1969, 313–60.

————. "A Small Fragment 'On the Collective Finding of Truth.'" *Theological Investigations* 6, 82–88.

————. "The New Image of the Church." *Theological Investigations* 10. Trans., David Bourke. New York: Herder and Herder, 1973, 3–29.

————. "On the Presence of Christ in the Diaspora Community According to the Teaching of the Second Vatican Council." *Theological Investigations* 10, 84–102.

————. "The Presence of the Lord in the Christian Community at Worship." *Theological Investigations* 10, 71–83.

————. "The Teaching Office of the Church in the Present-Day Crisis of Authority." *Theological Investigations* 12. Trans., David Bourke. New York: Seabury, 1974, 3–30.

————. "The Function of the Church as a Critic of Society." *Theological Investigations* 12, 229–49.

————. "The Two Basic Types of Christology." *Theological Investigations* 13. Trans., David Bourke. New York: Seabury/Crossroad, 1975, 213–23.

————. "Basic Observations on the Subject of Changeable and Unchangeable Factors in the Church." *Theological Investigations* 14. Trans., David Bourke. New York: Seabury/Crossroad, 1976, 3–23.

————. "The Faith of the Christian and the Doctrine of the Church." *Theological Investigations* 14, 24–46.

————. *Foundations of Christian Faith: An Introduction to the Idea of Christianity.* Trans., William V. Dych. New York: Crossroad, 1990.

Ratzinger, Joseph. *Church, Ecumenism, and Politics: New Essays in Ecclesiology.* New York: Crossroad, 1989.

————. *Called to Communion: Understanding the Church Today.* Trans., Adrian Walker. San Francisco: Ignatius Press, 1991.

————. "The Local Church and the Universal Churches." *America* 185, no. 16 (November 19, 2001) 7–11.

Rheingold, Howard. *The Virtual Community: Homesteading on the Electronic Frontier.* Reading, MA: Addison-Wesley, 1993.

Sanks, T. Howland, S.J. "Forms of Ecclesiality: The Analogical Church." *Theological Studies* 49 (1988) 695–708.

Schillebeeckx, Edward. "The Teaching Authority of All—A Reflection about the Structure of the New Testament." In Metz and Schillebeeckx, eds., *The Teaching Authority of the Believers. Concilium* 180, 12–22.

Schreiter, Robert J. *Constructing Local Theologies.* Maryknoll, NY: Orbis, 1985.

Schüssler Fiorenza, Elisabeth. "Claiming Our Authority and Power." In Metz and Schillebeeckx, eds., *The Teaching Authority of the Believers. Concilium* 180, 45–53.

————. *In Memory of Her: A Feminist Theological Reconstruction of Christian Origins.* Tenth Anniversary ed. New York: Crossroad, 1994.

Seaga, Edward. *Revival Cults in Jamaica: Notes Toward a Sociology of Religion.* Kingston: Institute of Jamaica, 1982.

Searle, Mark. "The Notre Dame Study of Catholic Parish Life." *Worship* 60 (1986) 312–33.

Sennett, Richard. *Authority.* New York: Alfred A. Knopf, 1980.

Siefer, Gregor. "Ecclesiological Implications of Weber's Definition of 'Community.'" In *The Church as Institution,* Gregory Baum and Andrew Greeley, eds., 148–60. *Concilium,* vol. 91. New York: Herder and Herder, 1974.

Simon, Yves. *Nature and Functions of Authority.* The Aquinas Lecture 1940. Milwaukee: Marquette University Press, 1940.

————. *A General Theory of Authority.* Notre Dame: Notre Dame University Press, 1962.

Skinner, John E. *The Meaning of Authority.* Washington, DC: University Press of America, 1983.

Sobrino, Jon. "The 'Doctrinal Authority' of the People of God in Latin America." In Metz and Schillebeeckx, eds., *The Teaching Authority of the Believers. Concilium* 180, 54–62.

Spiro, Herbert J. "Authority, Values, and Policy." In Carl J. Friedrich, ed., *Authority. Nomos* 1. Cambridge: Harvard, 1958, 49–57.

St. Joseph's Parish Staff. *Mémorial du Cinquantenaire de la Fondation de la Paroisse St-Joseph de Biddeford, Maine.* 1922.

————. *Paroisse St-Joseph, Biddeford, Maine, 75ᵉ Anniversaire Programme–Souvenir.* 1945.

————. *St. Joseph Parish Centennial, Biddeford, Maine.* 1970.

St. Matthew's Parish Staff. *Five-Year Parish Report.* Boston: St. Matthew's Parish, 1989.

Stagaman, David J. *Authority In the Church.* Collegeville: Liturgical Press, 1999.

Starkloff, Carl F. "Church as Structure and Communitas: Victor Turner and Ecclesiology." *Theological Studies* 58 (1997) 643–68.

Sweetser, Thomas. *Successful Parishes: How They Meet the Challenge of Change.* Minneapolis: Winston, 1983.

———. *The Parish as Covenant: A Call to Pastoral Partnership.* Franklin, WI: Sheed and Ward, 2001.

Tillard, J.-M. R. *L'église locale: ecclésiologie de communion et catholicité.* Paris: Cerf, 1995.

Toby, Jackson. "Introduction." In *The Evolution of Societies* by Talcott Parsons. Jackson Toby, ed. Englewood Cliffs, NJ: Prentice-Hall, 1977.

Tönnies, Ferdinand. *Community and Civil Society,* ed. Jose Harris. Cambridge Texts in the History of Political Thought. Cambridge: Cambridge University Press, 2001.

Turner, Victor. *The Ritual Process: Structure and Anti-Structure.* The Lewis Henry Morgan Lectures at the University of Rochester, NY. New York: Aldine, 1969.

Ulrich, Dave. "Six Practices for Creating Communities of Value, Not Proximity." In *The Community of the Future,* Frances Hesselbein, et al., eds., 155–65. San Francisco: Jossey-Bass, 1998.

Vandenakker, John Paul. *Small Christian Communities and the Parish.* Kansas City, MO: Sheed and Ward, 1994.

Vaskovics, L. "Theses on the Interdependence of Religious Organizations and Familial Sub-Systems." In Baum and Greeley, eds., *The Church As Institution. Concilium* 91, 139–47.

Vatican Council II. *The Documents of Vatican II.* Ed. Walter Abbot, s.j. New York: Herder and Herder, 1966.

———. *Vatican Council II: The Conciliar and Post-Conciliar Documents.* Vol. 1. Ed. Austin Flannery. Northport, NY: Costello; Dublin: Dominican, 1996.

Wackenheim, Gérard. "Ecclesiology and Sociology." In Baum and Greeley, eds., *The Church as Institution. Concilium* 91, 32–41.

Waldenfels, Hans. "Authority and Knowledge." In Metz and Schillebeeckx, eds., *The Teaching Authority of the Believers. Concilium* 180, 31–42.

Warren, Michael. *At This Time, In This Place: The Spirit Embodied In the Local Assembly.* Harrisburg, PA: Trinity Press International, 1999.

Warwick, Donal. "The Centralization of Ecclesiastical Authority: An Organizational Perspective." In Baum and Greeley, eds., *The Church As Institution. Concilium* 91, 109–18.

Weber, Max. *Economy and Society: An Outline of Interpretive Sociology.* 3 vols. Eds., Guenther Roth and Claus Wittich. New York: Bedminster Press, 1968.

Westley, Dick. *Redemptive Intimacy: A New Perspective for the Journey to Adult Faith.* Mystic, CT: Twenty-Third Publications, 1991.

Whitehead, Evelyn Eaton. "The Structure of Community: Toward Forming the Parish as a Community of Faith." In eadem, ed., *The Parish In Community and Ministry*. New York: Paulist, 1978.

Whitehead, James D., and Evelyn Eaton Whitehead. *Method In Ministry: Theological Reflection and Christian Ministry*. New York: Seabury, 1981.

Yarnold, G. D. *By What Authority*. London: A. R. Mowbray, 1964.

Yarnold, Edward J., and Henry Chadwick. *Truth and Authority: A Commentary on the Agreed Statement of the Anglican-Roman Catholic International Commission "Authority in the Church," Venice 1976*. London: SPCK, Catholic Truth Society, 1977.

Zizioulas, John. *Being As Communion: Studies in Personhood and the Church*. Contemporary Greek Theologians. Crestwood, NY: St. Vladimir's Seminary Press, 1985.

Index of Authors and Selected Subjects

catholicity (mark of the church), 58–59, 62, 122, 125 (n. 67), 138, 154–55, 184

Catlin, George E. Gordon, 108 (n. 8), 110 (n. 18), 125 (n. 66)

Chadwick, Henry, 101, 110 (n. 20), 111, 118 (n. 43)

charism/charismatic, 16, 27, 30, 62, 92, 95 (n. 71), 97–98, 125 (n. 67), 161, 177–78

Chopp, Rebecca S., 114 (n. 33), 193 (n. 4)

church (general): understood theologically xi–xii, xvii, 140; as local, xii, xvi–xx, xxii, xxiii, 1–2, 58, 69–70, 133–34, 137, 142–49, 150–53, 155, 157–62, 163–86; as universal, xviii, xxv, 58, 93, 124, 127–29, 131, 133–43, 148–50, 152–53, 157–62, 164, 169, 172–73, 177–82; and institutions/structures, xii–xvi, xx, 1, 23, 31, 104, 139, 142, 147, 150, 155, 163, 167, 172, 181, 194; relationship of whole and part in, xix, 164, 168–77; importance of concrete circumstances of, xxi, 146, 148, 151, 154, 181; relationship between local and universal in, xxii, 9, 105, 126–27, 129–30, 133–62, 163, 167–86, 193–94, 198–99; ownership of, 23–24, 33, 104; membership in, 23–24, 128, 140; and culture, 57–58, 92, 155–56, 166, 174; as human 69, 152, 178; and authenticity, 75, 161; sharing Jesus' intimacy with Father, 91; centralization of, 96–99, 126, 143, 150, 172, 185, 190–92; unity of, 97, 108, 122 (n. 55), 126, 130, 134, 136, 143, 147, 150–51, 158, 163, 171–79, 181, 184–85, 194; and popular devotion, 101–02; and authority, 129, 161, 166, 178; as divine, 134, 140, 151, 152; and apostolic

succession, 136; origins of, 138; pre-existence of, 139, 141, 148–49, 151; and diversity, 145, 146, 164; and divine intervention, 165–66 (*see also* "church, images and descriptions of," "church buildings," "community [local]," "ecclesiology," "mission of the church," "Roman Catholic Church")

church buildings: 5–6, 8, 10–11, 25–26, 32–33

church, images and descriptions of: visible society, xi; global community of faith, xii, 1, 24, 139, 181–86; sign of continuity, 5–7, 17; sign of change, 7–9; "helper," 17–22, 52; obstacle, 18, 20–22; relationship, 24, 70; place of gathering, 27–31; place of division, 27–31; teacher, 52, 59, 174, 177; community of disciples, 62, 139, 166; protector, 63; mystery, 87, 140, 144, 152; community of ministry, 122, 125 (n. 67); "palpably present," 134; sacrament, 153, 164–66, 171, 185, 199; event, 161, 164, 167, 169, 196; pilgrim, 164, 179–81, 200; source of grace, 166; *societas perfecta*, 167; presence of Christ to the world, 170, 199 (*see also* "Body of Christ" and "People of God")

Clement of Rome, Letter to Corinthians, 139

clergy: decline in vocations, 41, 105, 195; specialization of 41; role in parish, 43–44, 103–05, 191; spirituality, 55; relationship to diocese, 60; development in early church, 93–101; and mission, 129; difference from laity, 129; members of local communities, 131; response of laity to, 157; as *presbyterium*, 176

clericalism, xiv, xvi, xx, 12, 185, 189–91, 193–96